Toward a Global Business
Confederation

Praise for *Toward a Global Business Confederation*

"A contemporary 'classic' book on international business has finally arrived. *Toward a Global Business Confederation* vividly demonstrates the economic, geopolitical, and social implications of today's multinational companies and their conflicts and cooperation with the nation-states for welfare generation on a global basis. This is a must reading for international business scholars and policymakers."

—Masaaki Kotabe, The Washburn Chair Professor of International Business and Marketing, Temple University

"A strong, well-presented grasp and analysis of the reality of the power of multinational corporations in our globalized world. A clear and focused argument for the opportunity and need to harvest that power to bring about a mutually beneficial global economic prosperity."

—Robert D. Werner, former Chairman, Timex Watches Ltd.

"Eye opening and intriguing, *Toward a Global Business Confederation* is a wonderful book for all current and future international business people. It lucidly lays out the basics of globalization and proffers a Global Business Confederation as a link between today's multinational corporations and nation states and a bridge to a more equitable and peaceful world of the future. While one may or may not agree with this solution, one will definitely look at the path of globalization in a different and much more informed way."

—Gregory A. Boyko, Member of the Board of Advisors, University of Connecticut School of Business

"Subhash Jain has exposed many of the challenges facing business and nations in the coming decade, in both the developed and developing economies. With the increasing power of the multinational corporations and innovative technology, new approaches will be needed to handle the enormous growth of international markets. The author provides provocative ideas as to how these issues could be addressed. This book must be required reading for all who expect to survive and flourish in the globalized world."

—Marjorie D. Anderson, Executive Director, World Affairs Council, Hartford, Connecticut

"Jain's effort to define and promote a worldwide confederation of governments, companies, and interest groups that would set rules on multinational company activities is an admirable step toward development of needed global institutions. His analysis points out the many benefits produced by these companies, and the need to harness their positive contributions while responding to their activities that diverge from broad public interest. Jain has raised an excellent concept (of the Global Business Confederation), and one that should be explored in careful detail in today's globalized world."

—Robert Grosse, Professor of Economics, Thunderbird, The American Graduate School of International Management

TOWARD A GLOBAL BUSINESS CONFEDERATION

A Blueprint for Globalization

Subhash C. Jain

PRAEGER

Westport, Connecticut
London

Library of Congress Cataloging-in-Publication Data

Jain, Subhash C., 1942–
    Toward a global business confederation : a blueprint for globalization / Subhash C. Jain.
        p. cm.
    Includes bibliographical references and index.
    ISBN 1–56720–535–6 (alk. paper)
    1. International economic integration. 2. Globalization—Economic aspects.
    3. International business enterprises. 4. International economic relations. I. Title.
    HF1418.5.J35 2003
    338.8′8—dc21   2003052896

British Library Cataloguing in Publication Data is available.

Library of Congress Catalog Card Number: 2003052896
ISBN: 1–56720–535–6

First published in 2003

Praeger Publishers, 88 Post Road West, Westport, CT 06881
An imprint of Greenwood Publishing Group, Inc.
www.praeger.com

Printed in the United States of America

The paper used in this book complies with the
Permanent Paper Standard issued by the National
Information Standards Organization (Z39.48–1984).

10 9 8 7 6 5 4 3 2 1

CONTENTS

PREFACE

Enough evidence is available to support the fact that globalization leads to worldwide economic prosperity. It is the most powerful force for good the world has seen. The foundation of globalization is worldwide capitalism. Thanks to capitalism, life expectancy is up, infant mortality is down, education is richer, horizons are broader, environmental awareness is greater, and global cooperation is possible. Above all, capitalism is the reason we can provide reliable social welfare on a mass scale. The activities of capitalists generate the money to pay for education, medical research, and social welfare and help provide the incentives for people to invent things to make our lives better.

Measured either in terms of trade or direct investment, globalization has been highly uneven. A few developing countries have managed to increase their trade a lot. They are the same countries that have attracted the lion's share of foreign direct investment. And they have also seen the benefits of openness. According to the World Bank, 24 countries—home to 3 billion people and including China, India, Brazil, Argentina, and the Philippines—have substantially increased their ratios of trade to gross domestic product (GDP) in the past 20 years. These countries are the low-income globalizers. On average, their growth rates have improved as well. The GDP per head in these economies grew by an average of 5 percent a year during the 1990s, and their poverty rates declined. Rich countries in the same time period grew by 2 percent.

However, another 2 billion people live in countries that have become less, rather than more, globalized. In these countries, including Pakistan and much of Africa, trade has diminished in relation to national income, economic growth has been stagnant, and poverty has risen. Apparently, globalization has not been global. Much of the world, home to one-third of its people and including large tracts of Africa and many Muslim countries, has simply failed to participate. Thus, the process of globalization has not finished. Nonglobalizing developing countries must become a part of the process.

Over the next 20 years, the rich world's population will fall slightly, while the developing world will acquire 2 billion additional people, many of them in countries that are currently political and economic failures. Unless, with help from the rich countries and from one another, they can find ways to integrate into the global economy, much of the potential gains of globalization will continue to be limited to the rich and a few developing countries. Such a failure is good for neither rich nor developing countries. After the September 11, 2001, attacks on New York City and Washington, D.C., no country—least of all the United States—can believe it is immune from the effects of poverty and political collapse halfway around the world. Thus, the goal must be to spread the benefits of globalization more widely.

This book supports economic globalization because it leads to worldwide prosperity. Multinational corporations (MNCs) play a key role in making globalization feasible. Unfortunately, the movement toward globalization is too slow. To a large extent, this slowness can be attributed to the barriers that nation-states create in furthering globalization. To enhance the pace of globalization, it is essential that nation-states not force their national rules and regulations on multinationals. Rather, global rules and regulations must be enacted to allow MNCs to perpetuate globalization at full speed.

The book proposes the establishment of a global business confederation (GBC) to regulate and encourage MNCs to bring about global economic prosperity in a manner responsive to cultural, social, and human issues. This proposal amounts to a new type of capitalism, which may be called *globally shared capitalism*. Under such an arrangement, MNCs, following global rules and regulations established by the GBC, would seek global economic and business integration. The role of MNCs would expand while the roles of nation-states would decline. MNCs would work in full concert with other special interest groups such as labor, environmentalist, human rights, and other groups.

The GBC would be a unique, treaty-based, institutional framework that would define and encourage activities of MNCs around the globe in the greater interest of worldwide economic and social prosperity. The world-international markets were about $11 trillion in 1998, compared with almost $7 trillion of world exports in the same year. Year after year, both global output and sales of foreign affiliates have grown faster than world gross domestic product (GDP) and exports.[2]

Exhibit 1.1 shows the distribution of MNCs between developed and developing countries and among different nations in each group. An important dimension of MNCs is the predominance of large firms. Virtually one hundred MNCs have annual sales of more than $10 billion. The economic significance of these corporations as compared with other economic entities, including the economies of many nations, suggests that they are an important source of global power. Exhibit 1.2 shows that many MNCs have higher annual revenues than the gross national products (GNPs) of some countries. Approximately 70 percent of world trade is controlled by 500 corporations.[3] The largest 200 MNCs control almost one-third of the world's GDP.

Many MNCs derive a substantial portion of their net income and sales from overseas operations. About one-third of the top 100 U.S. companies generate over 50 percent of their annual sales in foreign markets. Put together, the world's 1,000 largest companies produce 80 percent of the global industrial output. MNCs play a dominant role in the economies of specific countries. Foreign firms account for almost half of Ireland's employment and two-thirds of that country's output. In Australia, each of the 10 biggest MNCs has annual sales larger than its government's tax revenue. As shown in Exhibit 1.3, the nondomestic earnings of many U.S. companies, such as ExxonMobil, Hewlett-Packard, Dow Chemical, Motorola, McDonald's, Gillette, Rohm & Haas, Avon Products, and others, exceed 50 percent of the total earnings.

Another important feature of MNCs is their predominantly oligopolistic character; that is, they operate in markets that are dominated by a few sellers. Their technological leads, special skills, and ability to differentiate their products through advertising are all factors that help sustain or reinforce their oligopolistic nature. Four companies—ConAgra, ADM Milling, Cargill, and Pillsbury—mill nearly 60 percent of all flour produced in the United States, and two of them—ConAgra and Cargill—control 50 percent of grain exports.[4]

An important aspect of the operations of MNCs is the business activity that is generated within the multinational companies themselves as they export and import among their own foreign-based subsidiaries. About 50 percent of U.S. exports and imports are goods that constitute intrafirm transactions.[5] A U.S. computer company ships design components to its

Exhibit 1.1

Number of Parent Corporations and Foreign Affiliates, by Area and Economy, Latest Available Year

Area/Economy	Year	Parent Corporations Based in Economy	Foreign Affiliates Located in Economy
DEVELOPED ECONOMIES		49 806	94 623
Western Europe		39 415	62 226
European Union		33 939	53 373
Austria	1996	897	2 362
Belgium	1997	988	1 504
Denmark	1998	9 356	2 035
Finland	1997	1 963	1 200
France	1996	2 078	9 351
Germany	1996	7 569	11 445
Greece	1991	--	798
Ireland	1994	39	1 040
Italy	1995	966	1 630
Netherlands	1993	1 608	2 259
Portugal	1997	1 350	5 809
Spain	1998	857	7 465
Sweden	1998	5 183	3 950
United Kingdom	1997	1 085	2 525
Other Western Europe		5 476	8 853
Iceland	1998	70	79
Norway	1997	900	3 000
Switzerland	1995	4 506	5 774
Japan	1998	4 334	3 321
United States	1996	3 382	18 711
Other developed		2 675	10 365
Australia	1998		2 550
Canada	1997		4 562
New Zealand	1998		1 106
South Africa	1997		2 147
DEVELOPING ECONOMIES			
Africa		43	429
Ethiopia	1998	--	21
Mali	1999	3	33
Seychelles	1998	--	30
Swaziland	1996	30	134
Zambia	1997	2	175
Zimbabwe	1998	8	36
Latin America and the Caribbean		2 594	26 577
Bolivia	1996	--	257
Brazil	1998	1 225	8 050
Chile	1998	478	3 173
Colombia	1998	877	4 468
El Salvador	1990	--	225
Guatemala	1985	--	287

Exhibit 1.1
(continued)

Guyana	1998	4	56
Jamaica	1997	--	156
Mexico	1993	--	8 420
Paraguay	1995	--	109
Peru	1997	10	1 183
Trinidad & Tobago	1998	--	70
Uruguay	1997	--	123
South, East, and Southeast Asia		6 067	206 148
Bangladesh	1997	143	288
China	1997	379	145 000
Hong Kong, China	1998	500	5 312
India	1995	187	1 416
Indonesia	1995	313	3 472
Korea, Republic of	1998	4 488	5 137
Malaysia	1998	--	3 787
Mongolia	1998	--	1 100
Pakistan	1993	57	758
Philippines	1995	--	14 802
Singapore	1995	--	18 154
Sri Lanka	1995	--	139
Taiwan Province of China	1990	--	5 733
Thailand	1992	--	1 050
West Asia		449	1 948
Oman	1995	92	351
Saudi Arabia	1989	--	1 461
Turkey	1995	357	136
Central Asia		9	1 041
Kyrgyzstan	1997	9	1 041
The Pacific		84	2 763
Fiji	1997	--	151
Papua New Guinea	1999	--	2 342
Tonga	1998	84	270
Central and Eastern Europe		850	174 710
Albania	1998	--	1 239
Armenia	1998	--	157
Belarus	1994	--	393
Bulgaria	1994	26	918
Croatia	1997	70	353
Czech Republic	1999	660	71 385
Estonia	1999	--	3 066
Hungary	1998	--	28 772
Lithuania	1998	16	1 778
Poland	1998	58	35 840
Romania	1998	20	9 195
Russian Federation	1994	--	7 793
Slovakia	1997	--	5 560
Slovenia	1997	--	1 195
Ukraine	1998	--	7 066
WORLD		59 902	508 239

Source: UN Conference on Trade and Development estimates.

Exhibit 1.2

GNPs of Various Countries Ranked with Sales of Selected Corporations, 2002

Country/Company	Billions of U.S. Dollars
Switzerland	284
Sweden	227
Austria	217
ExxonMobil	206
Turkey	201
Wal-Mart	191
General Electric	185
General Motors	184
Denmark	175
Ford Motor	170
Norway	152
Poland	151
Saudi Arabia	143
South Africa	137
Thailand	132
Indonesia	130
Finland	125
Greece	123
Citigroup	112
Portugal	106
Iran	102
Colombia	100

Source: World Bank and company annual reports.

subsidiary in Malaysia for assembly and then imports the finished machines back to the United States and exports them to other buyers around the world.

MNCs are mainly the product of developed countries. However, the relative importance of different home countries has changed in the last 15 years. The MNCs of Japan and the European countries have increased in significance, whereas the significance of MNCs of the United States has declined. The available evidence suggests that these shifts are due primarily to changes in the international competitiveness of companies based in different countries.

Foreign Direct Investment Patterns

The establishment of foreign affiliates involves costs in either cash or kind. Often these costs comprise a package of equity participation in the new venture, technology transfer, and sharing of managerial expertise. In addition, loans may be made to the affiliate with an agreement to reinvest

Exhibit 1.7

World Top 100 Nonfinancial MNCs: Assets, Sales, and Employment (billions of dollars and number of employees)

	Corporation	Country	Industry	Assets		Sales		Employment	
				Foreign	Total	Foreign	Total	Foreign	Total
1	General Electric	United States	Electronics	97.4	304.0	24.5	90.8	111 000	276 000
2	Ford Motor Company	United States	Automotive	72.5	275.4	48.0	153.6	174 105	363 892
3	Royal Dutch/Shell Group	Netherlands/ United Kingdom	Petroleum	70.0	115.0	69.0	128.0	65 000	105 000
4	General Motors	United States	Automotive	0.0	228.9	51.0	178.2	...	608 000
5	Exxon Corporation	United States	Petroleum	54.6	96.1	104.8	120.3	...	80 000
6	Toyota	Japan	Automotive	41.8	105.0	50.4	88.5	...	159 035
7	IBM	United States	Computers	39.9	81.5	48.9	78.5	134 815	269 465
8	Volkswagen Group	Germany	Automotive	...	57.0	42.7	65.0	133 906	279 892
9	Nestle SA	Switzerland	Food and beverages	31.6	37.0	47.6	48.3	219 442	225 808
10	Daimler-Benz AG	Germany	Automotive	30.9	76.2	46.1	69.0	74 802	300 068
11	Mobil Corporation	United States	Petroleum	30.4	43.6	36.8	64.3	22 200	42 700
12	FIAT Spa	Italy	Automotive	30.0	69.1	20.2	50.6	94 877	242 322
13	Hoechst AG	Germany	Chemicals	29.0	34.0	24.3	30.0	...	137 374
14	Asea Brown Boveri (ABB)	Switzerland	Electrical equipment	...	29.8	30.4	31.3	200 574	213 057
15	Bayer AG	Germany	Chemicals	...	30.3	...	32.0	...	144 600
16	Elf Aquitaine SA	France	Petroleum	26.7	42.0	25.6	42.3	40 500	83 700
17	Nissan Motor Co., Ltd.	Japan	Automotive	26.5	57.6	27.8	49.7	...	137 201
18	Unilever	Netherlands/ United Kingdom	Food and beverages	25.6	30.8	44.8	46.4	262 840	269 315
19	Siemens AG	Germany	Electronics	25.6	67.1	40.0	60.6	201 141	386 000
20	Roche Holding AG	Switzerland	Pharmaceuticals	...	37.6	12.7	12.9	41 832	51 643
21	Sony Corporation	Japan	Electronics	...	48.2	40.3	51.1	...	173 000
22	Mitsubishi Corporation	Japan	Diversified	21.9	67.1	41.5	120.4	...	8 401
23	Seagram Company	Canada	Beverages	21.8	22.2	9.4	9.7	...	31 000
24	Honda Motor Co., Ltd	Japan	Automotive	21.5	36.5	31.5	45.4	...	109 400
25	BMW AG	Germany	Automotive	20.3	31.8	26.4	35.9	52 149	117 624
26	Alcatel Alsthom Cie	France	Electronics	20.3	41.9	25.9	31.0	...	189 549
27	Philips Electronics N.V.	Netherlands	Electronics	20.1	25.5	33.0	33.5	206 236	252 268
28	News Corporation	Australia	Media	20.0	30.7	9.5	10.7	...	28 220
29	Phillip Morris	United States	Food/tobacco	19.4	55.9	32.1	56.1	...	152 000
30	British Petroleum (BP)	United Kingdom	Petroleum	19.2	32.6	36.5	71.3	37 600	55 650
31	Hewlett-Packard	United States	Electronics	18.5	31.7	23.8	42.9	...	121 900

11

Exhibit 1.7
(continued)

32	Total SA	France	Petroleum	...	25.2	23.4	31.9	...	54 391
33	Renault SA	France	Automotive	18.3	34.9	18.5	35.6	45 860	141 315
34	Cable and Wireless Plc	United Kingdom	Telecommunica-tion	...	21.6	7.8	11.5	33 740	46 550
35	Mitsui & Co., Ltd.	Japan	Diversified	17.9	55.5	52.3	132.6	...	10 994
36	Rhone-Poulenc SA	France	Chemicals/phar-maceuticals	17.8	27.5	11.5	15.0	...	68 377
37	Viag AG	Germany	Diversified	17.4	32.7	15.9	27.6	...	95 561
38	BASF AG	Germany	Chemicals	...	26.8	23.9	32.2	...	104 979
39	Itochu Corporation	Japan	Trading	16.7	56.8	48.7	117.7	2 600	8 878
40	Nissho Iwai Corporation	Japan	Trading	16.6	40.4	32.3	75.5	2 068	6 398
41	Du Pont (E.I.)	United States	Chemicals	16.6	42.7	20.4	39.7	...	98 000
42	Diageo Plc	United Kingdom	Beverages	...	29.7	17.6	22.6	63 761	79 161
43	Novartis	Switzerland	Pharmaceuticals/chemicals	16.0	36.7	21.0	21.5	71 403	87 239
44	Sumitomo Corporation	Japan	Trading/machin-ery	15.4	43.0	15.1	95.2	...	8 694
45	ENI Group	Italy	Petroleum	14.6	49.4	12.5	34.3	23 239	80 178
46	Chevron Corporation	United States	Petroleum	14.3	35.5	13.8	40.6	8 610	39 362
47	Dow Chemical	United States	Chemicals	14.3	23.6	11.3	20.0	...	42 861
48	Texaco Incorporated	United States	Petroleum	14.1	29.6	22.3	45.2	...	29 313
49	BCE Inc.	Canada	Telecommunica-tion	13.6	28.2	15.5	23.2	...	122 000
50	Xerox Corporation	United States	Photo equipment	13.5	27.7	9.0	18.2	...	91 400
51	Saint-Gobain SA	France	Industrial material	...	22.7	9.5	18.3	...	107 168
52	Thomson Corporation	Canada	Printing and publishing	13.0	13.3	8.3	8.8	46 300	49 800
53	Peugeot SA	France	Automotive	12.9	30.8	16.1	31.2	32 100	140 200
54	Montedison	Italy	Chemicals/agri-business	...	18.1	9.7	13.9	18 354	27 135
55	Matsushita Electric	Japan	Electronics	12.2	62.7	23.6	59.7	...	275 962
56	Hitachi, Ltd.	Japan	Electronics	12.0	76.6	19.8	63.8	58 000	331 494
57	Motorola, Inc.	United States	Electronics	11.7	27.3	17.4	29.8	70 000	150 000
58	Marubeni Corporation	Japan	Trading	11.6	55.9	38.5	103.3	2 827	8 868
59	Fujitsu Limited	Japan	Electronics	11.2	38.8	14.1	37.7	...	180 000
60	Imperial Chemical Industries (ICI) Plc	United Kingdom	Chemicals	10.6	15.2	14.7	18.1	51 400	69 500
61	Veba Group	Germany	Diversified	10.4	45.0	16.0	46.2	32 178	129 960
62	Volvo AB	Sweden	Automotive	...	20.7	21.5	24.1	29 250	72 900
63	RTZ Cra Plc	United Kingdom /Australia	Mining	10.2	16.7	5.8	9.4	27 297	50 507
64	Lafarge SA	France	Construction	10.1	16.0	5.1	7.0	28 936	37 097
65	Procter & Gamble	United States	Chemicals/cosmetics	10.0	31.0	17.9	37.2	...	110 000
66	McDonald's Corporation	United States	Restaurants	10.0	18.2	6.8	11.4	...	267 000
67	Ericsson LM	Sweden	Electronics	10.0	18.2	15.4	20.7	55 414	100 774
68	AMOCO Corporation	United States	Petroleum	9.9	32.5	8.0	31.9	...	43 451

12

Exhibit 1.7
(continued)

69	Johnson & Johnson	United States	Chemicals/pharmaceuticals	9.5	21.1	10.9	22.6	...	90 500
70	Mitsubishi Motors	Japan	Automotive	9.1	25.1	10.9	28.3	19 600	75 300
71	Glaxo Wellcome Plc	United Kingdom	Pharmaceuticals	...	13.6	12.1	13.1	...	53 068
72	Robert Bosch GmbH	Germany	Automotive	9.0	19.5	17.7	27.0	89 071	179 719
73	Petroleos de Venezuela S.A.	Venezuela	Petroleum	9.0	47.1	32.5	34.8	11 849	56 592
74	Electrolux AB	Sweden	Electrical appliances	...	10.1	13.6	14.3	...	103 000
75	Daewoo Corporation	Republic of Korea	Diversified	...	22.9	...	18.8	...	...
76	Michelin	France	Rubber and plastics	...	13.6	11.3	13.3	...	123 254
77	British American Tobacco Plc	United Kingdom	Food/tobacco	8.1	84.8	26.2	34.5	115 000	117 339
78	Crown Cork & Seal	United States	Packaging	8.1	12.3	5.1	8.5	...	40 985
79	Merck & Co., Inc.	United States	Drugs, cosmetics, and health	8.1	25.7	6.5	23.6	20 000	53 800
80	Generale des Eaux	France	Diversified /utility	...	43.1	9.2	28.6	...	193 300
81	AT&T Corp.	United States	Telecommunication/electronics	...	61.1	...	51.3	...	128 000
82	Solvay SA	Belgium	Pharmaceuticals/ chemicals	...	8.5	8.0	8.4	...	34 445
83	L'Air Liquide Group	France	Chemicals	...	9.3	4.7	6.6	...	27 600
84	GTE Corporation	United States	Telecommunication	...	42.1	...	23.3	...	114 000
85	International Paper	United States	Paper	7.8	26.8	5.8	20.1	28 000	82 000
86	Mannesmann AG	Germany	Engineering/telecommunication	...	16.4	12.6	22.5	41 290	120 859
87	Akzo Nobel N.V.	Netherlands	Chemicals	...	10.6	11.4	12.3	51 300	68 900
88	Danone Groupe SA	France	Food and beverages	7.5	16.5	8.8	14.8	...	80 631
89	Holderbank Financiere Glarus AG	Switzerland	Construction materials	7.5	12.0	6.9	7.8	37 302	40 779
90	BTR Plc	United Kingdom	Plastic and foam	7.5	12.7	11.5	12.3	90 878	110 498
91	Royal Ahold NV	Netherlands	Retailers	7.4	9.9	18.2	26.6	148 872	209 591
92	Atlantic Richfield	United States	Petroleum Exploration/refining/distribution	...	25.3	3.5	18.6	4 400	19 600
93	Bridgestone	Japan	Rubber and plastics	7.2	13.3	9.8	16.7	...	13 049
94	Smithkline Beecham Plc	United Kingdom	Drugs, cosmetics, and health	7.1	13.4	11.5	12.9	...	55 400
95	LVMH SA	France	Diversified	7.1	16.3	6.5	8.0	...	33 511
96	Canon Electronics Inc.	Japan	Electronics	7.0	22.0	14.6	21.2	41 211	78 767
97	American Home Products	United States	Pharmaceuticals	6.9	20.8	6.1	14.2	...	60 523
98	Toshiba Corporation	Japan	Electronics	6.8	44.9	14.6	41.3	...	186 000
99	Gillette Company	United States	Drugs, cosmetics, and health	6.8	10.9	6.4	10.1	31 600	44 000
100	Pharmacia & Upjohn, Inc.	United States	Pharmaceuticals	6.8	10.4	4.6	6.6	...	30 000

Note: The companies have been ranked by foreign assets.
Source: UN Conference on Trade and Development.

Exhibit 1.8
Industry Composition of Top 100 MNCs, 2000 (number)

Industry	
Chemicals and pharmaceuticals	21
Electronics/electrical equipment	18
Automotive	14
Petroleum refining/distribution and mining	13
Food and beverages	9
Diversified	7
Telecommunication/utilities	4
Trading	3
Machinery and engineering	2
Metals	-
Construction	3
Media	1
Other	5
Total	100

Source: UN Conference on Trade and Development.

employed about 6 million people in their overseas subsidiaries. These MNCs accounted for an estimated 15 percent of the foreign assets of all MNCs and 22 percent of their sales. A mere 1 percent of all MNCs own half the total stock of FDI.[7]

General Electric holds the first position among the world's 100 largest nonfinancial MNCs in terms of foreign assets. About 85 of the top 100 MNCs are firms that have been ranked in the top 100 over the last five years. Exhibit 1.7 identifies these 100 firms, along with their foreign sales, assets, and employment figures. Of the 100 companies, 89 originated in the United States, the European Union, or Japan. Only 2 companies among the global 100 companies came from developing countries: 1 company each from South Korea and Venezuela.

The industry classification of the top 100 firms is shown in Exhibit 1.8. Four industries account for two-thirds of the companies: chemicals and pharmaceuticals, electronics, automotive products, and petroleum. Chemicals and pharmaceuticals, with 21 companies, dominates the list.

Role of MNCs in OECD Economies

Multinational firms play on increasingly important role in the Organization for Economic Cooperation and Development (OECD) countries in

Exhibit 1.9
Share of Foreign Affiliates in Manufacturing Production

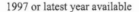

1997 or latest year available

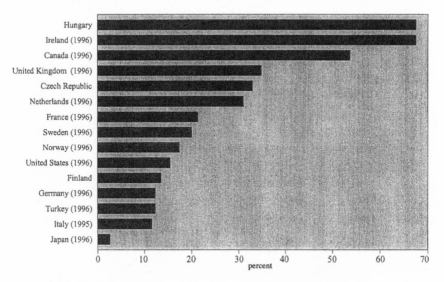

Source: Organization for Economic Cooperation and Development, Activities of Foreign Affiliates database.

terms of production and employment. The share of production and employment under foreign control in the OECD economies amounts to between 10 and 20 percent on average, but there are wide differences among countries. The share of foreign affiliates in manufacturing production ranges from 66 percent in Hungary and Ireland to 1 percent in Japan (see Exhibit 1.9). Foreign affiliates feature prominently in Canada, the Netherlands, France, the Czech Republic, Sweden, and the United Kingdom. Their presence is limited in Italy, Turkey, Germany, Finland, Norway, and the United States. The share of foreign affiliates depends on various factors, including the size and attractiveness of the country and the ease, from the institutional standpoint, with which such investments can be made.

The share of foreign affiliates in manufacturing production exceeds their share in manufacturing employment in nearly all countries. As shown in Exhibit 1.10, the mean wage paid by foreign affiliates in the manufacturing sector is also generally higher than the mean wage paid by national firms.

The share of foreign affiliates in research and development (R&D) varies widely across countries, ranging from less than 1 percent in the

Exhibit 1.10
Compensation per Employee of Foreign Affiliates in Manufacturing

National firms = 100

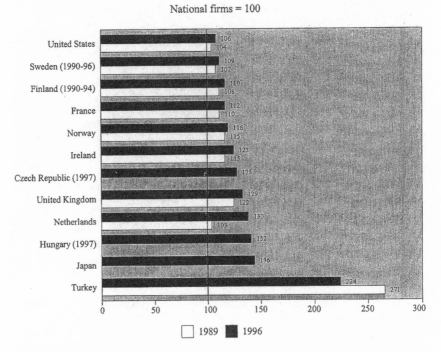

□ 1989   ■ 1996

Source: Organization for Economic Cooperation and Development, Activities of Foreign Affiliates database.

manufacturing industry in Japan to 68 percent in Ireland and 77 percent in Hungary. At over 30 percent, the share is very large as well in Spain, Canada, the United Kingdom, Australia, and the Czech Republic (see Exhibit 1.11).

In the European Union in 1998, a quarter of the total manufacturing production was controlled by foreign subsidiaries of bigger companies, compared with 17 percent in 1990. The figure has probably increased since then, and it is expected to climb further as the euro increasingly links member countries' economies.

MNCs from Developing Countries

MNCs from developing countries are a recent phenomenon. Their overseas subsidiaries have increased in number from dozens in the 1960s to

Exhibit 1.11
Share of Foreign Affiliates in Manufacturing R&D

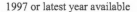
1997 or latest year available

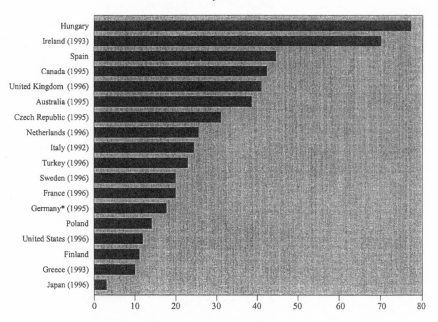

Note: Sample of the 500 most R&D–intensive firms.
Source: Organization for Economic Cooperation and Development, Activities of Foreign Affiliates database.

more than 9,000 today. They are successfully competing for a share of world markets.

Exhibit 1.12 lists the top 50 nonfinancial MNCs from developing countries, ranked by foreign assets. In general, the size (in terms of foreign assets) of MNCs from developing countries is relatively small; their median foreign asset holdings are about $1.3 billion, which is far below the median of the top 100 MNCs ($13.3 billion). A large number of these MNCs either were diversified or belonged to food and beverages, petroleum, or construction industries.

The strength of the developing world's MNCs comes from their special experience with manufacturing for small home markets. Using low technology and local raw materials, running job-shop kinds of plants, and making effective use of semiskilled labor, these MNCs are able to custom design products best suited to host countries. For example, a Chinese com-

Exhibit 1.12

Nonfinancial MNCs from Developing Countries (millions of dollars and number of employees)

	Corporation	Country	Industry	Assets		Sales		Employment	
				Foreign	Total	Foreign	Total	Foreign	Total
1.	Petroleos de Venezuela	Venezuela	Petroleum	9 007	47 148	32 502	34 801	11 849	56 592
2.	Daewoo Corporation	Republic of Korea	Diversified	--	22 946	--	18 802	--	--
3.	Jardine Matheson Holdings Limited	Hong Kong, China/ Bermuda	Diversified	6 652	11 970	7 983	11 522	--	175 000
4.	First Pacific Company Limited	Hong Kong, China	Electronics	6 295	11 386	7 416	8 308	40 400	51 270
5.	Cemex, S.A.	Mexico	Construction	5 627	10 231	2 235	3 788	10 690	19 174
6.	Hutchison Whampoa, Limited	Hong Kong, China	Diversified	4 978	15 086	1 899	5 754	17 013	37 100
7.	Sappi Limited	South Africa	Paper	3 830	4 953	2 419	3 557	9 492	23 458
8.	China State Construction Engineering Corporation	China	Construction	3 730	7 230	1 530	5 420	5 496	258 195
9.	China National Chemicals Import and Export Corporation	China	Diversified	3 460	5 810	11 240	17 880	625	8 905
10.	LG Electronics Incorporated	Republic of Korea	Electronics and electrical equipment	3 158	15 431	5 175	17 640	32 532	80 370
11.	YPF Sociedad Anonima	Argentina	Petroleum	3 061	12 761	911	6 144	1 908	10 002
12.	Petroleo Brasilie S.A. – Petrobras	Brazil	Petroleum	--	34 233	--	27 946	--	41 173
13.	Sunkyong Group	Republic of Korea	Diversified	2 561	24 572	9 960	31 692	2 600	32 169
14.	Hyundai Engineering and Construction Co.	Republic of Korea	Construction	--	8 063	--	5 405	--	30 981
15.	New World Development Co., Limited	Hong Kong, China	Construction	2 060	14 030	800	2 580	--	14 840
16.	Guangdong Investment Limited	Hong Kong, China	Diversified	1 898	3 053	676	924	15 080	16 500
17.	Citic Pacific Limited	Hong Kong, China	Diversified	1 834	8 733	912	2 154	8 262	11 800
18.	PETRONAS – Petroliam Nasional Berhad	Malaysia	Petroleum	--	20 990	--	10 055	--	13 000
19.	Shougang Corporation	China	Diversified	1 600	6 640	1 040	4 390	--	218 158
20.	Fraser & Neave Limited	Singapore	Food and beverages	1 578	4 273	1 230	1 912	11 461	13 131
21.	Samsung Electronics Co. Limited	Republic of Korea	Electronics and electrical equipment	--	16 301	--	13 050	--	57 817
22.	Singapore Airlines Limited	Singapore	Transportation	1 546	9 111	3 454	4 727	2 957	13 258
23.	Companhia Vale do Rio Doce	Brazil	Transportation	1 509	14 332	3 320	4 744	7 432	42 456

18

Exhibit 1.12
(continued)

24. Enersis S.A.	Chile	Electrical services	--	14 281	--	890	--	14 366
25. Acer Incorporated	Taiwan Province of China	Diversified	1 376	2 946	3 204	4 217	6 792	12 342
26. Orient Overseas (International) Limited	Hong Kong, China	Transportation	1 341	1 872	1 882	1 896	3 443	4 062
27. Companhia Cervejaria Brahma	Brazil	Food and beverages	--	3 854	106	2 490	--	10 955
28. China National Metals and Minerals Import and Export Corp.	China	Diversified	1 020	2 438	1 221	4 458	171	1 296
29. Gener S.A.	Chile	Electrical services	--	3 123	--	612	--	752
30. San Miguel Corporation	Philippines	Food and beverages	1 009	3 020	287	1 964	44 687	18 444
31. Tatung Co.	Taiwan Province of China	Electronics and electrical equipment	--	3 850	--	2155	--	19 570
32. Reliance Industries Limited	India	Chemicals and pharmaceuticals	--	6 175	--	1 982	--	17 375
33. Keppel Corporation Limited	Singapore	Diversified	889	4 490	346	2 078	1 700	11 300
34. Perez Companc S.A.	Argentina	Petroleum exploration/refining/distribution	875	4 450	191	1 370	527	4 446
35. Empresas CMPC S.A.	Chile	Pulp and paper	799	4 531	257	1 204	1 495	10 345
36. Compania de Petroleos de Chile (COPEC)	Chile	Diversified	791	6 368	138	3 147	493	8 277
37. China Harbor Engineering Company	China	Construction	770	2 210	240	1 530	1 889	76 460
38. Want Want Holdings, Limited	Singapore	Food and beverages	757	779	395	409	9 390	9 400
39. Sime Darby Berhad	Malaysia	Diversified	754	15 340	2 314	5 294	7 917	36 513
40. China National Foreign Trade Transportation Corp.	China	Transportation	740	2 160	440	750	488	57 368
41. South African Breweries Plc	South Africa	Food and beverages	--	3 757	1 923	5 244	8 579	47 902
42. Hong Kong and Shanghai Hotels Limited	Hong Kong, China	Tourism and hotel	654	3 242	85	356	3 247	6 008
43. Barlow Limited	South Africa	Diversified	--	2 597	--	4 125	--	27 804
44. Dong-Ah Construction Ind. Co. Limited	Republic of Korea	Construction	--	3 926	--	1 785	--	6 403
45. Souza Cruz S.A.	Brazil	Diversified	--	2 157	620	1 692	--	8 250
46. Gruma S.A. de C.V.	Mexico	Food and beverages	565	1 696	736	1 344	6 676	12 384
47. SABIC – Saudi Basic Industries Corp.	Saudi Arabia	Chemicals and pharmaceuticals	536	18 187	2 011	6 406	300	14 238
48. Sadia S.A. Industria e Comercio	Brazil	Food and beverages	--	1 799	--	2 569	--	25 375
49. Vitro S.A. de C.V.	Mexico	Other	481	3 290	458	2 474	4 203	33 136
50. Wing on International Holdings Limited	Hong Kong, China	Diversified	461	1 406	65	369	1 066	3 165

Source: UN Conference on Trade and Development.

pany has managed projects in countries from Indonesia to Nigeria. Its managers have drawn on their ability to make paper from inexpensive, locally available materials. In addition, they run a very efficient job-shop operation, with printing, folding, and cutting machinery selected or built in-house to make very short runs of a wide range of packaging for cigarettes, candy, and other items. Managers of MNCs from developed countries usually have forgotten these types of skills.

Although small-scale manufacturing remains the unique strength of MNCs in developing countries, these MNCs also are moving in other areas that are particularly suited for local conditions. A Thai company uses rice stalks for paper and plantain products for glue. A Brazilian company has developed sun-resistant dyes, as well as household appliances that withstand high humidity and survive the fluctuating voltages common in the developing world.

The rapid growth of developing countries' MNCs presents both a threat and an opportunity to MNCs from developed countries. The developing countries' MNCs can be tough competitors in building plants and chemical complexes that do not require high technology. But these MNCs also offer profitable opportunities to Western companies for joint operations. They lack marketing skills and thus may share their special know-how with traditional MNCs in exchange for the use of brand names and techniques for promoting new lines.

BACKLASH AGAINST MNCS

MNCs expanded relatively quietly during the 1950s and 1960s. The idea of both producing and selling abroad was welcomed by most countries, whether they were involved as investors or as hosts. The international transfer of capital, management, and technology created new jobs and helped develop natural resources. Within the prevailing world economic order, a favorable business environment grew in scores of countries. The system of fixed exchange rates, a downward trend in tariff barriers, and an expansive world economy encouraged companies—large and small—to join in and do business globally.

However, as the upsurge in international business gained strength during this period, questions began to be raised as to the economic, political, and social significance of the change, first in Europe and then elsewhere in the world. In France, the idea was advanced that the spread of U.S. business throughout Western Europe was generating a basic challenge to European societies, as well as to European corporations.[8] A second wave of concern, which gained momentum in the developing countries during the

1960s, arose within the UN Conference on Trade and Development (UNCTAD). A new world bloc emerged, urging improved terms of trade between developed and developing regions of the world and a redistribution of labor and wealth on an international scale. Its members—sometimes referred to as the Group of 77—began to view the rising strength of the MNCs as a threat rather than a benefit to their newly proposed world economic order.

This organized questioning of the concept of multinational business led, in the early 1970s, to passage of the UN Charter on Economic Rights and Duties of States. The charter was, and still is, viewed by business as an attempt at a basic reordering of the international economic environment. The impetus behind the charter soon led to the creation of the UN Commission on Transnational Corporations and the beginning of a code of conduct for international business dealings and international enterprises.

These movements and others around the world—fueled by recent revelations of questionable practices of some MNCs—have focused new attention on the fundamental concept of multinational enterprises. In many respects, the rising storm of criticism centers on basic social considerations more than on the economics of MNCs. The fundamental issue is the extent to which these enterprises are contributing to or threatening national economic and social development programs.

The criticism of MNCs does not come only from host countries. Domestic labor unions in the United States have decried MNCs for transferring jobs overseas and for entering into shady deals through bribery and politicking. Similarly, MNCs have been blamed for environmental decay and for ignoring the interests of the people in the United States. The major charges leveled against MNCs are discussed in following paragraphs.

MNCs Lack Transparency

One of the main concerns with MNCs is their invisibility. The most important source of information about MNCs is their annual reports. In addition, a torrent of information is available from public and private sources. Most often, however, these data are incomprehensible, incapable of being compared, incomplete with missing critical data sets, and frequently changing.[9] It is therefore not easy to make much sense out of them. Investors, regulators, legislators, and the general public end up confused about the true state of affairs of MNCs. Society is forced to depend on secondhand information, filtered data that cannot be audited. As Janet Lowe points out:

Unfortunately, for almost every meganational, it takes extra digging to find the information that casts a company in a lesser light. In most annual reports the situations where the society has decided the corporation has been remiss can be found buried in the footnotes to financial information under "other liabilities" or "contingencies," or some other ambiguous heading. The sentence or two that spells out the trouble often is inadequate. There is no question that further frankness is needed.[10]

MNCs Undermine Workers at Home

A buzzword, *stakeholders,* has become increasingly popular in the corporate world. It conveys the notion that stockholders are not the only proprietors of a company; a company also owes allegiance to customers, employees, and society at large. Opponents of this view claim that although all four kinds of proprietors are essential to a company's survival, business activity begins with those who take the risk and provide capital—that is, the stockholders—and that the most important purpose of a company is to maximize the stockholders' return.

It has been asserted that capital was claiming a large share of the return from production at the cost of employees, especially the production workers. In the United States, the earnings share of the value-added production had fallen over 20 years from 45 percent to 35 percent. In Germany, though wages remained high, the wage share of production returns had declined from 47 percent to 42 percent. A similar trend was observed in Japan.[11]

In developing countries, MNCs resist unions, arguing that local wages rise rapidly with or without unions as workers' productivity improves. Critics of MNCs question this claim and the evidence from the World Bank's tables did not support such an assertion. In places like Malaysia and Indonesia wages were indeed rising but the workers' share of the value-added returns kept falling, just as was happening with their better-off counterparts in U.S. and European factories.[12]

MNCs Destroy Local Culture

MNCs have been cited for the so-called McDonaldization of the world, that is, the standardization of all facets of peoples' lives globally. This standardization devalues the preservation and promotion of ethnic qualities, making the world less colorful and varied. MNCs seek standardization to realize scale efficiency, reduce costs, and make operations easier. David Korten has noted:

The architects of the corporate global vision seek a world in which universalized symbols created and owned by the world's most powerful corporations replace the distinctive cultural symbols that link people to particular places, values, and human communities. Our cultural symbols provide an important source of identity and meaning; they affirm our worth, our place in society. They arouse our loyalty to and sense of responsibility for the health and well being of our community and its distinctive ecosystem. When control of our cultural symbols passes to corporations, we are essentially yielding to them the power to define who we are. Instead of being Americans, Norwegians, Egyptians, Filipinos, or Mexicans, we become simply members of the "Pepsi generation," detached from place and any meaning other than those a corporation finds it profitable to confer on us. Market tyranny may be subtler than state tyranny, but it is no less effective in enslaving the many to the interests of the few.[13]

MNCs Exert Political Influence to Their Advantage

MNCs have too much power, which they use to influence local, national, and world events. Gerald Zilg illustrates the point with reference to Du Pont:

The du Ponts own the state Delaware. They control its state and local government; its major newspapers, radio, and TV stations; university and colleges; and its largest banks and industries, with four exceptions: Getty Oil, Phoenix Steel, and the Chrysler and General Foods plants, and even with these they have made profitable deals. The Du Pont Company alone employs more than 11 percent of Delaware's labor force, and when the family's other holdings are included, the percentage rises to over 75 percent. Throughout the United States, over a million Americans work to increase the du Pont fortune, and tens of thousands more work overseas at lower wages. Through one or more of their corporations, every nation in the "free" world is touched by the silver hand of the du Pont family.

Predictably, the long arm of Du Pont can also be found in Washington, D.C. Du Pont family members represent Delaware in both houses of Congress. In the last 25 years Du Pont lieutenants have served as representatives, senators, U.S. Attorney General, secretaries of defense, directors of CIA, and even Supreme Court justices.

With their power, "The Armorers of the Republic," as they like to call themselves, have helped drive America into world war, sabotaged world disarmament conferences, built deadly arsenals of atomic weapons and nerve gas, flirted with Nazis, and according to charges brought before a congressional committee, once were even implicated in an attempt to overthrow the U.S. government—at the same time managing to avoid their share of taxes. A family ambition that was once limited to a total American monopoly, their vision of domination has now been extended to every corner of the world.[14]

It is argued that in many countries, governments, at the demand of MNCs, prohibit all attempts to organize independent unions in order to prevent workers from collectively demanding higher wages. If unions are allowed, companies threaten to move their factories to nations where wages are even lower. As a matter of fact, some companies left Malaysia for Vietnam and China when the government did not cooperate.[15]

MNCs Take Advantage of Legal Loopholes

In theory MNCs are accountable to the governments of the countries in which they are registered and do business. But accountability is limited to particular areas, specified in the law. MNCs are quick to take advantage of legal loopholes, particularly in such critical areas as environmental damage and consumer protection. As Walter Adams and James Brock have said:

Through separation of ownership from management it [the MNC] has emancipated itself from the control of stockholders. By reinvestment of profits, it has eliminated the influence of the financier and capital market. By massive advertising, it has insulated itself from consumer sovereignty. By possession of market power, it has come to dominate both suppliers and customers. By judicious identification with the manipulation of the state, it has achieved autonomy. Whatever it cannot do for itself to assure survival and growth, a compliant government does on its behalf—assuring the maintenance of full employment, eliminating the risk of and subsidizing the investment in research and development, and assuring the supply of scientific and technical skills required by the modern techno structure. In return for this, the industrial giant performs society's planning function.[16]

MNCs Engage in Creative Accounting

MNCs have been found to use creative accounting practices to deprive governments of tax revenues.[17] BMW, for instance, claimed in 1993 that 95 percent of its profits (DM 1.5 billion) were made overseas. From 1988 to 1992, BMW reduced the taxes it paid to German authorities from DM 545 million to DM 31 million. The company was able to do so because it incurred as many expenditures as feasible in Germany, where taxes were highest. Similarly, IBM reported that one-third of its profits in 1987 were earned in operations in the United States, yet it paid no taxes. By deducting its worldwide

R&D expenditures against its U.S. income, IBM wiped out its federal tax liability. Intel treated profits from chips made in the United States as Japanese income for U.S. tax purposes by transferring the title of the goods to Japan. The result was that half of Intel's export income was exempt from U.S. tax. That income became so-called nowhere income—that is, income not taxable in any country—although the tax treaty between the United States and Japan explicitly required that such profit be treated as U.S. income.

MNCs Transfer Jobs Overseas

MNCs have no commitment to local communities. They abandon them when the economics of doing business at a particular place become unfavorable. Volkswagen closed its plant in Westmoreland County, Pennsylvania, despite the millions it had received in benefits. Similarly, U.S. companies conveniently trade away industrial jobs offshore if business wisdom suggests such a step. When Boeing announced a $5 billion order from China, President Clinton personally celebrated the deal at the White House. In Seattle, however, Boeing machinists and engineers were not excited about the deal, because it required that the tail sections of Boeing's most popular model, the midrange 737, be designed and manufactured in China.[18] Similarly, to seek entry for its European-made Opel in India, General Motors sold the business of its U.K. subsidiary to a company in India to manufacture about half the worldwide supply of Opel radiator caps. Jobs moved from Britain.

MNCs Squeeze Money from Communities for Locating Business

MNCs use their flexibility in shifting manufacturing from one nation to another to seek benefits from the public treasury to locate jobs at a particular location. Ford's chief executive officer (CEO), Alexander Trotman, himself British, threatened that if the British government did not provide an additional $150 million in state aid for its Jaguar plant in the United Kingdom, the company would move the production of a new Jaguar model and a thousand jobs to the United States.[19] Ohio paid $16 million in direct incentives to Honda for a plant in Marysville in 1982. Kentucky spent $125 million to lure Toyota to assemble its cars in the state. The price for jobs continues to rise. The package that wins the last factory becomes the opening bid for the next plant. Tennessee gave Nissan $11,000 per job for a plant in Smyrna. South Carolina put up $79,000 per job for a BMW plant, and Alabama committed $100,000 per job to Mercedes-Benz.[20]

MNCs Treat Labor Unfairly in Developing Countries

MNCs are held responsible for the unfair treatment of labor in developing countries. Harley Shaiken observed that the productivity of Mexican automobile workers was up 40 percent since 1990, but that real wages in pesos were down 40 percent.[21] Similar divergences have been noted in the Asian labor market. Consider the case of shirts. U.S. workers could make a shirt with 14 minutes of human labor, whereas workers in Bangladesh took 25 minutes. The average U.S. wage in the industry has been $7.53 an hour, whereas in Bangladesh it has been $.25, an edge that would not be erased if Bangladesh wages were doubled or quadrupled.[22] *Business Week* has described the filthy conditions in overseas factories:

> In foreign-funded factories, which employ about 6 million Chinese in the coastal provinces, accidents abound. In some factories, workers are chastised, beaten, strip-searched, and even forbidden to use the bathroom during work hours. At a foreign-owned company in the Fujian province city of Ziamen, 40 workers—or one-tenth of the work force—have had their fingers crushed by obsolete machines. According to official reports, there were 45,000 industrial accidents in Guangdong last year, claiming more than 8,700 lives. Last month 76 workers died in Guangdong factory accident.[23]

CONCLUSION

There are as many arguments that favor MNCs as there are arguments that oppose them. MNCs, on the whole, have made significant positive contributions to economic and social progress throughout the world. Through their technological and managerial capabilities, MNCs have helped develop the material and productive resources of many nations and have worked to meet the world's growing needs for goods and services. Their investments have stimulated the diversification of local national economies. Their capital input has helped host governments fulfill nationally defined economic development goals. They have provided jobs and helped to raise living standards in many areas.

But in the 1970s, in response to the various criticisms of MNCs, significant changes occurred that affected the world environment in which MNCs must operate. Many MNCs responded appropriately by adopting new perspectives for doing business overseas. A number of MNCs issued codes of ethical conduct for transacting business abroad.[24] Many governments around the world took measures to regulate MNC operations in their countries. The measures adopted by the United States and other individual governments and the voluntary acts of the corporations have mitigated several problems. At the same time, as developing countries gain experience, they should be able to negotiate with the MNCs from a new vantage point. Still, some problems need to be addressed, especially problems relating to workers' living conditions in developing countries, protection of the environment, and respect of local cultures.

NOTES

1. United Nations, *World Investment Report* 2001: Promoting Linkages (Geneva: United Nations Conference on Trade and Development, 2001), p. xvii.

2. Ibid., pp. 3–6.

3. *World Trade Organization Newsletter*, March 2002.

4. A.V. Krebs, *The Corporate Reapers: The Book of Agribusiness* (Washington, D.C.: Essential Books, 1992).

5. World Bank, *World Development Indicators* (Washington, D.C.: World Bank, 2000).

6. United Nations, *World Investment Report,* pp. 77–84.

7. Figures in this section are taken from Organization for Economic Cooperation and Development, *Measuring Globalization: The Role of Multinationals* (Paris: OECD, 2000).

8. See J.J. Servanschreiber, *The American Challenge* (New York: Atheneum, 1968).

9. David J. Saari, *Global Corporations and Sovereign Nations* (Westport, Conn.: Quorum Books, 1999).

10. Janet Lowe, The *Secret Empire: How 25 Multinationals Rule the World* (Homewood, Ill.: Business One Irwin, 1992), p. 204.

11. William Greider, *One World, Ready or Not: The Manic Logic of Global Capitalism* (New York: Touchstone, 1998), p. 75.

12. The World Bank tables, 2000.

13. David C. Korten, *When Corporations Rule the World* (San Francisco: Berrett-Koehler Publishers/Kumarian Press, 1995), p. 158.

14. Gerard Colby Zilg, *Du Pont: Behind the Nylon Curtain* (Englewood Cliffs, N.J.: Prentice Hall, 1974), p. 28.

15. G-Pascal Zachary, *The Global Me* (New York: Public Affairs, 2000), p. 53.

16. Walter Adams and James Brock, *The Bigness Complex* (New York: Pantheon Books, 1986), pp. 73–75.

17. For the BMW, IBM, and Intel examples discussed in this section, see Greider, *One World, Ready or Not,* p. 95.

18. Reported by Reuters, 21 March 1996.

19. *Financial Times,* 6 January 1995.

20. U.S. Congress, Office of Technology Assessment, *Bidding War: Multinationals and National Interest: Playing by Different Rules* (Washington, D.C.: Office of Technology Assessment, September 1993).

21. Remarks made by Harley Shaiken at the Economic Strategy Institute Conference, Washington, D.C., 9 March 1994.

22. Richard Rothstein, *Workforce Globalization: A Policy Response* (Washington, D.C.: Brookings Institution, 2000).

23. "Damping Labor's Fires," *Business Week,* 1 August 1994, pp. 40–41.

24. "A New Partnership between Businessmen and Diplomats," *Nation's Business,* September 1974, pp. 74–75.

Chapter 2

FORCES AT WORK

The powerful forces of technology, economic liberalization, and deregulation surround us in a historic convergence. These forces are sudden and radical, and they necessitate a basic reorientation of all institutions. They are not mere trends but large, unruly forces: the deregulation of economies worldwide, the liberalization of global trade, and the technological development in the fields of communications and transportation.

None of these transformations is a passing phenomenon. All are happening at the same time and at a fast rate. They cause and influence one another, and they thus give birth to a new era, nourishing a feeling that business and society are in the midst of a revolution comparable in scale and consequence to the Industrial Revolution.

DEREGULATION

In the post–World War II period, nations assumed a significant role in controlling economic activity within their borders. Even in the Western countries, such as Great Britain and France, a number of industries—airlines, banks, broadcasting, and utilities—were government owned and run as public sector enterprises. The developing countries everywhere went much further by creating a huge public sector of business enterprises in both manufacturing and service industries. Most of these businesses produced goods of mediocre quality at high cost and thus incurred heavy losses. Inasmuch as the deep pockets of the government could be used to absorb those losses, public sector companies were considered essential to prevent private business from making easy money at the expense of the people.

In the 1980s, governments in Western countries began to have second thoughts about the public sector. With Margaret Thatcher at the helm in Great Britain, a number of companies previously owned by the government were privatized. Other countries followed Britain's lead.

After the breakdown of the Soviet Union, governments in developing countries started raising questions about the vitality of public sector enterprises. In the 1990s, practically all developing countries initiated privatization programs for business.

While public ownership prevented individual citizens from participating in many industries, governments imposed a variety of rules and regulations to keep foreign companies at bay. Some industries were totally banned for foreign involvement. In other industries, foreigners could hold only subordinate positions. In addition, the freedom of foreign companies was curtailed in various ways. Foreign companies could not import machinery, parts, or inputs freely. Their marketing decisions, which extended to which products to manufacture, as well as their pricing, distribution, and promotion, required government permission. Moreover, in other areas they had to overcome many hurdles to run a business. For example, they could not raise capital freely or lay off workers at will. To be concise, in the name of establishing a national base of industries, governments erected huge barriers to discourage entry of foreign companies.

In the past decade, the legitimacy of the role of governments in running national economies has come under question. As a consequence, regulations have been relaxed, and barriers—such as foreign exchange controls; ownership restrictions; and access to capital, infrastructure, and information—have been dismantled. The creed of national interest and ownership that had discouraged international competition was swept away. Today, most nations welcome foreign investment. As a matter of fact, many governments have promotional programs to attract overseas investment. Foreign delegations of political and business leaders from developing nations often call on CEOs of large MNCs to woo them to their countries.

The widespread decision during the 1990s to open markets, allow foreign investment, and otherwise liberalize business has led to a large-scale political revolution. Politics in earlier years kept a considerable part of the world separate, thanks to ideology and beliefs about self-sufficiency. The demise of these economic barriers has brought many nations closer to one another.

The scope of the deregulation varies from nation to nation. Western nations, particularly Great Britain, Germany, and France, have gone much further than the developing nations. They have privatized many companies; undertaken programs to abandon numerous older regulations and modify rules in the fields of environment, health, banking, and insurance; and reduced corporate taxes. Economies in transition, such as the economies of the Central and Eastern European nations of Poland, Hungary, the Czech Republic, Romania, Bulgaria, and others, have adopted privatization programs and enacted laws to attract foreign investment and create a favorable business climate. Among the developing countries, Mexico, Brazil, Turkey, Thailand, and South Africa have been more forward-llooking than Argentina, Egypt, and Indonesia. The latter countries have been cautious in their deregulation programs. Eager to be full-fledged members of Western international institutions, large countries such as China, India, and Russia strive to adopt the rules by which those institutions operate. Given the sheer weight of these countries, each one can reasonably hope for a major role in international affairs once it has developed the economic capability to play such a role.[1] Therefore, these countries may further deregulate their economies.

At the threshold of the new century, practically all nations are opening their economies to the world, and this process is likely to continue. Take the case of the telecommunications industry. Fifteen years ago, most member countries of the OECD and almost all developing nations held in state ownership the telecommunications sector, power, a large proportion of banking, and the entirety of the education and health care systems. What the state did not own, it regulated. Today, these sectors are fast becoming local and private domains.

According to UN data, between 1990 and 2000, governments made 980 changes in the regulating regimes relating to FDI. Of these changes, 95 percent concerned deregulation and liberalization. The number of countries deregulating FDI regulatory regimes increased from 35 in 1991 to 76 in 1997, and to 98 in 2000. Even the Asian financial crisis did not hinder the deregulation process.[2] Although Malaysia did impose strict capital control measures, it had to relax them a year later.

The deregulation process allows developing nations to benefit from inward (and outward) FDI, as well as from the accompanying transfer of technology, easier access to foreign markets for differentiated goods, and the realization of the need for high-quality socioeconomic infrastructure (a need made apparent by close integration with more advanced economies). The impact of deregulation on inward FDI is shown in Exhibit 2.1, which

Exhibit 2.1
Ratio of Inward FDI Stock to GDP (in billions): 1980, 1985, 1990, 1995, 1998, and 2000 (in percentages).

Country	1980	1985	1990	1995	1998	2000	Multiple
Argentina	6.90	7.50	6.40	15.80	15.80	22.10	2.05
Brazil	7.50	11.50	8.00	17.10	17.10	21.60	3.67
Chile	3.30	14.00	33.30	39.30	39.30	55.30	2.12
China	3.10	3.40	7.00	28.10	28.10	30.80	1.55
Costa Rica	14.50	25.50	24.50	30.00	40.00	42.30	1.40
Egypt	10.00	16.40	25.50	23.40	20.20	19.70	0.86
Indonesia	13.20	28.70	34.00	25.00	72.70	46.20	1.84
Malaysia	21.10	23.70	24.10	32.90	62.30	65.40	1.97
Morocco	1.10	3.10	3.50	9.10	13.50	15.90	1.78
Philippines	4.00	8.50	7.40	8.20	14.30	14.90	1.87
Republic of South Africa	2.00	15.70	8.20	9.90	11.70	13.00	1.30
Slovenia	-	-	-	9.60	14.90	14.50	1.40
Thailand	3.10	5.10	9.60	10.40	18.30	21.40	2.10
Tunisia	6.60	8.20	5.90	6.60	6.00	5.70	0.80
Turkey	0.15	0.60	0.90	3.00	3.80	4.50	1.33
Vietman	-	0.00	4.60	3.10	4.90	5.20	1.68
Average	12.50	16.90	14.60	20.00	30.00	31.00	1.73

Note: The column marked "Multiple" gives the ratio of the value for 2000 to the value for 1995.
Source: Based on *World Development Indicators* (New York: Oxford University Press, 2001) and UN Conference on Trade and Development.

examines the ratio of inward FDI stock to GDP for 16 countries from 1980 through 2000. A clear majority of the 16 countries have positive ratios of inward FDI to GDP, showing that with deregulation, more FDI has flowed into these nations.

TRADE LIBERALIZATION

Commerce is older than recorded history. Archaeological discoveries give evidence of the antiquity of trade. Thousand of ancient commercial documents indicate that a considerable commercial class existed many centuries before any European or Mediterranean city attained a high degree of civilization. In the ancient world, people had even developed a system of payment of precious objects for traded goods—a forerunner of the modern system.

Trading has evolved through the ages in response to altering needs spurred by changes in technology and philosophy. Growth in trade was particularly stimulated by the discovery and use of metals and by the global horizons provided by advances, first in transportation and later in communication. Trade has evolved from exchanges between isolated peoples, to trade through conquest, to trade among friendly neighbors, to a system of silent barter among both adversaries and friends. World trade is not a new phenomenon. Groups of people have always traded.

As civilization progressed around the world, however, trading became more organized and productive. For example, ancient seaborne commerce was inefficient and proportionately insignificant. Piracy and ship raids were commonplace. Such hazards discouraged trade expansion and required that harbors be fortified for protection. In modern times, although nations still go to war, piracy and raiding have been virtually eliminated by a variety of treaties, arrangements, and other international laws.

World trade requires that nations be willing to cooperate with one another. Countries naturally trade with those nations with whom they are on friendly terms. Nonetheless, trading often goes on among nations even when political relations are not amicable.

The Theory of Comparative Advantage

The classical economists—Adam Smith, David Ricardo, and John Stuart Mill—are credited with providing the theoretical economic justification for international trade. In simple terms, modern trade takes place because a foreign industry is able to provide a material or product cheaper than native industry can. For example, if the landed cost of a Japanese-made television is less than the cost of a television made in the United States, it makes economic sense for the United States to import televisions from Japan. Likewise, if U.S. computers can be sold at lower prices in Japan than computers manufactured in Japan, Japanese businesses will find it economically desirable to import U.S. computers.

Ricardo advanced the concept of relative or comparative cost as the basis of international trade. He emphasized labor costs more than other aspects of production. He thought such aspects as land and capital either were of no significance or were so evenly distributed overall that they always operated in a fixed proportion, whereas labor did not. The theory of comparative advantage states that even if a country is able to produce all its goods at lower costs than another country can, trade still benefits both countries, based on comparative, not absolute, costs. In other words, countries should concentrate on producing goods that have advantage compared with the goods of other countries and then export those goods in exchange for goods that command advantage in their native countries. The key to the concept is the word *comparative,* which implies that each and every country has both a definite advantage in some goods and a definite disadvantage in other goods.

No matter how we look at it, the internationalization of trade appears to perpetuate worldwide prosperity. Despite that finding, no country permits international trade dealings without some conditions. Governments impose all sorts of barriers to restrict trade across national boundaries. But there are reasons for trade barriers and for the international efforts to liberalize trade.

The real purpose behind barriers is to protect national interests. Arguments that countries advance for such protection include the following:[3]

- *Keep money at home.* Barriers prevent national wealth from being transferred in exchange with another nation for goods.
- *Help home markets.* Barriers help perpetuate home industry.
- *Equalize costs of production.* Barriers allow local goods to compete fairly against imports, which otherwise may be cheaper because of technological advantages or similar reasons.
- *Protect against low wages.* Barriers protect home industry from imports from low-wage countries.
- *Protect employment.* Barriers protect the level of home employment.
- *Protect against dumping.* Barriers protect against dumping of foreign products.
- *Allow bargaining and retaliation.* Barriers allow a country to seek reduction of tariffs by other countries or to retaliate against another country.
- *Promote national security.* Barriers allow a country to be on its own for national security reasons during events such as war or natural calamities.
- *Help infant industries.* Barriers encourage new industry in a country.
- *Promote diversification.* Barriers promote a broad spectrum of industries in a country.

Countries use two types of barriers, tariff and nontariff barriers, to restrict trade. Tariff barriers are taxes such as customs duties levied on goods moved between nations. Different nations handle tariff barriers differently. A country may have a single tariff system for all goods from all sources, called a *unilinear* or *single-column tariff.* Another type of tariff is the general-conventional tariff. This tariff applies to all nations except countries that have tariff treaties (or conventions to that effect) with a particular country. A tariff may be worked out on the basis of a tax permit, called *specific duty,* or as a percentage of the value of the item, which is referred to as *ad valorem duty.* Sometimes both specific and ad valorem duties may be levied on the same item as a combined duty.

Nontariff barriers include quotas, import equalization taxes, road taxes, laws giving preferential treatment to domestic suppliers, and administration of antidumping measures that impede trade. Subsidies, quotas, and monetary barriers are the most common nontariff barriers. Many nations provide direct payments (i.e., subsidies) to select industries to enable them to compete effectively against imports. For example, in 2001, the U.S. government agreed to a kind of subsidy for the steel industry to strengthen its position against Japanese imports. Quotas impose a limit on the quantity of one kind of good that a country permits to be imported. A quota may be applied on a specific-country basis or on a global basis without reference to exporting countries. The United States, for example, has established quotas for textile imports from particular countries. Monetary barriers are exchange controls, of which there are three widespread types: blocked currency, differential exchange rates, and government approval to secure foreign exchange. Currency blockage totally cuts importing by completely restricting the availability of foreign exchange. This barrier often is used politically against one or more nations. The differential exchange rate barrier describes setting different rates for converting local currency into the foreign currency needed to import goods from overseas. A government can set higher conversion rates for items whose imports it wishes to restrict and lower rates for imports it desires. Finally, a government may require specific approval before it allows the import of any goods. Most developing countries that are working toward maintaining a secure foreign exchange position only grudgingly grant such approval, which often is accompanied by a variety of hindrances and bureaucratic headaches. Additionally, many nations define their nontariff barriers in broad terms, leaving much to the interpretation and discretion of government officials. This tendency makes assessment of certain countries difficult.

The Perpetuation of Free Trade

Internationally, systematic efforts to promote free trade started after World War II. A keen awareness of the need to achieve economic prosperity grew among nations. The war years had shattered Europe and Japan, and they needed reconstruction. A number of countries were wresting independence from colonial rulers, particularly from Great Britain. It did not take long for these countries to realize that political freedom alone was not sufficient. Economic prosperity was necessary not only for existence but also for long-term survival and growth. Countries realized that planned international cooperation fostered economic development and prosperity. Thus, immediately after the war, nations agreed to a framework of international rules to maintain monetary discipline and reduce trade barriers.

Monetary Discipline

After long and careful deliberations, a monetary system was decided upon at the UN Monetary and Financial Conferences held at Bretton Woods, New Hampshire, in 1944. Member countries agreed to control the limits of their exchange rates in a predetermined way. The exchange rates were permitted to vary by 1 percent above or below a par. As a country's rate of exchange attained or approached its limit, called an *arbitrage support point,* its central bank intervened in the market to prevent the rate from passing the limit. Market intervention required a nation to accumulate international reserves of gold and foreign currencies, above normal trading requirements. An institution called the International Monetary Fund (IMF) was established at Bretton Woods to oversee the newly agreed upon monetary system.

More and more nations joined the original 55 IMF signatories; today the IMF has over 200 members. With the passage of time, various changes have been made in the IMF system to ameliorate the difficulties that nations faced or to respond to emerging issues.

Tariff Reduction Programs

In 1947, the United States and 22 other major trading countries met in Geneva, Switzerland, to find ways to reduce tariffs and remove trade barriers. The General Agreement on Tariffs and Trade (GATT) resulted. The intention of the participants at the Geneva gathering was to establish a permanent body like the IMF to oversee tariff reduction on an ongoing basis. Unfortunately, the members maintained wide differences on the structure and power of such a body; therefore, they decided to enter into an ad hoc tariff reduction agreement and postponed the idea of a permanent organi-

Exhibit 2.2
Dimensions of Agreements under GATT

Major Agreements	Number of Contracting Parties	Value of World Trade Involved (Billions of Dollars)	Percentage of Average Tariff Reduction
1947 Geneva	23	$10.0	-
1949 Annecy, France	33	-	-
1951 Torquay, England	37	-	-
1956 Geneva	35	2.5	4
1962 Geneva (Dillion Round)	40	4.9	7
1967 Geneva (Kennedy Round)	70	40.0	35
1973 Tokyo (Tokyo Round)	85	115.0	50
1986 Punta del Este (Uruguay Round)	117	450.0	70

zation for the future. But since the ad hoc agreement (that is, GATT) worked out to be a great success, member countries made GATT a permanent office for global tariff reduction endeavors. Since then, seven additional major efforts to reduce trade barriers have been undertaken under the auspices of GATT (see Exhibit 2.2).

The first two rounds of meetings, the 1947 Geneva and 1949 Annecy, France, meetings, are considered significant, both for tariff reduction and for structuring GATT's organization. The 1951 Torquay, England, and the 1956 Geneva meetings are regarded as less important. Insurmountable differences arose among nations over the issue of tariff disparities, that is, the imbalance between the high tariff of one country and the low tariff of another. In 1962, the Dillon Round resulted in further reduction of average world tariff rates. But it fell short of its goals: an across-the-board 20 percent reduction of tariffs and the resolution of problems unsolved since the 1956 meeting, especially problems involving trade agreements with less developed countries.

The Kennedy Round, sixth in the series, was the most comprehensive round of negotiations in terms of the number of participating countries, the value of the world trade involved, and the size of tariff reductions. The negotiations were concluded in 1972, with tariffs reduced on some sixty thousand commodities valued at $40 billion in world trade. Despite its success, the Kennedy Round did not quite meet all the ambitious goals set for it. A major goal of the Kennedy Round had been a 50 percent across-the-board reduction in tariffs of industrial products. However, overriding national interests forced exceptions for such commodities as chemicals, steel, aluminum, pulp, and paper. The question of tariff disparities, linked with the 50 percent goal, also yielded to exceptions because many Western European countries raised objections. Overall, the Kennedy Round negotiators agreed to tariff cuts that averaged about 35 percent on industrial products. The round was also meant to resolve the problem of nontariff barriers, but the results were rather modest except for the adoption of an antidumping code.

The principal objective of the Tokyo Round in 1973, seventh in the negotiation series, was the expansion and ever-greater liberalization of world trade. The Tokyo Round recognized that the scope of exceptions should be limited, and it supported the general feeling that the special interests of the developing countries should be borne in mind in the tariff negotiations. The Tokyo Round, concluding in 1978, was the most complex and comprehensive trade-negotiating effort attempted up to that time. It tried to develop a substantially freer world trading system with balanced opportunities for countries with different economic and political systems and needs. Although the actual achievements of the Tokyo Round fell short of the goals, the overall results were very encouraging.

During its existence, GATT had some successes: average tariffs in industrial countries tumbled to around 5 percent in 1986 from an average of 40 percent in 1947. The volume of trade in manufactured goods multiplied 20-fold. GATT's membership increased fivefold. But the growing protectionism nurtured by the economic difficulties that had beset the world since the 1970s undermined the credibility of GATT and threatened the open trading system it upheld. Cars, steel, videocassette recorders, semiconductors, and shoes have followed textiles and clothing into the category of managed trade. The United States, the European Community, and Japan were spending a total of $70 billion a year on agricultural subsidies, and GATT rules proved unworkable. GATT did not cover services (nearly 30 percent of all world trade), investment abroad, or intellectual property (patents, copyrights, and so on), which were of growing importance to the rich countries as the centers of manufacturing increasingly shifted to the developing countries.

Protectionist forces had been gaining momentum, particularly in the United States. In Europe, where half of all economic activity related to trade, U.S. protectionist sentiments created uneasiness. The Europeans had warned that they would retaliate if the United States adopted protective measures. The developing economies did not know what to do, because the Western nations constituted a big market for their limited exportable products. Individual efforts by different nations to meet the protectionist threat did not succeed. One of the achievements of the post–

World War II trade liberalization had been the expansion of world trade, which was being challenged in the 1980s. What countries could not accomplish unilaterally, however, they thought they might be able to accomplish under the GATT umbrella.

The conditions for another round of trade talks were ripe. In November 1985, 90 countries unanimously agreed to a U.S. proposal to launch a new round of global trade talks, the eighth in the negotiation series. Thus, the Uruguay Round began in September 1986 in Punta del Este, Uruguay. The focus of this round was on agricultural exports, services, intellectual properties, and voluntary trade limits.

In December 1993, after tortuous negotiations, trade officials from 117 nations wrapped up a Uruguay Round trade pact that slashed tariffs and reduced subsidies globally. It was intended to reduce barriers to trade in goods, including tariffs and such nontariff barriers as quotas, export subsidies, and anti-import regulations. It was also intended to extend the 47-year-old GATT, which functioned as the rule book for international trade, to cover agriculture, financial and other services, and intellectual property such as patents. The Uruguay Round agreement met some of these goals, but negotiators jettisoned several controversial issues at the last minute. The agreement created the World Trade Organization (WTO) to replace the GATT secretariat. The WTO has more authority to oversee trade in services and agriculture than the GATT did.

The delegates from nations met again in Doha, Qatar, in November 2001 and agreed on beginning a new round of trade talks. If the agenda set for this round is accepted, global trade will be further liberalized, which could increase growth by as much as $600 billion and be a welcome boon to developing countries. Although these gains would take several years to achieve, just starting negotiations would strengthen the rule-based trade system and restrain protectionist impulses.

Liberalization of trade has played a major role in creating worldwide economic prosperity. Practically all nations have gained significantly from trading across borders. Overall, since the 1950s trade has been expanding faster than world output. As a matter of fact, even in the midst of the Asian financial crisis, merchandise exports grew at 9.5 percent in 1997. At the end of 2001, the total value of world merchandise trade was estimated at over $5.8 trillion. It is forecast to continue to rise at a higher rate in the coming years as nations further liberalize broad areas of economic activity, particularly within service sectors.[4]

Trade is a vital part of development strategy. Should the newly launched global trade negotiations, the Doha development agenda, succeed in halving trade barriers in agriculture and textiles alone, developing countries would gain more than $200 billion a year in additional income by 2015.[5]

TECHNOLOGY

Technological developments result from research efforts. Two types of research can be distinguished: basic and applied. Research is funded either by governments or by companies themselves. In most countries, the government plays a crucial role in sponsoring basic research. Companies mainly concentrate on applied research, although large MNCs often engage in basic research as well.

Technology has three different aspects: the type, process, and impetus for development. Technology itself can be grouped into five categories: energy, materials, transportation, communications and information, and genetics (which includes agronomic and biomedical). The impetus for technological breakthroughs can originate from any or all of three sources: defense needs, the common welfare, and the commercial market. The three stages in the process of technological development are invention, the creation of a new product or process; innovation, the introduction of that product or process into use; and diffusion, the spread of the product or process beyond its first use.

Since World War II, technology has made headway in all categories. Advances in areas such as materials, energy, and medicine have all contributed toward bringing together people from across the planet. However, the advances with the greatest impact are in transportation and communications and information, and it is with these two areas that this book is most concerned.

Transportation

In 1956, a hauler from North Carolina converted a vessel sailing from Newark, New Jersey, to Houston, Texas, so that it could carry trailers. This process eliminated the need to unload goods from trucks into warehouses at the port and then reload the goods from the warehouses to ships. A few years later, ships carrying detachable trailers were plying the seas carrying manufactured goods of all kinds. Companies were more willing to import sophisticated goods, because they could be fully protected in shipment. Meanwhile, shipping costs declined tremendously, because containers could be transported from a company's plant to the ship without the need for other handling in between. The greatest impact of this development has been the shift in the nature of goods being shipped overseas. Manufactured goods replaced raw food and crude materials by a huge margin. Soon container transportation spread to railways and airlines as well. Thus, boxes are switched rapidly from one kind of carrier to another with little human labor. A typical ship today spends about 24 hours in a port instead of 3 or 4 weeks, as was the case previously.[6] Cheaper, quicker, and safer transportation opened new markets for all sorts of goods, encouraging even small firms to enter the foreign trade.

Communications and Information

In the past, electronic communication was largely confined to the traditional definition, which included voice (telephone), pictures (television), and graphics (computer), three different kinds of communication devices. Now, electronics can produce total communications. It is possible to make simultaneous and instantaneous electronic transmission of voice, pictures, and graphics. People scattered over the globe now can talk to one another directly; see one another; and if necessary, share the same reports, documents, and graphs without leaving their offices or homes.

The real revolution in communications began in the 1990s as the use of the personal computer (PC) became widespread, declaring the arrival of the information age. Today there are about half a billion PCs in the world, 1 for every 12 people. It is true that as many as 40 percent of the PCs are in the United States, but this percentage has been declining slowly as families in large developing countries such as China and India begin to acquire PCs.[7]

PCs alone, however, would not have meant much if not for two other developments: digitalization and the Internet. Today, virtually everything—voices on telephones, pictures on screens, and human decisions—can be converted into 0s and 1s, and then stored or transmitted. John Micklethwait and Adrian Wooldrige note: "Indeed, if there is such a thing as a universal language, it is not English but binary: A Chinese computer speaks exactly the same language as a Spanish one, as well as the same one as a Spanish digital phone."[8]

In 1990, the concept of the Internet was at the talking stage, limited to academics. In 2001, half a billion people use the Internet. The World Wide Web allows people access to a vast amount of information from virtually anywhere in the world. In coming years, the Internet will change how people live, work, play, and learn. As the Industrial Revolution brought together people with machines in factories, the Internet revolution will bring together people with knowledge and information in virtual environments worldwide. The Industrial Revolution took place over the course of a hundred years; the Internet revolution will encompass the globe in one-fourth the time.[9]

The real potential of the Internet has yet to be realized. Today it is more or less a hobby for people in the United States, with white-collar workers from advanced nations and a few educated urbanities in developing countries also using it. Lack of infrastructure and hardware has slowed down its universal application. For example, the entire continent of Africa has fewer telephones than either Tokyo or Manhattan.

But the Internet is bound to triumph with the help of further technological developments. For example, fiber optics will make information transfer much faster and cheaper. A pair of fibers, no thicker than a human hair, can carry all the voice traffic passing across the Atlantic at any moment. Rather than going from switch to switch, packets of digital or voice data will float through connectionless networks, based on Internet protocols with small access fees. According to Craig Barrett, an Intel executive, the Internet ultimately will create a seventh continent—a world of 1 billion connected computers.[10]

Along with the Internet, another noteworthy development has been the emergence of the mobile phone. A surprising shift between the developed and developing countries has occurred. In the latter, the mobile phone is a necessity, because traditional telephone infrastructure is highly inadequate; in the developed world, in contrast, the mobile phone is only one advancement among many. But the result is that the mobile phone permits individuals in developing countries to connect to the outside world. This point may be illustrated with reference to Bangladesh. There is 1 phone for every 300 people, and 90 percent of the nation's 68,000 villages have no traditional telephone connection. But the mobile phone has changed the situation. A new group of entrepreneurs, called *the phone ladies,* using loans from a private firm specializing in microlending, buy state-of-the-art cell phones and rent out telephone time. Farmers are the major customers. With the cell phones, farmers are able to find out the fair value of their crops instead of accepting whatever the intermediaries have offered. Today, practically everybody in the country is within two kilometers of a mobile phone.[11]

As further developments permit the compatibility of three devices— mobile phones, computers, and personal organizers—a single handheld device may be created. As the number of wireless devices with Internet access increases, there will be a dramatic expansion of Internet use in places like New Delhi, Beijing, Djakarta, and Rio de Janeiro.

The result of the technological developments discussed above will be the death of distance, reducing the importance of geography. Examples abound. Netscape has been selling its software around the globe without ever leaving California. Amazon.com became a global bookseller without setting foot outside Seattle. Most of the clients of Infosys, an Indian software firm, are in the United States. Toward the end of a workday, customers in the United States e-mail their problems to the Infosys office in Bangalore, India, whose technicians work on them and e-mail the solutions back to the United States by the beginning of the next day. Technicians at Infosys work while Americans slumber, and vice versa. In other words, by taking advantage of the time differences between different regions of the world, information technology has made a 24-hour work shift feasible. The possibilities are unlimited.

THE BIRTH OF A NEW ERA

The forces discussed in the previous section have transformed the global business environment profoundly. The power and influence of institutions that shape market functions and structures has shifted. Assumptions related to the role of the nation-state and MNCs have been radically revised. Furthermore, interdependencies among nations have increased so that economic downturns and crises are not limited to a nation or a region but have an impact on the entire globe. The implication is that the global business environment is complex and interconnected. It appears that a new era is taking shape. The characteristics of this emerging reality are clustered under three headings, each of which will be addressed in this section: the mobility of capital, the new consumer class, and the leveraging of knowledge and talent. The impact of any one of these groups of characteristics is powerful enough in its own right, but what has given them their invincibility in recent years is the fact that they all fit together neatly. Free-flowing capital is readily available to companies, even in remote places. A new class of customers constitutes a tremendous market opportunity. Finally, knowledge and talent can be easily located and used on a global basis.

The Mobility of Capital

One impact of the forces discussed in this chapter has been the growth and integration of the world's capital markets. In the 1980s, many governments abandoned capital controls; that is, currency rates have been determined by demand and supply rather than by the central banks. Because owners of capital want to place their money where they get the maximum return with the least risk, capital flows freely around the globe searching for better returns and opportunities. Deals can be struck and concluded electronically in a split second.

With foreign exchange and bonds becoming integrated, one price prevails throughout the world. In turn, equity markets begin to integrate, making capital more mobile. Capital flows across borders increased from about $.5 trillion in 1991, to about $1.3 trillion in 1995, and to $5.6 trillion in 2000, excluding foreign direct investment. The world's stock of liquid financial assets grew from $10.7 trillion in 1990, to $41.5 trillion in 1994, and to $90.2 trillion in 2000.[12]

A significant proportion of these capital flows goes to developing countries that traditionally depended on international institutions such as the IMF and the World Bank for financing. For example, 50 percent of FDI over 10 percent of portfolio capital flows is directed toward these markets, even though such markets account for less than 25 percent of world GDP.[13] Furthermore, these flows are directed more toward long-term financing.

The capital market trends affect global business and trade in a variety of ways. First, they are forcing a convergence of economic policy worldwide. Nations that the capital markets perceive as fiscally responsible and politically committed to market-based policies are asked to attract capital they need to finance growth and infrastructure development. Second, companies anywhere in the world are able to obtain capital as long as they generate high returns. A virtually limitless supply of relatively inexpensive capital is available to fund corporate growth. Finally, capital markets are focusing on shareholders' value and market capitalization as the dominant factors for measuring corporate performance.

Overall, the world's capital markets now possess both the power and the instruments to globalize the world economy. Countries that get rid of capital controls and liberalize their banking systems see more efficient investment, because markets allocate money better than bureaucrats do. Economies fare best when capital is cheap, plentiful, and just as important, allocated fairly.

The amount of capital in circulation is greater than ever before, and it is expected to expand hugely as more people learn to invest in the stock market. About 45 percent of people in the United States owns shares or mutual funds, whereas in Great Britain one in four owns shares. In France, the figure is 15 percent, whereas in Italy it is about 10 percent and in Germany, slightly less.[14] In 1990 there were probably about 100 million people on the planet who owned a share of stock or had a pension plan. By 2010, that number is likely to rise to 1 billion. China's stock market is only 10 years old, but the country already has more than 60 million retail stockholders—a larger number than the Communist Party can boast.[15]

If more and more people in developing countries learn to invest in capital markets and the number of shareholders on the European Continent increases to British levels, the capital market will be three times as large in 2010 as it is today. As time passes, more and more money will be invested outside the home country, bringing the world closer together.[16] This trend will occur because long-term prospects for growth in developing countries confidently outstrip prospects in the United States or Europe.

The New Consumer Class

Traditionally, MNCs depended on their customer base in the developed countries. To an extent, they still do. After all, the triad market—the United States and Canada, Japan, and Western Europe—accounts for approximately 14 percent of the world's population, yet it represents more than 70 percent of the world gross product. As such, these countries absorb the major proportion of capital and consumer products. However, some markets in these countries are becoming saturated far faster than new buyers are being found. Staple consumer goods such as cars, radios, and televisions already outnumber the triad households, and other products are fast approaching the same levels. The slowing growth of the population in triad countries means that the number of households is likely to grow at less than 1 percent to the year 2010, and the demand for consumer goods is unlikely to grow any faster.[17]

MNCs in many industries face the challenge of finding new markets to continue to operate successfully. International markets, especially in those areas where market saturation is still a distant threat, provide an attractive alternative.

Thanks to the forces discussed above, the world is changing fast, resulting in the emergence of new markets. In the 1990s, new business opportunities developed from the European Union, enhanced by the reunification of Germany and the thriving economies in the Pacific Rim countries. In the twenty-first century, China, India, Latin America, and the emerging market-based economies in Eastern Europe promise new opportunities.

In the next 50 years, as the developing world begins its time-bending leap into the modern era, billions of consumers will begin an equally rapid transition from rural to urban, from agrarian to industrial, from feudal to contemporary society. As the rural populations of more of these nations travel to the cities to shop, the demand for goods and services, from the most basic household commodities to sophisticated technical devices, will soar.

The growth in credit card use is one of the most conspicuous signs of the budding consumer revolution. Visa International, Asia's biggest credit card issuer with an estimated 50 percent of the market, increased the number of cards in the Asian region by 25 percent, to 160 million in 2001. South Korea, Thailand, India, and Indonesia all had big increases in sales, turning Asia into Visa's fastest-growing region. In 2001, the volume of retail sales and cash withdrawals using Visa cards grew by 44 percent, to $310 billion.[18] As the Asian nations climb the development ladder, the expansion of consumer demand is the result.

The new consumer class is taking shape in an environment where knowledge is exploding. Today, a typical consumer in emerging markets is more aware than was a consumer in the developed world in the 1950s. The worldwide spread of television and other sources of communication has been creating a revolution in which information travels fast. This knowledge explosion has resulted in three phenomena: First, people have a greater awareness and understanding of the world around them. Second, everyone has a full plate; there are so many things to do, but there is no time. And third, the level of individual aspiration has increased. People want to pursue their own agendas and be entrepreneurial, creative, and different.

Another interesting circumstance has been the birth of a global culture. Communications, finance, and other developments have homogenized outlook and understanding and have resulted in a global culture. Three types of global cultures can be found: professional culture, intellectual culture, and mass (or popular) culture. Professionally, a physicist in the United States has more in common with physicists in other parts of the world than, say, with a banker in the United States. This situation applies to virtually any profession. Intellectuals throughout the world will continue to opt for what they perceive as the best of what is being offered in the sciences, arts, literature, and other fields. Availability will increase, and a great number of cultures will be represented, but people considering themselves intellectuals will still strive to be global masters.

The influence of the United States in creating a global culture is obvious. About a million foreign students study in the United States. They return to their home countries fully equipped with the values that describe U.S. society. They become agents for change in their own nations as they occupy leadership positions in business, government, and universities. The point may be illustrated with reference to three Latin Americans who studied at Harvard University in the 1970s and developed a close friend-ship. When Pedro Aspel of Mexico, Domingo Cavallo of Argentina, and Alejandro Foxley of Chile returned home, each man became finance min-ister of his country. All have developed and applied similar free-market policies to open up the economies of their nations.

The intellectual culture will be a mixture of the perceived best from all cultures. Professional culture will be most heavily affected by the cultures that have the greatest influence within each profession. Popular culture in the post–World War II period has been dominated by U.S. culture. As worldwide communications accelerate and U.S. marketing techniques and institutions grow, the global popular culture will be an extension of the U.S. culture. Culturally, then, the new markets represent a global village whose residents have common needs. They want the same goods and ser-vices they have seen or heard about to satisfy their new appetites. They are willing to work hard and acquire them.

The Leveraging of Knowledge and Talent

Advances in information and communications technologies have pro-vided managers new tools and infrastructures to capture knowledge globally. Worldwide deregulation of the telecommunications industry and evolving technologies have reduced the marginal cost of computing and communications to almost zero. The upgrading of the industry infrastruc-ture has increased rapidly. Information flows freely across borders, reduc-ing the risks related to unfamiliarity, speeding up the arbitrage of price anomalies, and stimulating demand for world-class products and services. In a few years, services that now require a physical presence could be delivered electronically, making it feasible to reach customers globally.

The service sector is likely to undergo a fundamental shift in global trade. It has the potential to lift hundreds of thousands of people out of poverty and to cut costs for companies that ride the phenomenon. Already, a number of developing countries are exporting billions of dollars in ser-vices that range from answering 1-800 (toll-free) telephone calls to soft-ware coding to Ph.D.-level risk-modeling work. Consider the following:

- General Electric (GE) Corporation hired 6,000 people in India in 2001—bringing its head count there to 10,000—to handle accounting, claims processing, customer service, and credit evaluation and research for GE around the world. This year it expects to hire roughly a thousand scien-tists. The firm is so gung ho on India that eventually it plans to transfer a major part of its R&D to that nation.

- More than two thousand Moroccans speak to Spanish and French consumers from call centers near Rabat and Tangiers built by outsourcers and a unit of Spain's phone giant, Telefonica. India, the Philippines, Jamaica, Estonia, Hungary, and the Czech Republic also are establishing themselves as low-cost call center sites. Ireland used to be a call center favorite, but wages there now are on par with the rest of Europe.

- Hong Kong Shanghai Bank Corporation (HSBC) has 2,000 people in India handling back-office work, and it is expected to triple its head count by 2005. HSBC joins companies such as British Airways (accounting), American Express (finance and customer service), America Online (customer service), and McKinsey & Company (research), which already enjoy savings of up to 60 percent in low-wage markets. Services trade has the potential to dwarf previous waves of globalization, because services account for 60 to 70 percent of global gross domestic product.

Consider a Barbie doll, which in the mid-1990s was selling for about $10 in the United States. An estimated $.35 of the $10 was paid for the Asian labor to assemble the doll. Most of the debate on globalization is focused around those $.35. Until now, poor countries largely have been unable to compete for the pricey stuff that goes into the doll—the legal, design, transportation, consulting, marketing, accounting, and other services—that together cost about $7, or 20 times the cost of the labor.[19]

What's enabling all this change? The Internet explosion and Moore's Law (the power of microchips doubles every 18 months) have played a spectacular part—transforming fields such as logistics, design, marketing, engineering, and law into computer inputs and outputs. Eastern Europe, China, and India, with their immense labor forces and sophisticated schools, are opening up to the world economy. And there is a technological leapfrog effect. Thanks to powerful fiber optics, businesses that could hardly get a dial tone a decade ago can link into the world.

A service trade boom could create significant wealth in the Third World. It's unlikely that the result of globalization will be to depress U.S. wages to Third World levels, as the trade unions argue. If productivity in the United States keeps increasing, wages will as well. And the ability to buy inexpensive services from low-cost locations increases productivity.

In addition, technology increases the value of all kinds of intangible assets, such as brand name, company reputation, intellectual property, software, media content, and talent worldwide. Many of these assets have tremendous scale effects, when leveraged globally, encouraging intangibles-rich companies to shape their industries worldwide. For example, companies like Coca-Cola, Microsoft, Glaxo, and Marriott Hotels follow strategies

Exhibit 2.3
How Knowledge and Talent Shape the World

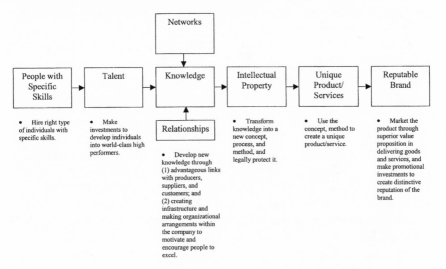

intended to minimize investment in fixed assets and maximize the ability to leverage brands, standards, management skills, and intellectual property across the globe. They are able to derive synergies and perform better than companies that have not pursued such a business approach.[20]

As Exhibit 2.3 shows, intelligent individuals are the heart of any successful business. Traditionally, MNCs looked for resourceful individuals in the home country or in other industrialized countries. Of the 6 billion people in the world, about 1 billion live in the industrialized world. Assuming the top 1 percent of these 1 billion people are the most desirable employees, MNCs depended on a total pool of 10 million individuals. Today, MNCs have the opportunity to locate talent worldwide. Instead of 10 million people, the total pool has expanded to 60 million smart individuals.

Two factors are responsible for this change. First, a larger number of younger people are seeking higher education, made possible by the investment that developing countries have made in postsecondary education. Second, the educational standards in the non-Western world have been advancing along the same lines as in developed countries. Students in less developed countries have available the methods, techniques, and materials that their counterparts in rich countries use. The Internet has opened the door for all people to have easy access to information, wherever it is generated. Students in India read the same scientific journals and textbooks as U.S. students do. Up until 1960, formal higher education in business administration was limited to the United States. In the 1960s, six business schools were established outside the United States—three in developed countries (the United Kingdom, France, and Switzerland) and three in developing countries (India, Iran, and Peru). Since then, schools of business administration have mushroomed worldwide. In 2001, five thousand business schools outside the United States offered bachelor's and master's degrees.

Today companies can develop powerful global talent and continue to convert specific opportunities into an uninterrupted profit stream. If nation-states create hurdles by imposing outdated immigration laws for foreign workers, companies can ship work to the people. As a matter of fact, this option offers advantages in many other ways as well. GE, for example, transferred a major portion of its research work to Bangalore, India. The company hires more individuals with Ph.D.'s in India than in the United States. They keep in touch with their counterparts through e-mails and faxes 24 hours a day. The sun never sets on the GE empire. When U.S. offices close, Indian offices open, and the work never stops. What a way to enhance productivity! In addition, as is true nowhere else, in India GE can hire an English-speaking individual with a Ph.D. in physics, chemistry, or engineering at a salary of $12,000. This situation results in further savings. GE is not exploiting such individuals, because by India's standards they earn more than a decent salary.

Furthermore, the Indian scientists can be moved from a GE laboratory in India to a GE laboratory in the United States, because the labs use the same equipment. The talent belonging to other cultures adds to the cultural diversity, which not only is healthy in creating viable relationships among employees but also is a great source for generating new ideas.

CONCLUSION

The globalization process is driven by global capital seeking profits across national borders. Economic deregulation and falling trade barriers have opened up tremendous opportunities. Suddenly and simultaneously, world markets are accessible to any company with a little patience and foresight. As companies capture these opportunities, they spur the globalization movement. Jane Fraser and Jeremy Oppenheim note:

> The combination of capital market developments, broader market access, and knowledge intensification is driving an exponential change in the pace, scale and scope of globalization. Pace is increasing because the globaliza-

tion process is fueling itself—and because the infrastructure for diffusing technology and ideas globally has become much more powerful. Scale, because the share of world GDP that is effectively globalized is set to rise from around 20 percent today to well over 50 percent in the next 10 to 15 years. And scope, because as globalization's footprint expands, so do opportunities to combine resources and segment markets in new ways.[21]

Globalization leads to a worldwide convergence of supply and demand. More countries want the benefits of foreign trade, investment, and technology; multinational firms—desperate for new markets—supply those benefits. Developing countries represent the last frontier for many multinationals. The world's new consumers, new builders of infrastructure, and new investors are located outside the United States, Europe, and Japan. Nothing governments do will suppress these powerful forces. Companies work around trade and investment barriers.

NOTES

1. Jane Fraser and Jeremy Oppenheim, "What's New about Globalization?" *McKinsey Quarterly,* 1994, no. 2: 168–79.

2. Abbas J. Ali, *Globalization of Business* (Binghamton, N.Y.: Haworth Press, 2002), pp. 23–24.

3. See Subhash C. Jain, *International Marketing,* 6th ed. (Cincinnati: South-Western College Publishing, 2001), pp. 36–39.

4. "2001 and Beyond," *Financial Times,* 25 January 2001.

5. Mike Moore, "Development Needs More Than Trade," *Financial Times,* 18 January 2002, p. 15.

6. John Micklethwait and Adrian Wooldrige, *A Future Perfect* (New York: Crown Publishers, 2000), pp. 34–35.

7. "Sheltering from the Storm," *Economist,* 8 September 2001, p. 63.

8. Micklethwait and Wooldrige, *Future Perfect,* p. 36.

9. Peter Dicken, *Global Shift,* 3d ed. (New York: Guilford Press, 1998), pp. 149–51.

10. Craig Barrett, quoted in Paul Taylor, "The Revolutionary Shape of Things to Come: Survey of Information Technology," *Financial Times,* 13 January 1999.

11. Micklethwait and Wooldrige, *Future Perfect,* p. 43.

12. Frank Rose, "Think Globally, Script Locally," *Fortune,* 8 November 1999, p. 156.

13. Glenn Yago and David Goldman, "Capital Access Index: Emerging and Submerging Markets," (Aspen, CO: Milken Institute, 1999).

14. "Capital Goes Global," *Economist,* 25 October 1997, p. 38.

15. *Fortune,* 22 November 1999, p. 140.

16. "2001 and Beyond."

17. Jain, *International Marketing,* p. 7.

18. John Thornhill, "Asia Awakes," *Financial Times,* 2 April 2002, p. 14.

19. Douglas Lavin, "Globalization Goes Upscale," *Wall Street Journal,* 1 February 2002, p. 18.

20. Lowell Bryan et al., *Race for the World: Strategies to Build a Great Global Firm* (Boston: Harvard Business School Press, 1999), pp. 177–205.

21. Fraser and Oppenheim, "What's New about Globalization?" p. 174.

Chapter 3

THE RISE OF BUSINESS GLOBALIZATION

Confronted with the forces of change discussed in the previous chapter, firms find widespread scope for conducting business globally. There is a great deal of anecdotal evidence describing how companies, once strictly limited to their neighborhoods, now find it convenient to strike deals with foreign counterparts without traveling to their locations. The world economy appears to be integrating rapidly. Industries, companies, customers, and countries are increasingly connecting with one another in surprising and often inscrutable ways at an incredible pace. Furthermore, the scope of integration is expanding such that all economic and social institutions of our time are affected.

As globalization spreads, companies face new challenges. For most firms, even large multinationals, foreign business traditionally meant modest aspirations to gain market share outside the home country. But globalization is much more than that. It forces companies to broaden their views of markets and competition, which requires a lot of new learning—including figuring out how to find the right country in which to build a plant, how to coordinate production schedules across borders, and how to absorb research wherever it occurs. Companies must learn what sort of people to hire, how to inculcate a global mentality in the ranks, and when to sell standardized products instead of customizing them for local markets. Only a few managers are capable of handling the competitive rigors of the new global marketplace.

The purpose of this chapter is threefold: first, to examine the concept of globalization of business; second, to explore various dimensions of globalization; and finally, to discuss the implications of globalization for businesses and nation-states. The chapter concludes with the challenges that firms face in becoming global.

CONCEPT OF BUSINESS GLOBALIZATION

Globalization has become a buzzword. There is hardly any business or economic discourse, writing, or speech that does not touch on globalization. National economies have shifted toward globalization, markets are converging globally, business has become global, firms are competing in a global market, and many other changes are taking place.

The term *globalization* is commonly applied when countries are interdependent. The interdependence comes in the form of seeking new markets for existing products or new products, human resources, raw materials, or technology, among other things. Finance, legal incorporation, taxation, and low-cost production facilities often have provided motivation to venture out of home countries. The important unresolved issue is how to measure the levels of interdependence. For example, how do we determine the degree and speed of globalization? At the firm level, how do we assess the extent of globalization? Business globalization is too vast a concept to be captured fully by today's still-limited set of available information.

Defining Globalization

Although academics and practitioners use the word *globalization,* the term has no standard definition. A consensus definition is needed but has not emerged. Most scholars seem to view globalization from their own perspectives and backgrounds. Presently, a clear and coherent articulation of globalization is missing, and it has no scholarly paradigm to support it.

There are three major approaches to defining globalization: the economic, the social, and the political. Writers use a combination of these approaches to view globalization. Economically, globalization is defined as the expansion of production, distribution, and marketing of goods and services across national boundaries. Considered from the point of view of MNCs, the term *globalization* refers to a process of making investments overseas to create foreign subsidiaries, which add value across national boundaries.[1] Globalization has also been mentioned as the elimination of trade and other economic barriers among nations. Adopting a social perspective, globalization is a process of linking nations together to form a worldwide community.[2] In this sense, globalization fosters oneness among people worldwide through connectivity, interdependence, and integration.[3] In terms of politics, the term *globalization* refers to interconnectedness of different nations, making a single unit in which national boundaries are obsolete.[4] This process requires the redefinition of roles, possibilities, and risks of different nations. When viewed from economic, social, and political viewpoints together, globalization is a complex process of linking people's lives in all spheres: cultural, economic, political, technological, and environmental.

Essentially, scholars have adopted different perspectives of globalization, depending on their backgrounds and experiences. The result is the lack of a single definition of the concept. This makes the discourse on globalization subjective and vague.

In this book, globalization is considered to be a concept of international political economy that is founded on the belief that all economic activity, whether local, regional, or national, must be conducted with a worldwide perspective. The expectation of this view is that a new world of greater production, trade, and wealth, as well as high standards of living, will emerge. The multinational firm has the primary role in delivering these gains by creating wealth through the transfer of technology, market making, and global employment. The nation-states play a secondary role that supports and supplements the needs of the firms. Thus, globalization is the process by which the world's economy is transformed from national and regional markets to one market that operates without regard to national boundaries.

The process comprises both economic and social development simultaneously; human welfare and environmental protection are important responsibilities, along with development and economic gains. The globalization process provides high-value global products and services that are designed, manufactured, and marketed by global talent for global markets using global resources in a manner that ensures that social concerns are fully addressed at all levels. This definition of *globalization* is based on economic, political, and social approaches and highlights the roles of two important institutions—MNCs and nation-states—in the progression toward globalization.

Ideally, truly global companies would have access to the world's finest resources: the most talented labor, the largest markets, the most advanced technologies, and the cheapest and best supply of goods and services. They would serve the global consumers with due concern for social development through support from nation-states. Globalization through the combination of market forces, diminished government interference, ingenious technologies, and a truly universal customer base would allow MNCs to double or triple income levels of the entire planet within a few decades and still maintain social quality.

Emergence of Global Markets

The European period of exploration was the beginning of globalization. The ventures to find profitable supplies and to market goods allowed Western powers to expand their geographic domination and maritime trade. However, when the interests of a local population and the controlling authority were at odds, nationalism grew and colonialism declined. Globalization can be seen to be a reversal of this isolating process, as separate parts fit together like pieces of a giant jigsaw puzzle and willingly work toward a unified whole.

The world power at this time, the United States, will benefit most from globalization of markets. Hence, in some quarters, globalization is perceived as a synonym for U.S. economic expansion. But all nations that participate in globalization benefit from it, provided they create the conditions that enable globalization to work profitably.

Currently, global markets account for 20 percent of world GDP, that is, about $6 trillion of the planet's GDP of $28 trillion. Although this sum is substantial, the potential for the future looks even better. Within 30 years, assuming 4 percent overall real growth, the world GDP is expected to expand to $91 trillion, while the global market could multiply 12-fold to reach $73 trillion.[5] If this forecast holds true, global markets would amount to more than 80 percent of the world output. The forces described in the previous chapter promote the explosion and emergence of global markets in countless industries. For example, the global personal financial services industry, at $300 billion in 1997, is expected to double to $600 billion by 2008.[6] Geographic expansion has been the key to the evolution of human societies and economies. The reduction of tariff barriers, new means of communication and transportation, and the adoption of liberal policies all help in geographic expansion and global commerce.

The Logic of Globalization

Any business will attempt to maximize the wealth of its owners. Large companies have sought opportunities outside the home country since colonial days, but their objective has always been to increase their shareholders' wealth over the long term. After World War II, the pace of business

Exhibit 3.1
Logic of Globalization

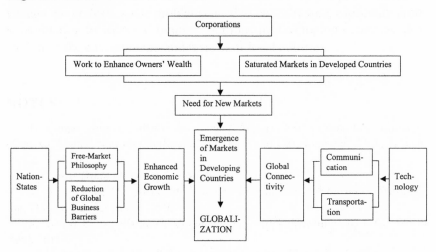

access across national boundaries grew greatly, partly because of the Marshall Plan for Europe. This aid package was an important seed and structurally followed the cultivation of new markets for U.S. goods and ideas. Japan is following a similar strategy with its foreign aid policy, particularly in the Pacific Rim countries, and is a major donor in the world today.

Traditionally, most large corporations have hailed from developed countries, and they have looked for opportunities in other developed nations first. In the 1990s, as markets were becoming global and countries of all dimensions began to emerge as viable markets, corporations, whether or not they were already multinational in their operations, expanded their market horizons to become truly global. Global corporations seek greater internal integration to capture global specialization and scale advantages, and they follow local approaches to gain privileged market access. Globalization of markets benefited corporations that had saturated traditional markets in developed countries and thus needed new markets to maintain their growth rates.

The globalization of markets and the simultaneous response of business enterprises to become global have sowed the seeds of a new world order, as shown in Exhibit 3.1. If globalization triumphs and continues to flourish, it should lead to worldwide prosperity. Billions of people in developing countries stand to gain more, because it would be their first chance to live decently.

Primarily motivated by a desire to increase their own shareholders' prosperity, corporations drive globalization. The point may be illustrated with reference to Nike. Nike shareholders want to boost profits by holding down production costs, which means sending manufacturing overseas to low-cost production sites. Indonesian workers want to elevate their incomes by moving from farms to work in Nike factories. As both parties try to upgrade their benefits, the invisible hand of globalization obliges by enmeshing them in an ever-larger, ever-denser web of investment, R&D, production, and marketing. Interdependencies that have been created need to be protected, and all parties benefit.

GLOBALIZATION DIMENSIONS

Globalization has many dimensions; it affects all facets of corporate life. Although the interests of stockholders are central to a company's working, companies must simultaneously pay attention to the concerns of other stakeholders if they are to survive and prosper. Although creating profit must remain of central importance within the corporate culture, that goal has to be balanced by other values that help define the limits of activities designed to achieve profits and may include other important ethical and socially responsible behaviors.

Abbas Ali suggests classifying globalization dimensions under five headings: the trade dimension, the international politics and relations dimension, the organizational dimension, the intellectual dimension, and the moral dimension. Aspects of these dimensions are given in the following discussion.[7]

The Trade Dimension

Businesses should conduct their operations across borders in an open market to achieve the greatest benefit without inflicting social damage or violating the rights of people from other countries. The global organization should do the following:

- Develop marketing and production strategies that span nation-state borders to make the best use of resources and skills.
- Tap the globe through trade and direct investment.
- Design products with attention to cultural and operational needs.
- Work with the best suppliers to improve local managerial and technological capabilities, as well as local working conditions.

- Respect the integrity and autonomy of local cultures and business practices by maintaining a proper contractual relationship with local suppliers.
- Minimize the impact on the affected workforce and community when dislocations occur, and plan well to avoid drastic shifts in direction.
- Derive maximum advantages without exploiting workers or communities when entering new markets or establishing new facilities.
- Make safe products and services available to the people of the world.
- Advance the idea of free and fair trade and economic operations across the globe.

The International Politics and Relations Dimension

Businesses should accept and participate in the development and refinement of their practices and norms across cultures while respecting national sovereignty and cultural identities. The global organization should follow these guidelines:

- Be flexible in dealing with a wide range of environments and their peculiarities.
- Accommodate business styles that are different from the organization's own style.
- Be conscious of, and plan for, alternatives needed because of political risks and upheaval throughout the globe.
- Establish a local network of contacts to facilitate understanding of one another's viewpoints.
- Hire talented local advisers to help meet new challenges.
- Join industry associations and support industry publications (or start them if they do not exist).
- Keep informed about local political affairs and regulatory changes.
- Be careful and thorough in assessing political stability and risk and their potential to cause expropriation of company assets abroad.
- Choose the best ideas and practices from each culture to transmit throughout the global organization.
- Focus on the shifting competitive structures locally and globally.
- Ascertain the standards for good corporate citizenship in each host country and respect them.
- Find means to operate while maintaining cultural elements that are important in the host value system.
- Work with local business partners to identify culturally sensitive business practices.

- Cope with situations of uncertainty and instability; be flexible in reacting to different and changing environments.
- Understand foreign environments well enough to begin to anticipate broad political, social, and cultural trends and to deal with them before they become crises.

The Organizational Dimension

Businesses should have the ability to set forth organizational structures and human resource systems that can mobilize managers and employees to implement globalization visions. The global organization should take care to do the following:

- Attract the best personnel without prejudice toward nationality.
- Encourage the development of global teams working collectively on projects.
- Have systems in place that allow input from employees globally on major functional activities and projects.
- Accord the same degree and respect of organizational citizenship to all employees.
- Have managers from around the world meet and interact regularly.
- Obtain understanding, in both the host country and the home country, of the purposes and objectives of the business or project.
- Accommodate cultural differences with respect to decision making, participation, and communication.
- Base rewards on a combination of individual, unit, and global performance.
- Have a truly globalized board of directors and executive management team.
- Assign and train expatriate managers carefully so that they can adjust to local environments.
- Ensure that organizational structures are flexible.
- Hire and promote employees who have a global vision.
- Share information about hazardous waste management, job safety, and other threatening consequences of the product's presence, including risks inherent in local product or service manufacture.
- Provide financial and administrative support to facilitate expatriation of talent from all sources.
- Offer appropriate training to enable employees to aspire to, and compete for, higher positions.
- Offer promotion and advancement opportunities to the best-qualified employees, regardless of individual background.

- Have the vision to detect the talents of its people without prejudice.
- Develop the capacity to manage changes that will invariably occur.
- Empower local managers who are closest to the marketplace to act in a manner that is responsive to local customer groups.
- Have a culture and flexible structure that respond quickly and effectively to global and local host market changes.
- Identify and develop core competencies essential for globalization.

The Intellectual Dimension

Businesses should treat globalization as an outlook that broadens and energizes the human mind and perspective—that is, as an opportunity to create a culture in which knowledge and a sense of belonging are transmitted and embedded in organizational life. Consequently, the global organization should have these goals:

- Sponsor and nurture global networks of the organization's professionals in their disciplines.
- Promote cross-cultural organizational transfers of employees at different levels in the company.
- Create a corporate culture that is friendly and open to all members of all cultures, genders, religions, and ethics.
- View foreigners simply as people.
- Share ideas and knowledge with employees and customers.
- Create a community feeling among people in the host country to break down some of the barriers.
- Ensure that executive managers demonstrate in their behavior the values and visions they espouse.
- Recognize that knowledge must be translated into internationally competitive products and services.
- Establish and implement the principles of the learning organization to the degree that learning transcends functional, organizational, and national boundaries.
- Institute policies that show respect for knowledge (such as foreign language competency).
- Be sensitive to the risks of interracial hostilities that might ignite old conflicts and be counterproductive as individuals are hired from neighboring nations.
- Encourage expatriate managers to assimilate into local society, to better understand local expectations and more effectively advocate legitimate local interests in the larger corporation.

- Provide expatriate managers with the means for remaining effectively integrated into the organizational life of the parent organization.
- Reserve international responsibilities for those managers who have international breadth, technical and organizational competence, and the personal flexibility needed to perform effectively in an international context.
- Create interpersonal appreciation and acceptance of international differences.
- Educate employees on the benefits of acquiring and using global-based knowledge for personal and organizational purposes.
- Reward innovations relating to globalization of the organization.
- Create systems that facilitate the gathering and dissemination of relevant information to the interested parties.
- Develop systems and structures that allow for the sharing of knowledge in a way that does not compromise proprietary technology.

The Moral Dimension

Businesses should stress objectivity in treating issues across the globe and have the courage to confront, on a timely basis, biases and prejudices. To achieve these objectives, the global organization should do the following:

- Promote cross-cultural awareness (e.g., through sensitivity seminars).
- Promote an organizational culture that disdains and rejects stereotyping.
- Look for similarities in cultures, as well as understand differences.
- Set the standards for itself and for others to follow.
- Ensure environmental responsibility and safety.
- Value local traditions and cultural activities, and respect their importance.
- Clearly understand the local laws and practices with regard to human rights.
- Manage the company for the long-term benefit of all stakeholders.
- Include ethical performance in the evaluation of individuals.
- Develop an explicit statement of corporate global values.
- Be guided by the highest standards of conduct that are generally accepted in both the parent company's home and host societies.
- Remain in compliance with the general standards of local custom or local law.
- Protect consumers around the globe.
- Lead on the basis of character and an ethic of fairness, honesty, and integrity.

- Support due process through the law.
- Create a culture whereby moral and ethical business practices are a top priority.
- Reduce sources of cultural conflict.

The globalization dimensions underscore the point that the role of an MNC has shifted from that of an economic institution solely responsible for its stockholders to that of a multifaceted force owing its existence to different stakeholders to whom it must be accountable. As one of the most progressive institutions in the global society, the MNC is expected to provide balanced prosperity in all fields.

IMPLICATIONS FOR MNCS

Globalization changes the competitive game. It forces worldwide companies to develop three strengths simultaneously: global efficiency, an ability to be locally responsive, and the vision to develop and diffuse innovations internationally.[8] In the past, companies could survive if they were strong in any one of these areas, but globalization requires that all three be developed and used at the same time. Furthermore, the three strengths must be balanced in a way that takes account of the specific industry. In this endeavor, some large, well-established worldwide companies have been forced to take large losses or even abandon businesses.

Global Efficiency

In some industries, such as consumer electronics and integrated circuits, it is feasible to develop and manufacture products on a global basis. This way, world-scale plants produce standard products very efficiently. Technology permits realization of production efficiencies, and global convergence of consumer preferences and tastes guarantees large markets for such products of technology. The introduction of quartz technology in watch making is an example of realizing global efficiency.

Global economies are achieved by rationalizing product lines, standardizing parts design, and specializing manufacturing operations. In industries in which consumer requirements do not vary, it is easier to implement global efficiency. But even in industries that have been traditionally local, it is possible to achieve substantial scale economies by restructuring and specializing plant configurations.

Globalization forces companies to manage their businesses in a globally integrated manner to capture the benefits of efficiency. Successful implementation of global efficiency strategy becomes a principal source of competitive advantage.

Local Responsiveness

The claim that customer needs are converging globally may be only partially true. A variety of impediments and countertrends require localization of products. The classic barrier to globalization of products has always been rooted in cultural differences. In addition, economic, political, and structural differences among nations make it difficult to successfully sell standardized products.

Thus, local consumers require that an organization not market standardized products manufactured in world-scale plants fully realizing scale economies. Standard products must be adapted to local differences. In other words, although it is important to achieve global-scale economies, they must be developed in a manner that gives managers enough flexibility in producing differentiated products to be locally responsive. In an environment where standard products do not suffice, a company focused on achieving the most scale-efficient global operation may be at a disadvantage compared with a company that develops products to meet local requirements.

International Vision

The third demand that globalization makes on MNCs is the need to develop and diffuse innovations on a worldwide basis. As competitors achieve parity by achieving scale economies through rationalizing their operations globally and judiciously meeting local requirements, the ability to link and leverage global learning offers a company the extra strength it needs to succeed.

The importance of global learning is based on three factors. First, R&D costs have been increasing, and no company can afford to duplicate R&D efforts in several places. Second, national governments want local involvement in the leading-edge products sold in their markets. Third, human skills are in short supply, so they must be used sparingly and only where most needed. All this means that some parts of R&D must be decentralized and that knowledge development must be spread out to several locations. Such an effort at dispersal must be fully coordinated so that people at different locations work as a team, feeding one another their progress on a timely basis. The coordination may require frequently moving people from one research center to another to discourage the development of a local mentality. In addition, these employees must be provided with intercultural training so that people belonging to different cultures are able to work together. They must be made to think of themselves as IBMers, for example, and not as citizens of different nations.

IMPLICATIONS FOR NATION-STATES

Globalization makes demands on nation-states as well. Nations that have agreed to join in the move toward interdependency become members of an elite club. The members must observe the rules of the club to enjoy the membership privileges. Some of the expectations from nation-states are examined in this section.

Transparency

Nation-states should be open in sharing the true economic perspectives of the country. Complete transparency is needed on both fiscal and monetary matters, enabling the outsiders to decide the range of their economic activity with the country.

Lack of transparency may encourage outside interests to invest in a country under optimistic illusions and thus create a bubble. False optimism forces these interests to pump more and more money into nontransparent countries, confident that they could provide the same high returns they did in the past, even though the early money might have been invested in, say, productive factories and the later money was going into luxury condominiums for which there was no demand. The investors finally learn that their optimism was based on an illusion. The attitude changes, and the country's ratings take a dip in the global economic community, making the country a basket case. Thomas Friedman remarked:

> The opaqueness that drives the optimistic illusionists to bid up prices to exaggerated levels also empowers the paranoid illusionists to bid them down to exaggerated levels when sentiment shifts. Because on the way down all of the stories that you as an optimistic illusionist told yourself, all the assumptions you made about the country's foreign currency reserves or forward obligations, collapse. You go from believing everything to believing nothing.[9]

The outsider cannot do any serious analysis on opaque systems.

Standards

Globalization demands that countries set and follow high standards of accounting. Traditionally, U.S. accounting standards have been well regarded, although in the aftermath of the Enron fiasco they are questioned. But the fact remains that every nation should follow high accounting standards, which probably could be set internationally. Auditors must adhere to these standards to report the true state of financial affairs of any institution in the country, be it a company, agency, or government department.

As a matter of fact, high standards of behavior and conduct should be observed by all participants in all affairs. Public officials, as well as corporate executives, should set the examples by following accepted norms in their day-to-day activities. In other words, they should not take advantage of their privileged position in any way.

Furthermore, standards should be set to match the highest in the world. If a country has weak standards, adhering to them is not enough. The government should impose new standards if it wishes to be a part of the global village. Even a single company in a developing country can set itself apart by following high standards not common in the country but comparable with standards in industrialized nations, and the company thus can gain international recognition. The strong example of India's Infosys, the fastest-growing software company in the world, makes this point.

The key to Infosys's success has been abandoning the Third World policies and practices that hobble many subcontinent companies and has been forging a connection to the First World that permits the utmost in customer convenience: "We decided from the outset that there would be no blurring of corporate and private resources," says Narayana Murthy, the company's visionary founder and chairman. This decision means that no one uses a company car for a personal errand—a radical break from traditional Indian business practice. Indian corporate officers frequently make personal use of company assets. Company electricians work in executives' homes. Employees pick up their supervisors' children from school and baby-sit them. Corporate accounts finance purchases of homes. Employees put up with such practices because they have no choice. Nevertheless, these perks lead to growing alienation and a rebellious withdrawal of creative input. That problem does not occur at Infosys. Infosys is the first Indian company to announce audited annual results within a week of the close of the financial year, the first to publish quarterly audited financial statements, and the first to publish statements in compliance with U.S. generally accepted accounting principles (GAAP) and the disclosure requirements of the U.S. Securities and Exchange Commission.[10]

Corruption

One reason why globalization leads to economic prosperity is because it encourages competition among companies, as well as among nations. For example, investors have a choice of making investments in their own country or outside, and outside in countries A to Z. The investor will choose the nation that promises the best return and the fewest headaches. Why would anyone invest in a country where officials must be bribed if equally good opportunities exist elsewhere and eliminate the need to make under-the-table payments? Thus, a nation hoping to become part of the globalizing trend must control corruption at all levels. Friedman stresses the importance of controlling corruption under globalization:

> As U.S. ambassador in Finland it was my job to go around to Finnish business leaders and encourage them to invest in Russia on the argument that this was the best way to produce stability across the border from them. But these Finns would say back to me: "Sure, we'll do business with the Russians. They can bring their trucks in here and fill them up with whatever they want, as long as they bring a bag of cash to pay for it. But we're not going over there to do business. It is way too corrupt and dangerous. And why should we? We can go to Hungary or Estonia, or The Czech Republic and make money and be assured of being able to get our profits out. Why should we bother with Russia in the condition it's in?" I would say, "Yes, yes, but you should think about investing there for regional stability." And they would just give me a blank stare. Well, now I'm out of government and I am advising several investment firms on Wall Street. They were asking me the other day about investing in Russia and I just told them, "No way." If I look at it not from a policy maker's point of view, but from a businessman's point of view, you would be crazy to invest in Russia now. The Finns had it right.[11]

Freedom of the Press

In addition to requiring transparency at all levels in a country, globalization forces a free press. A free press represents an independent, unbiased view of different events and actions in a society on a day-to-day basis. While government makes policies and corporations make decisions, somebody must play the devil's advocate by raising issues, both positive and negative, relative to these policies and decisions. A free press has this responsibility.

A press controlled by a government represents only the viewpoint of politicians and bureaucrats. It shares with the public the information the government wants the people to have. The comments of a government-controlled press are always biased. The press is responsible only to the government and not to the people. A controlled press cannot provide an unprejudiced and balanced view of things.

As a nation adopts globalization, a free press is born as people become aware. For example, under a controlled press, a government may shield a company that has knowingly made bad investments and cheated people out of the money they invested in the company's stock. In the future, people will refuse to invest their savings in the stock market for fear of being cheated again. This situation will lead to the drying up of an important source of cheap capital. The people themselves will demand a press that keeps them informed on such matters as a company's performance and potential. The government will be forced to accept this openness.

Bond Markets

Another effect of globalization is the development of bond markets in a country. Bond markets, along with mutual and pension funds, are necessary for people to invest their savings and, probably, earn a better return. The bond market also provides so-called patient capital to corporations— that is, long-term loans so that businesses are not subjected to the vagaries of short-term lending from banks. Corporate bonds, assuming they are rated by a credible agency such as Moody's or Standard and Poor's, are a safe vehicle to attract foreign capital.

Of course, there are always risks involved in depending on foreign capital, because it flows in and out rapidly. For example, in 1999 Serge Tchruk, one of the best-known business executives in France, told a breakfast meeting of international investors that profits of his company, Alcatel, the French telecommunications giant, would be considerably lower than the company had forecast just a few weeks earlier. The same day, the Alcatel stock fell 38 percent, the largest one-day decline on the French stock exchange, as mainly U.S. and British pension and mutual funds sold their Alcatel holdings. In the past few years, foreigners have pushed many companies to change management, reform accounting systems, initiate international mergers, and replace local language with English in corporate affairs.[12] Briefly, the bond market is a desirable route to seek foreign capital, but it requires ongoing acceptable performance failing which investors are quick to withdraw their holdings.

Democratization

Globalization forces democratization of a nation for the sake of flexibility, legitimacy, and sustainability. A democratic regime in a nation introduces flexibility in policies and their implementation. The more democratic, accountable, and open a government is, the less likely it is to be exposed to economic shocks and surprises. Even if it is exposed to shocks and surprises, it can adjust more quickly to changing circumstances and demands. Furthermore, the more democratic a nation is, the more feedback it will receive, which increases its opportunity to make midcourse corrections before it is too late.

In addition, the more democratic a government is, the more legitimacy it will have if painful reforms have to be introduced as a corrective measure to set the house in order. Authoritarian governments lack legitimacy. Therefore, no matter what they say or do, their actions are never taken by the public at face value.

Finally, any reforms that a government undertakes will not be sustainable in the long run if the society is not democratic. Nations that try to conduct their business through the rule of law and accountability but that offer no regular free elections will not be able to sustain reforms in the long run. No nation can long sustain the rule of law and accountability with an authoritarian regime that it is not itself accountable, does not allow an independent judiciary to pursue corruption, and does not permit free elections so that the political management can be changed. The best way for the rule of law to prevail is for the politicians overseeing it to know that an electorate is always watching them and can always remove them.

GLOBALIZATION'S CHALLENGES FOR MNCS

The previous section noted that as companies go global, they need to seek efficiency, become locally responsible, and coordinate knowledge development on a worldwide basis. This section considers some of the important factors that will affect their global strategy.[13]

Management of Foreign-Dominated Liquid Assets

MNCs conduct business in a number of foreign currencies whose exchange rates are subject to great upheavals, with far-reaching consequences for earnings. These changes result from disturbances in international, social, political, and economic environments. Thus, in addition to protecting a business from competitive inroads, the management of foreign funds has an impact in other areas—for example, deciding on the best currency mix to maintain on a short-term basis.

Limits to Growth

Traditionally, MNCs have pursued expansion or growth overseas as an important corporate objective. Growth per se, however, may be problematic. The trade deficits of many countries (among both industrialized and developing nations) and a common desire among nations for self-sufficiency may render achievement of perpetual growth in foreign markets difficult. Even where opportunities abound, an entry should be clearly earmarked with the possibility of retrenchment or exit forced by economic nationalism or other political reasons. It may become virtually impossible to raise capital in a host country, the traditional source of long-term funding, and such a situation would certainly block growth.

Decentralization of the Production Process

For both political and economic reasons, more and more industries may follow the strategic lead of the electronics industry and seek component specialization. If not all components of a product can be efficiently manufactured by an MNC in one host country, the corporation may opt for specialization in a few components while depending on other sources for other components. The decentralization of the production process is attractive to host nations because it could encourage local involvement in the manufacturing of the product.

Automation of Assembly Lines

In advanced countries especially, many routine tasks on the assembly line might be performed by robots. Japan is way ahead in this area. The United States will probably move in the same direction in the coming years. Such automation of assembly lines will result in substantial cost reductions and uniformity in product quality, which in turn will favorably affect the competitive position in the world markets.

Corporate-Labor Relationships

The developing nations' MNCs, able to depend on an abundance of cheap labor for their factories, may emerge as a newly significant competitive force. This new competition is likely to have a far-reaching impact on corporate-labor relationships in the industrialized countries. Increased understanding and harmony among traditional adversaries will become necessary for mutual survival. The change in labor-management agreements for the U.S. auto industry bears testimony to the emergence of this trend.

Globalization of Consumer Tastes

Another interesting phenomenon concerns the development of a common worldwide preference for a variety of consumer goods. The global craze for designer jeans and fast foods illustrates the point. However, the commonality of demand does not mean that the same marketing strategies will be effective in every overseas market. The marketing strategies must be appropriately customized to local customs and traditions.

As the new century evolves, the world marketplace will be quite different from what it was in the past. Although opportunities should abound, international marketers will need new strategic perspectives to capitalize successfully on these opportunities. Traditional policies and strategies may no longer result in big growth and profits. Corporations will need to develop new marketing strategies that not only enhance their competitiveness but also fit the needs of the future.

Businesses as Good Citizens

Environmental issues and problems, such as waste disposal and pollution, are becoming more and more important. Businesses will be expected to play an important role in solving these problems. Improving the quality of education will be another significant social issue affecting global organizations. It is commonly believed that business can make a very useful contribution to basic literacy skills.

People Power

In the coming decades, a dramatic convergence of demographic, technological, competitive, and global forces is likely to shift power from employers to employees and from the boardroom to the workplace, the point where value is added and wealth is created. Throughout North America, Europe, and Asia, these forces will converge in a strikingly similar manner—the power of the twenty-first century will be people power.

Shared Service Centers

Shared service centers (SSCs) are rapidly gaining momentum world-wide. An SSC is a separate unit, sited in a centralized location, into which a company bundles its supporting processes and nonstrategic activities. In addition to creating basic economy-of-scale savings, an SSC in theory eliminates much of the distraction of managing replicated business functions across the world, in turn allowing greater focus on strategic operations and the core business.

Having expanded massively across the globe, giving little thought to the duplication of support processes and staff in each new country, companies are now realizing the need to hasten new administrative and decision-making efficiencies and to rein in back-office costs. New technologies are fueling the process: the Internet and better telecommunication infrastructure are helping companies communicate more quickly, effectively, and safely with branch offices.

Companies tend to begin using an SSC for finance functions. Over time, an SSC can expand to engulf other processes as varied as administration, human resources, and information technology services.

CONCLUSION

Globalization makes sense because it forces efficient use of resources within the bounds of democracy. In doing so, however, globalization could be brutal and chaotic. Both companies and nations that refuse to play by the globalization rules lose. Such loss destroys jobs and makes processes obsolete. All institutions must undergo changes as globalization makes inroads. This shift requires enormous adjustments on the part of people. Once the adjustments are completed, the positive impact of globalization becomes much more visible.

Globalization does not claim worldwide commonality among people. There will always be rich and poor people, smart and not-so-smart individuals, risk takers and risk-adverse people. What globalization does promise is economic prosperity for all the participants compared with what they had before. In the foreseeable future, citizens of Western nations will certainly be ahead of South Asians or Latinos. But the life of a South Asian or a Latino in 2020 will be more prosperous than, say, it was in 2000.

Unfortunately, globalization is the convenient scapegoat when anything goes wrong. For example, when a U.S. company transfers manufacturing offshore, many workers lose jobs. They attribute their plight to globalization. But when they buy a Toyota made in the United States, they forget that the decision by the Japanese company to assemble cars in the United States rather than exporting them from Japan was also a globalization decision, and that strategy provided jobs to people in the United States. In other words, there are always losers and winners under globalization, but there are more winners. The losers are the people who refused to see that the world is changing and to prepare themselves ahead of time. If a company is not competitive, sooner or later it will go out of business. All that globalization does is to expand the scope of competition worldwide.

Globalization promises much. But before delivering positive results, it imposes responsibilities on both governments and companies. Governments need to examine their role and determine what existing policies are worth pursuing, what policies require scrapping, and what new policies must be instituted. Companies also must be willing to change the perspectives of their business—that is, to look again at which products and services they provide, where manufacturing should be done, where to conduct R&D, and whom to hire. If the government and businesses of a nation fail to take their responsibilities seriously, globalization might become counterproductive.

At the same time, it is not easy for companies and governments to respond to huge changes on a timely basis and on all fronts. Some decisions makers do not have the breadth of vision, the wisdom, and the outlook to change their perspectives from a narrow focus to a global focus. Consider large MNCs. They may have been doing business internationally for years, but they may be nearsighted and therefore see what they know best—the customers and competitors close to home. In reality, their customers are spread all over the globe, and their competitive landscape stretches to a global horizon. But their perspective is dominated by home country customers and the organizational units that serve them. For globalization to spread, political and business leaders with a global mentality are needed to integrate the globalization process fully. Partly, this challenge must be shared by the business schools. Students should not be allowed to earn an M.B.A. degree without proper insights into history, geography, and the politics of global business. They must learn to perceive the planet as a borderless world.

NOTES

1. Raymond Vernon, *In the Hurricane's Eye: The Troubled Prospects of Multinational Enterprise* (Cambridge: Harvard University Press, 1998), p. 12; also see Alan Rugman, *The End of Globalization* (New York, AMACON, 2001).

2. A.G. McGrew and P.G. Lewis, *Global Politics: Globalization and the Nation-States* (Cambridge, England: Polity Press, 1992), p. 319.

3. Abbas J. Ali, *Globalization of Business* (Binghamton, N.Y.: Haworth Press, 2002), p. 8.

4. Bhoutros Ghali, "Global Leadership after the Cold War," *Vital Speeches of the Day* 75, no. 2 (1987): 87.

5. Lowell Bryan et al., *Race for the World: Strategies to Build a Great Global Firm* (Boston: Harvard Business School Press, 1999), chap. 1.

6. Ibid.

7. Ali, *Globaliztion of Business,* pp. 97–102.

8. Christopher A. Bartlett and Sumantra Ghoshal, *Managing across Borders: The Transnational Solution,* 2d ed. (Boston: Harvard Business School Press, 1998), chap. 1.

9. Thomas L. Friedman, *The Lexus and the Olive Tree* (New York: Farrar, Straus and Giroux, 1999), p. 146.

10. *Hemispheres* (United Airlines magazine), December 1997, p. 48.

11. Friedman, *Lexus and the Olive Tree,* p. 151.

12. *Washington Post,* 20 February 1998, p. 14.

13. Subhash C. Jain, *International Marketing,* 6th ed. (Cincinnati: South-Western College Publishing, 2001), pp. 516–58.

Chapter 4

THE MYTH OF GLOBALIZATION

The previous chapter examined the rise of globalization. Indeed, globalization has become a popular topic during the past decade. To the business community, globalization means an increasing ability to operate as though the entire world were a single locale, creating products and selling them wherever is best for the producer. Globalization permits free flow and free creation of information: for example, it means being able to import talent from India and China to companies in Finland or the United States that will create software to be bought in Mexico and Israel. What globalization implies is that the world has moved toward an age of unprecedented international economic integration in which markets, technology, telecommunications, and faster transportation have shrunk the world and borders have dissolved.

This chapter argues that in practice, globalization is a myth. Available economic information on world commerce does not support the globalization thesis. Instead, the world is heading toward regionalism, a breaking of the world economy into blocks. Most manufacturing and service activity is organized regionally, not globally. The MNC is the principal institution that promotes international business, and its modus operandi is regional.

Essentially, international business comprises two types of activities: international trade and foreign direct investment. Based on the analysis of foreign trade data and direct investment flows, it appears that regionalism is increasing, whereas globalization remains a distant vision among its proponents. Cross-border acquisitions and mergers, as well as cross-border branding, do not support globalization either.

FOREIGN TRADE PATTERNS

Exhibit 4.1 shows the intraregional and interregional trade for the United States, the European Union, and Asia for 1990 and 2000. More than one-third of U.S. trade is within North America, and in the period 1990–2000 this situation did not change significantly. The intraregional exports of EU members in 2000 were 69.1 percent, much higher than in 1990. In other words, the geographic scope of EU exports has not changed over the 10 years. For Asia, the intra-Asia exports in 2000 were slightly less than 50 percent of all exports. Here again, the situation did not register any significant change over the 10 years. The imports in the three regions show a similar pattern. Further, imports of most countries are dominated by the nearest giant. Some 75 percent of Mexico's imports are from the United States, and 65 percent of the Czech Republic's imports are from the European Union. Likewise, Japan is the single largest exporter to South Korea, Malaysia, Indonesia, Hong Kong, and China.[1] Overall, the data provide evidence that the world is forming into regional trade blocks, and moving toward greater regionalism.

Notwithstanding the progressive opening of the world economy over a long period, integration has not developed significantly, either in relation to the mass of domestically oriented economic activity or by historical standards. Between 1950 and 2000, the volume of world production rose more than 6-fold, whereas the volume of world merchandise exports rose more than 19-fold. International trade has grown more quickly than output in virtually every year since 1950, and the ratio of world trade to world output has tripled. Even so, gross world trade, at $6.8 trillion in 2000, remained less than one-quarter of world output.

Much more business is still conducted within countries than between them. Moreover, slightly over half of merchandise trade is conducted within regions of the world rather than between them. Despite the rapid growth of world trade over the past half-century, many countries are not much more open to trade today than before World War I.

FOREIGN DIRECT INVESTMENT FLOWS

In today's world economy, FDI plays a more significant role than foreign trade. For example, in 1998, the global sales of MNC affiliates were worth $11 trillion, compared with worldwide exports of goods and services of $7 trillion in the same year. Moreover, an estimated one-third of world trade is intrafirm trade within MNCs.[2]

However, most FDI flows from a few developed economies into other developed economies, in particular, in the triad countries (Japan, the

Exhibit 4.1
Intraregional and Interregional Trade Patterns

| | Asia Intraregional and Interregional Trade | | | |
| | EXPORTS | | IMPORTS | |
	2000	1990	2000	1990
Intra Asia	46.6	46.7	56.7	50.8
North America	26.3	26.1	17.2	17.1
Latin America	2.5	1.4	1.6	2.3
EU	18.1	14.4	15.4	13.9
Other Europe	0.9	4.2	1.4	4.8
Rest of World	5.6	7.2	7.7	11.1
	100	100	100	100

| | EU Intraregional and Interregional Trade | | | |
| | EXPORTS | | IMPORTS | |
	2000	1990	2000	1990
Inter EU	69.1	59.7	67.6	57.2
Other Europe	5.1	14.8	5	13.7
North America	9.9	8.6	8.4	8.8
Latin America	2.4	1.9	1.9	2.7
Japan	1.8	2	3.6	4.5
Other Asia	5.7	4.6	8.6	5.4
Rest of World	6	8.6	4.9	7.8
	100	100	100	100

| | U.S. Intraregional and Interregional Trade | | | |
| | EXPORTS | | IMPORTS | |
	2000	1990	2000	1990
Canada	23.7	21.5	19	18.6
Mexico	12.6	6.9	10.5	5.7
Latin America	7.8	6.6	5.8	6.4
EU	23.9	23	20.7	16.3
Other Europe	0.8	6.1	1.2	5.7
Japan	8.3	12.3	12.7	19.8
Other Asia	18	18.8	25.9	23.5
Rest of World	4.9	4.8	4.2	4.1
	100	100	100	100

Source: World Trade Organization.

European Union, and the United States). Flows to developing nations have recently increased but are still smaller, and the world stock of FDI is very unevenly spread. In fact, the FDI concentration of the triad increased between 1988 and 1998.

In 1988 the total outward stock of the triad was $1.02 trillion, of which $626 billion, or 61 percent, went to the triad. Ten years later, of the total

Exhibit 4.2
FDI Stocks among Triad Nations

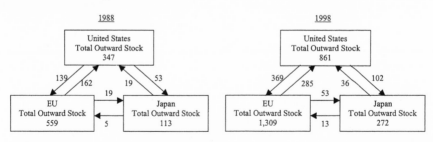

Source: UN Conference on Trade and Development.

triad outward FDI stock of $2.44 trillion, 63 percent, amounting to $1.54 trillion, ended in triad nations (see Exhibit 4.2).

As far as developing countries are concerned, their share has increased from about 30 percent in 1988 to 35 percent in 1998. But in 1998, one developing country, China, was the second largest recipient of FDI after the United States, with inflows of $46 billion, compared with $81 billion into the United States. China received 40 percent of all FDI attracted by the developing world. The rest of the developing world had to share the remaining 60 percent. Additionally, FDI inflows into developing countries are very unevenly distributed; the Asia-Pacific region absorbs 70 percent of all inflows, and the 10 most popular countries account for about two-thirds of total FDI stock in developing countries. This finding is not surprising, because FDI is privately owned funds looking for profit, and it is directed at nations that have the most viable environment for meeting the profit objective. Nevertheless, there is a problem for those developing countries that would welcome FDI inflow to boost their economic development but are unable to attract it.

From the point of view of globalization, FDI mainly flows between developed countries. Developing countries are brought into the loop based on ad hoc opportunities in a few nations. This situation has not changed for more than a decade. Thus, based on FDI perspectives, globalization has not advanced.

CROSS-BORDER MERGERS AND ACQUISITIONS

In the second half of the 1990s, mergers and acquisitions (M&As) involving firms located in different countries increased significantly, and

Exhibit 4.3
Total Value of Cross-Border Mergers and Acquisitions (in millions of dollars)

	By Economy of Seller			By Economy of Buyer		
	1988	1991	1998	1988	1991	1998
Developed economies	65,648	71,439	467,758	69,380	79,900	526,713
Developing economies	5,960	10,659	67,760	4,342	5,199	16,635
Share of developing economies	8%	13%	13%	6%	6%	3%

Source: United Nations, *World Investment Report,* 1999; and U.S. Department of Commerce.

M&As are now a popular mode of foreign entry. Cross-border M&As are primarily concentrated in developed countries, but there is also a trend toward higher M&A activity among developing countries.

As shown in Exhibit 4.3, during 1988–1991 the share of developing nations as sellers in cross-border M&As increased from 8 percent to 13 percent. To a large extent, the interest of developing nations in M&As is related to privatization programs of the telecommunications industry. Between 1991 and 1998, the developing countries maintained their share of cross-border M&As at 13 percent. The share of developing nations as buyers declined from 6 percent to 3 percent between 1991 and 1998. This finding may be partly attributed to the Asian crisis.

The cross-border M&A data reveal a pattern similar to FDI. Most transactions take place between the rich nations. Once in a while, countries like Mexico or one or two of the newly industrialized countries of Southeast Asia are invoked as sellers, especially in the wake of privatization of state-owned enterprises The cross-border M&A data do not show increased movement toward globalization.

Even within developed nations, where cross-border mergers have been on the rise, global companies that transcend business worldwide are not emerging. Consider the combination of Daimler-Benz and Chrysler. It was billed in 1998 as a merger of equals, but it turned into a German takeover, causing considerable bitterness and shareholder lawsuits in the United States. German executives have taken control of the U.S. operation in an attempt to stem its losses. Many of Chrysler's most senior executives have left or been forced out.[3] Take another example: Pharmacia and Upjohn, the pharmaceutical company formed through the 1995 merger of a Swedish and a U.S. company, also started life with global aspirations. The head-quarters were to be in the United Kingdom, and operational and R&D facilities were to be divided between the United States and Europe. But this plan did not materialize. Different centers of the company turned into squabbling fiefdoms. The company eventually moved its headquarters to New Jersey and has since been taken over by the Monsanto Company.[4]

Several companies that started out as British-French are now dominated by French executives, with British managers playing junior roles. These companies include Alstom, the transport and power engineering group; Eurotunnel; and Messier-Dowty, which makes aircraft undercarriages.[5] A number of other European companies billed as pan-European with global intentions are in fact coalitions of national interests, paying scrupulous attention to the sensitivities of their constituent nationalities.

Many companies have worldwide operations. Some even have multinational boards and executive teams. But almost without exception, none of these companies is truly global. The world's most successful companies remain clearly identified with their country of origin. General Motors and Microsoft are unmistakably American. Toyota and Sony are indisputably Japanese. Advocates of the global company may hope these national demarcations will decline, producing true transborder global organizations. But experience of cross-border M&As suggests a different outcome: one nationality will take clear control.

GLOBALIZATION OF BRANDS

Strong brands have the power to increase global sales and earnings. For companies in almost every industry, brands are important. A known brand name acts as an ambassador when companies enter new markets or offer new products.

It is interesting to note, however, that although global markets are emerging, only a few brands have permeated them. A recent study showed that of the 85 U.S. consumer nondurable brands, 29 (34 percent) were not marketed outside the United States at all. Others were only marginally marketed abroad.[6]

The companies surveyed showed a clear preference for selling their goods in markets culturally similar to the United States: Canada and the United Kingdom. Although one might argue that Canada was targeted so frequently because of its geographic proximity to the United States, the choice of the United Kingdom cannot be explained so easily. The United Kingdom is as far away as many other foreign countries, and its population and economy are smaller than those of several other foreign markets. The following are other key findings of the study:

- *Canada is the star.* Canada was the largest foreign market by far for U.S. brands (33 of the 56 brands sold abroad). In fact, Canada was the only foreign market for 13 brands. The United Kingdom was a distant second, being the largest foreign market for 5 brands. Mexico was next, with 4 brands, followed by Germany, with 3.

- *Few megabrands exist.* There were only 14 megabrands—brands that could be termed truly global in that they were marketed in more than 50 countries. The most internationalized brands were soft drinks, cleaning products, and over-the-counter drugs. Food products relied less on standard branding worldwide.

- *Older products are more international.* An interesting finding was that a majority (57 percent) of the brands sold abroad were launched before 1960. This finding challenges the notion that new brands are more likely than older brands to be designed for global markets.

- *No name changes exist.* One might expect the limited distribution of U.S. brands overseas to be offset somewhat by the distribution of foreign produced goods under different brand names, but this was not the case. Few survey respondents indicated that they sold similar items abroad under different brand names.

People worldwide have different needs. Thus, a brand popular in one nation may not be relevant in another country. For some products, limited discretionary income in some nations may prevent a company from taking its brand global. Consider photograhic film. Over one-half of the world has yet to take its first picture. In China, only about four-tenths of a roll of film is used each year per household, compared with about seven rolls of film per household in the United States and Japan.[7] It might appear that there is a huge unsatisfied demand for cameras and film in China. But a vast majority of people there don't have the income to engage in the luxury of taking pictures. By the same token, the infrastructure for getting photographs developed is not in place. Until economic conditions improve and people see the value of photography, there is no reason for Kodak to market its brand among the middle-class consumers in China.

RESPONSE OF MNCS TO GLOBALIZATION

With few exceptions, most MNCs are basically flag planters—domestic companies with foreign trading operations, manufacturing operations, or both. Overseas manufacturing operations might be very profitable, but they remain adjuncts to domestic business. Even Asea Brown Boveri (ABB), a Swedish-Swiss electrical engineering giant and a company often mentioned as an example of a real global company, is not truly global. The company's board of eight directors represents four nationalities, the executive committee has eight people from five countries, the corporate language is English, and the financial results are reported in dollars; and yet, as Jerry Wind and Jeremy Main have said, "at this point, ABB is more an experiment than a new business model."[8] Despite all its globalization efforts, more than half its business still remains in Europe.

Many factors discourage MNCs from going global. First, cultural differences in the marketplace play a significant role. These differences mean that companies cannot follow a standardized marketing strategy across the world. Unfortunately, although the demand for many products has become more homogeneous across countries, the product features that customers require and differences in technical standards among nations continue to hinder globalization. Consider the television industry. The international industry remains dominated by three broadcast standards: one for Europe, one for North America, and one for the Pacific region and Japan. The development of high-definition television was expected to homogenize those standards, but political pressures have become a stumbling block.

In addition, the ability of MNCs to manage far-flung operations through tight central control does not come easily, given that subsidiaries historically have demanded unique products, processes, services, and labor practices. Over time, subsidiaries develop cultures, systems, and structures that are incompatible with those of the parent. Thus, subsidiary managers are apprehensive about globalization and vehemently oppose it. The parent does not want to alienate and lose subsidiary managers, who might quit. Procter & Gamble endured a series of painful product failures because of its policy of imposing managers from headquarters on overseas subsidiaries.[9]

From the viewpoint of MNCs, regional strategies involve cross-subsidization of market-share battles in pursuit of regional production, branding, and distribution advantage. A company following regional strategies locates strategic decision making within the region, and its operations are organized toward regional-scale requirements. A regional strategy offers many of the efficiency advances of globalization while more effectively responding to the organizational barriers the company finds. Further, regionalism allows for faster delivery, greater customization, and smaller inventories than would be possible under globalization.

Above all, MNCs are reputed to be strongly attached to their home environment. Their strategies and organizational designs, as well as their relationships and interests, are invariably tied to the national interests and goals of their country of origin.[10] The underlying ideologies of MNCs are necessarily the economic, political, and cultural orientation of the home environment. Therefore, MNCs are incapable of playing global roles.

CHALLENGES AHEAD

For MNCs, the need to combine global clout with local savvy leads to two challenges: one organizational, the other motivational.

The Organizational Issue

Many firms try to organize their operations to be locally responsive but at the same time seek advantages of both scale and speed through central control. This combination has been accomplished by adopting matrix structures, wherein each unit reports simultaneously to a product group at headquarters and to a country manager. Many companies, such as Dow Chemical and Citibank, found that the matrix structure leads to frequent conflicts between the country group and the product group. Sometimes, even small differences of opinion end up as heated arguments. So the companies have gone back to their conventional structures, with clear lines of responsibility given to geographic managers.

The Motivational Issue

Motivating diversified workforces is even harder than implementing global structuring. It becomes difficult to motivate mangers with different cultural backgrounds to cooperate with one another. Companies have adopted two measures to motivate people: training and incentives. Training is needed at all levels to reorient thinking. Incentives encourage people to practice what they have learned. Philips, for example, has begun to open its top ranks in Holland to some non-Dutch individuals. Citibank and the Royal Dutch/Shell Group rotate managers. IBM has introduced performance measures to reward managers who are good global team players.

In the end, running a global company means trying to resolve a number of apparent contradictions. Firms have to be responsive to national needs, but they must also seek to exploit know-how on a worldwide basis; at the same time, they must strive to produce and distribute goods as efficiently as possible. Many companies manage to achieve one, or maybe even two, of these objectives. It is hard to think of any company that has yet managed to accomplish all three objectives simultaneously.

The concept of globalization has been made too simplistic. Although there are some economic drivers of globalization, extremely strong cultural and political barriers are preventing the development of a single world market. In only a few industries, such as consumer electronics, does globalization work, with homogeneous products being sold using a common worldwide marketing strategy. For most other kinds of manufacturers and services, market integration at a regional level is more relevant and feasible than globalization.

Attempts at Globalization—The Case of the Beer Industry

Dutch-based Heineken, the world's second biggest brewer, boasts that its beer is drunk in more than 170 countries and thus is the most international beer brand in the world. Belgium's Interbrew calls itself "the world's local brewer." In the past five years, it has made 17 acquisitions in 11 countries. Then there is the U.S. Budweiser, the world's largest brewer. A new entrant on the world scene is South African Breweries, which in 2002 acquired Miller Brewing Company to become the second largest beer company in the world. Despite the global consolidation of the industry, beer is one of the least global consumer goods of all. Nine out of every 10 cans of Budweiser are still drunk in the United States. About two-thirds of Heineken's and Interbrew's brands are drunk in the European Union. Furthermore, the industry is highly fragmented. Budweiser has only 3.6 percent of the world market, and the top 20 brands combined have barely more than a quarter of the market.[11]

The problem is common. People are deeply attached to their favorite brands, making beer an industry in which small local brands can continue to prosper. Besides, it is uneconomic to transport large quantities of beer across borders, where it is often heavily taxed. Building a local infrastructure, including a brewery and a distribution network, requires huge amounts of capital. Yet most beer tastes remarkably similar, making it a commodity business (95 percent of beer is pilsner). It is difficult to charge a premium price to differentiate a brand.

In addition, local regulations hold back firms with global ambitions. The beer industry might not enjoy the strategic importance of national airlines or car companies, but it is still important enough in the eyes of many governments to make it difficult for companies from different countries to invade one another's turf. The beer industry clearly demonstrates the difficulties involved in becoming global.

From the viewpoint of the MNCs, the advantages of globalization are more theoretical than real because of the following:

1. Industry standards remain diverse.
2. Customers continue to demand locally differentiated products.
3. Insider status remains critically important, especially in developing countries.
4. Global organizations are difficult to manage.
5. Globalization often circumvents subsidiary competencies.
6. Many managers believe that regional strategies increasingly are the primary determinant of competitive advantage.[12]

OBSTACLES THAT LIMIT GLOBALIZATION

Globalization means doing business all over the globe as one market with no barriers. This activity is neither realistic nor practical. Socioeconomic, cultural, and political differences among people make global integration difficult, at best.

World Poverty

Forty-eight percent of the world's population (about 3 billion people) live below the poverty line. Globalization has nothing to offer them, and vice versa. Ameliorating poverty is not an agenda item among the supporters of globalization, even though world poverty continues to grow. They conveniently assume that everyone on this planet wants the same material goods and that cultural differences have no significance.

The problem is that people in the West simply do not understand poverty. The picture is stark: any one of these statistics really is sufficient:[13]

- The richest 20 percent of the world population share 82 percent of the world income.
- The poorest 20 percent of the world population share 1.4 percent of the world income.
- The richest 50 million people, mainly in Europe and North America, have the same income as 2.7 billion poor people. The slice of the cake taken by 1 percent is the same as that allowed to the poorest 57 percent.

- And of course, the richest 20 percent cause the vast majority of the problems for the environment. The inhabitants of the industrialized countries constitute only one-fifth of the world population but consume—per inhabitant—nearly nine times more energy of commercial origin (mainly carbon based) than the inhabitants of developing countries.

Frankly, it is a moral problem. We should raise our children to find it intolerable that we who sit behind desks and punch keyboards are paid a hundred times more than the people who fabricate our keyboards in the Third World. Social justice is the only basis for worthwhile global economic integration.

Labor Mobility

If free trade and free movement of the elements of production are so good for the world, why not also encourage labor mobility as an equilibrium strategy? In Western capitals this idea is not subject to debate.

Economic Limits

The term *global economy* suggests that a worldwide fully equalized system of money, commerce, and trade exists. In reality, the global economy is an aggregation of multiple economic systems, driven by political states. At a macroeconomic level, the fact that no single global economy exists means that MNCs must select those areas in the world where the local economy supports profitable operations. For this reason, a company with a broad international presence may not be truly global. An international presence may be limited to the essentials of serving the local markets: maintaining sales and service centers and distribution operations. In other countries, manufacturing operations may exist primarily to take advantage of low labor rates.

Using labor rates as an example, let's say that there is a job building wire harnesses for automobiles, which is labor intensive. The price for this job in a unionized U.S. plant may be $28 per hour. Additionally, the fringe benefits and overhead of hiring an employee (i.e., training) in this job bring the rate to around $80 per hour. In a developing country, this job may be priced at $.75 per hour and, with overhead cost, at about $1.50 per hour. Traditionally, companies have moved operations to such locations to take advantage of the cheaper labor, which offsets the cost of shipping in raw materials and shipping out finished products. Today, in fact, there is a worker in the United States doing this wire harness–building job and a worker overseas doing the same job, with the same skill, and with the same quality and productivity, but the two work at different rates of pay. On a global basis, what is this job worth? One might think that a single job in a true global environment might command a single rate, but there is another socioeconomic factor here. The quality of life for each of these workers is quite different, and societies move to protect high standards of living and to improve low standards of living. Standards of living may also restrict the market opportunities. Luxury items may be limited to economically rich countries and may prevent global expansion.

Inflation

Inflation is another variable that partitions the global economy. In countries where runaway inflation exists, the climate for investment and commerce is unfriendly. Currency values and interest rates may limit or deter MNCs from investing in some countries. Capital investments in plants, facilities, and machinery must retain their value over time. Local costs of labor and materials, the valuation of inventories, and market prices must also be subject to reasonable inflationary escalation. The development of the euro as a common currency for the European community is a step toward facilitating trade and investment in the member countries. In theory, a true global economy would operate with a global currency and be subject to a global inflation rate. But this may never happen.

Value Systems

Another limitation to globalization is the differences in value systems. Different societies embrace differing value sets regarding business and commerce that reflect the values of their cultures. Value sets may involve business ethics, fair trade, human rights, environmental accountability, and intellectual property. The values embraced by a company may prevent or limit the extent to which that company is willing to globalize. For example, a company may refuse to extend its operations into China, despite the lucrative market potential, because of the human rights issues in that country. Many companies similarly refused to operate in South Africa under apartheid. Often a company's image is at stake, and the values held by the employees, shareholders, and other stakeholders are reflected in a company's actions. Many companies have adopted so-called green values, aimed at protection of the environment, as a company policy and also as a marketing strategy and have incorporated their policies, products, and financial support of the environment into their advertising. Differences in values can prevent or deter the presence of certain companies and products in a nation or region.

Benefits to the Developing Countries

A number of studies have concluded that MNC activities in developing countries do not do much for the hosts. For example, research on Pakistan by Ashfagne Khan and Yun-Hwan Kim showed that a 10 percent increase in the inflow of FDI increases imports by 1.8 percent, and that a 10 percent increase in FDI does not increase exports significantly. This finding led the authors to conclude: "When these two sets of results are taken together, it appears that FDI has worsened the country's trade balance."[14] Similar results were obtained by Jesus Felipe, who argued that FDI is not a panacea for economic development in poor countries.[15]

Political Constraints

Because of political influence driven by economic goals and policies, entry into some foreign markets may be possible only through joint ventures with private domestic firms or government-subsidized firms. Here the corporate investor may be allowed to have less than 50 percent of the joint venture, with control being retained within the country. Additionally, the terms of the deal might require supply localization, meaning that a specified percentage of materials and components must be purchased locally within the country. For some industries, the availability of quality local goods is limited, and the maintenance of multiple local sources may hamper the leverage a global corporation has on a single-source supplier. Furthermore, in many cases globalization is not acceptable to host governments. To them, globalization means minimal commitment to local markets.

Technology Transfer

Another obstacle to globalization might be the need for some forms of technology transfer to build up the industrial capabilities of the country. Investing firms may not want to transfer critical technologies that could be used to create competitors. It may be illegal to export some technologies from one country to another. The United States, for example, limits the export of technology to certain countries.

The One-World Fallacy

Proponents of globalization are idealists who look at one world as one market, fully efficient and capable of providing economies of scale. They forget that nationalism, racism, regionalism, religion, and caste are strongly embedded in human societies. To proponents of globalization, these concerns are managerial problems subject to ad hoc solutions.[16]

Global Corporation **Is a Misnomer**

According to Yao-Su Hu, the concept of a global or stateless corporation is misleading. The idea of nationality, home state regulation and taxing, the advent of bankruptcy and ownership, and control of voting stock suggest the significance of stateness, not statelessness.[17] In legal terminology, there is no international law under which an MNC can be formed and have legal existence in several nation-states.

The Elite Focus

The supporters of globalization comprise a few managers of large companies who are in the big league themselves and who try to enlist elites in other nations. In that process, they make assumptions that are entirely subjective. The point may be illustrated with reference to China. The globalists continue to be guided by a number of myths about China's economic potential.[18]

The first myth is that the People's Republic of China is a huge market. Although the large cities present a modern perspective, overall the Chinese market is quite limited. Foreign companies cannot distribute their own products unless they are made locally. Furthermore, with an average per capita income in China of at most $800 a year, few Chinese have the discretionary income to afford a PC or a car. U.S. exports to China are at the same level as exports to Belgium and Luxembourg, and much less than exports to Taiwan.

The second myth is that China will become the world's largest economy. China claims it has averaged economic growth of 10 percent annually. That pace has led to widespread predictions, among them that China's GDP could overtake Japan's by 2025 and the U.S. GDP by 2050. This scenario may not be realistic. Western estimates of Chinese growth are much lower, and the World Bank analyses project less than 5 percent growth for China beginning in 2005.

The third myth is that the key to modernizing China is foreign investments. Chinese industries have made progress over the past few years.

They have picked up some state-of-the-art technology and managerial know-how from select companies. However, the biggest outside investors in China are the overseas Chinese from Hong Kong, Taiwan, and the rest of Asia, who have mainly focused on low-tech industries in southern China, such as garments, toys, and shoes. Those labor-intensive operations created needed jobs and exports but did not bring in cutting-edge technology.

Fourth is the myth that China is immune from the Asian crisis. Actually, China suffers from many of the familiar symptoms, namely a lack of transparency, government interference in the economy, and shoddy business arrangements. Thus, China is as susceptible to bad economic management as any other nation unless steps are taken to straighten things out.

The last myth is that market forces have taken over the Chinese economy. Only some 40 percent of the industrial output in China is attributed to private ventures. The economy is dominated even today by state corporations and collectives. Essentially, the bureaucrats run the country.

CONCLUSION

It is evident that the limits of globalization are multidimensional and that each dimensional limit may interact with one or more other limitations. In the ideal world of true globalization, these limits might not exist. A theoretically ideal global economy and business environment might have more of the following characteristics:

- No trade laws or barriers.
- Open markets.
- A single currency.
- Inflation measured on a global basis.
- Consistent regulation regarding banking, taxes, labor, fair trade, the environment, and intellectual property.
- A common spoken and written language.
- A single ideology of culture and values.
- Worldwide availability of all technology.
- Equal access (at cost or by bid) to all geographic and natural resources.

This ideal world is only somewhat approximated in the definition of a country. Within a single country, many of these characteristics are evident or could potentially be put into place. It is inconceivable that the world could exist as a single country, but the map of the world will have to be redrawn to reflect the true global business environment. The redrawn map of the world might not show the United States or Germany or Japan. Instead, it might show Matsushita, ExxonMobil, Boeing, IBM, and Daimler-Benz. Through economic sovereignty, these giants might become the true superpowers of the future; their shareholders and employees would be their citizens, and their empires might comprise global partnerships and alliances. Will it be more important to be a citizen of France or a citizen of Airbus, of the United States or of Microsoft? Perhaps the destiny of globalization will be decided by these superpowers of industry. Their strength is influential and pushes every major government toward the creation of a more globalized business environment.

NOTES

1. *Economist,* 2 December 2000, p. 106.

2. United Nations, *World Investment Report,* 2001.

3. Michael Skapinker, "Global Brands with National Identity," *Financial Times,* 25 January 2001, p. iv.

4. Michael Skapinker, "Worlds Apart," *Financial Times,* 1 March 2001, p. xii.

5. Ibid.

6. Erdener Kaynak, "Who Sells, What, Where?" *International Marketing Review* 6 (1989): 7–19.

7. Ibid.

8. Jerry Yoram Wind and Jeremy Main, *Driving Change* (New York: Free Press, 1998), chap. 2.

9. *Economist,* 30 July 1994, p. 58.

10. "The Discreet Charm of the Multicultural Multinational," *Economist,* 30 July 1994, p. 57. Also see Paul N. Doremus et al., *The Myth of the Global Corporation* (Princeton, N.J.: Princeton University Press, 1998).

11. "This Euro Brew Is for You," *Business Week,* 24 July 2000, p. 120; and "The Big Pitcher," *Economist,* 20 January 2001, p. 63.

12. Allen J. Morrison, David Ricks, and Roth Kendall, "Globalization versus Regionalism: Which Way for the Multinational?" *Organizational Dynamics,* Winter 1991, pp. 27–29.

13. World Bank, *Global Economic Prospects and the Developing Countries* (Washington, D.C.: World Bank, 2002), pp. 4–6.

14. Ashfagne Khan and Yun-Hwan Kim, "Foreign Direct Investment in Pakistan," *EDRC Report* 66 (July 1999).

15. Jesus Felipe, "Globalization, Anything New?" working paper, Georgia Tech CIBER, Atlanta, 1999.

16. Robert S. Spich, "Globotalk: A Different View of Globalization," working paper, UCLA CIBER, Los Angeles, 1996.

17. Yao-Su Hu, "Global or Stateless Corporations Are National Firms with International Operations," *California Management Review,* Winter 1992, pp. 107–26.

18. "Five Chinese Myths," *Fortune,* 10 May 1999, p. 30.

Chapter 5

THE FUTURE OF GLOBALIZATION

In chapter 4, it was argued that globalization at this time is a myth. It has a long way to go to become a reality. Still, many groups in the industrialized nations are raising a hue and cry against globalization. Even when fears of recession were on the horizon in 2001, workers and government officials in nations as diverse as China, Mexico, and Hungary felt that the movement toward open markets had paid off. The tumultuous street drama of angry young middle-class westerners vilifying globalization and all its institutions seems bizarrely detached from the real-life concerns in countries that are supposed to be victims of globalization. Yet it would be a mistake to dismiss the uproar against globalization that began in 2000 in Seattle and has since gained further momentum at other places such as Washington, D.C.; Prague; and Genoa, Italy. It is time to reexamine the pros and cons of globalization as it affects different sections of society across the world. This reexamination will require a much more sophisticated look at the losses and benefits of open markets. Whatever hazards globalization does create must be addressed as it moves into the next stage.

CONDITIONS NECESSARY FOR GLOBALIZATION

Conceptually, globalization brings a good life to all. But globalization by itself is not enough. A number of conditions must be present in a nation before this process can deliver. In other words, globalization is not a magic formula that brings prosperity to all countries at the same rate in the same time frame. The dictum that all countries should open their markets to trade, direct investment, and short-term capital as quickly as possible, the inevitable result of which will be economic prosperity, may not hold true in all situations. Such an outcome depends on some enabling conditions: (1) the quality of a nation's macroeconomic management, (2) the efficiency of the administrative machinery, (3) the level of education of a nation's citizenry, (4) the anticorruption measures in place, and (5) a cultural motivation toward economic achievements.

Macroeconomic Management

A country that manages its economic affairs according to sound economic principles will benefit from global capitalism more than a country governed by political emotions and abrupt practices. The *macroeconomic management* refers to a country's ability to do the following:

- Sustain its internal and external debt.
- Pursue stable and diversified economic growth.
- Generate an adequate amount of foreign exchange.
- Legislate adequate regulations pertaining to the banking sector.
- Undertake appropriate fiscal and monetary means to steer the economy on a growth path.
- Follow business-friendly policies that allow MNCs and local companies to invest in modern technology, train workers, and nurture local suppliers and managers.
- Design a legal system that protects property rights.

Efficiency of Administrative Machinery

Every country has its own administrative scheme. The scheme emerges from such factors as experience, culture, systems of reward and punishment, availability of qualified administrators, and style of leadership. Additionally, the availability of modern means of transportation and communication helps to streamline government administration. A nation with efficient administrative machinery will benefit from globalization more than a nation bogged down with unnecessary administrative procedures and red tape. Adopting globalization policies will not help a nation in which senior administrators are not available, telephones do not work, files are forever lost, decision making is slow, and nobody seems to be in charge.

Exhibit 5.1
Relationship between Stronger Educational Systems and Globalization

Country	Gross Domestic Product (average percentage growth, 1990–98)	Education (% males completing 5th grade)	Poverty (% population below $1/day)
Chile	7.9	100	4.3
China	11.2	93	18.5
Malaysia	7.4	98	5.6
South Korea	6.1	98	2.0
Guatemala	4.2	52	39.8
India	6.1	62	44.2
Nigeria	2.6	70	28.9
South Africa	1.9	72	23.7

Source: World Bank.

The Level of Education

The quality of education at different levels distinguishes the countries whose workers thrive under globalization from countries that seem stuck in a screwdriver-assembly stage. As Exhibit 5.1 shows, China has fared better than India, and public education stands out as an important factor that separates the two giants. Whereas almost everyone in South Korea, Taiwan, Singapore, and Hong Kong received a high school education when their countries' export drives began decades ago, in much of Central America half of the population was never schooled beyond the fifth grade. It is not surprising, then, that Central America has been mired in horrific poverty.[1]

Anticorruption Measures

Nations where business deals are made on merit rather than on favoritism prosper under globalization. Where corruption influences decision making, globalization may not be much help. If a bank in a nation is forced to advance millions to a close relative of the president or the prime minister without proper scrutiny, the nation will suffer, globalization or no globalization. Similarly, when investment projects are undertaken on emotional grounds instead of sound economics, the results will be discouraging.

For globalization to work, governments must adopt measures to abolish corruption. They must start at the top so that people in power do not strike deals based on money payments, political favors, or other personal gains.

Individuals who succumb to bribery must be adequately punished. This policy will set an example for people in lower ranks.

A Cultural Motivation for Economic Prosperity

Not all nations attach the same importance to economic growth. Attitude toward growth can be explained in part by cultural differences among people. In Western societies, maximization of wealth is a common goal. Everybody likes to earn more and is willing to take risks and be enterprising. In Eastern societies, wealth is considered a means to an end and not an end in itself. Therefore, risk taking and entrepreneurship are not as common as in the West. Global capitalism generates and spreads economic growth more in nations where cultural orientation places a higher value on wealth accumulation and materialism.[2] Thus, if wealth maximization is not something that is favored in some nations, these countries may never be as prosperous as the United States, no matter how endowed they are by other enabling conditions.

Summary

Governments everywhere are at the center, playing the dominant role in creating conditions that spread economic growth with global capitalism. If governments are to gain from wide-open markets, they must understand the importance of delivering political stability, sound economic management, and educated workers. Asia's Tigers had many of these features or conditions when they began their export drives; most Latin American and African countries did not. To get the benefits of trade and capital flows, a nation needs a broad base of development. There is no automatic link between openness and growth in developing countries. Some countries face such immense challenges that they might not benefit for decades after lifting trade and financial barriers. Consider Africa, whose growth has fallen from 3.5 percent in the 1970s to 2.2 percent in the 1990s. MNCs have nothing against Africa, but the necessary stability, infrastructure, and skills are not there.

If globalization proceeds, whether it will fulfill its potential to be an equalizing force will depend on whether poor countries manage to integrate themselves into the global economic system. True integration requires not just trade liberalization but wide-ranging institutional reform. Many of the nonglobalizing developing countries, such as Myanmar, Nigeria, Ukraine, and Pakistan, offer an unattractive investment climate. Even if they do decide to open themselves up to trade, not much is likely to happen unless they also pursue other reforms. It is not easy to predict the reform paths of these countries; some of the relative successes in recent years, such as China, India, Uganda, and Vietnam, have come as quite a surprise. But as long as a location has weak institutions and policies, people living there are going to fall further behind the rest of the world.

The point may be illustrated with reference to Guatemala.[3] In 2000, a decade after Guatemala began to diversify its agricultural economy, the apparel industry generated $440 million in annual exports. Yet up to half of Guatemala's workers still earn less than $3 a day, the minimum wage, and a third of the adults are illiterate. Why has the export push not brought prosperity as quickly to Guatemala as it did to East Asia? The answer starts with Guatemala's being a fractured, strife-ridden society and includes its neglect of investment in its own people and its poor economic policies. Half of all Guatemalans are indigenous Indians, many of whom still speak little Spanish. The country is just beginning to recover from a 36-year civil war in which the military massacred entire villages. Unlike in most of East Asia, where land reform and far-thinking public housing policies helped peasants rise above the subsistence economy, in Guatemala just 2 percent of the people own 70 percent of the land. Small wonder that the rate of savings is about a third of Asia's rate, meaning Guatemala must depend heavily on foreign investors to grow. The country's business class, which is dominated by a handful of families, has thwarted most reform efforts. It is not surprising that the country is rife with sweatshops.

THE BACKLASH AGAINST GLOBALIZATION

In the last few years there have been numerous protests against globalization. The protesters are a diverse lot, as shown in Exhibit 5.2. They come mainly from rich countries, and their coalition has not always been internally consistent. They have included trade unionists who are worried about losing jobs and students who want to help the underdeveloped world gain them; environmentalists concerned about ecological degradation; and anarchists, who object to all forms of international regulation. Some protesters claim to represent poor countries but simultaneously defend agricultural protectionism in wealthy countries, whereas others accept the benefits of international markets but worry that globalization is destroying democracy. In recent years, the protesters as a group have come to be known as nongovernment organizations (NGOs).

Exhibit 5.2
Listing of Selected Groups against Globalization

A. Think tanks
  - Institute for Policy Studies
  - Economic Policy Institute
  - International Forum on Globalization
B. Consumer groups
  - Public Citizen's Global Trade Watch
  - Citizen's Trade Campaign
C. Human and civil rights groups
  - National Labor Committee for Human Rights
  - United Students Against Sweatshops
  - Human Rights Watch
D. Environmentalists
  - Friends of the Earth
  - Sierra Club
  - Humane Society
  - Greenpeace
E. Unions
  - American Federation of Labor–Congress of Industrial Organizations (AFL-CIO)
  - UAW
  - Teamsters
  - United Steel Workers
  - Unite
  - Mechanists and Aerospace Workers
F. Farmers
  - National Farmers Union
  - Family Farm Coalition
  - Institute for Agriculture and Trade Policy
G. Religious groups
  - United Methodist Church
  - U.S. Catholic Conference
H. Law firms
  - Center for International Environmental Law
  - Earth Justice Legal Defense Fund
I. Street theater groups
  - Earth First
  - Direct Action Network
  - Global Exchange
  - Ruckus Society

Overall, there are four major areas of concern relative to globalization: labor and human rights, the environment, democratic deficit, and ethical behavior.

Labor-Related Issues

In the area of labor, NGOs have two complaints. One complaint is that MNCs do not treat labor in developing countries humanely. They pay the workers extremely low wages and make them work in inhuman conditions. The other complaint is that MNCs transfer jobs overseas without considering the plight of displaced workers at home.

Investigators for U.S. labor and human rights groups estimate that thousands of sweatshops make products for U.S. and European companies. Often, when accused by activists of buying from sweatshops, MNCs dismiss the claims. But case studies and evidence show that sweatshops are all too common. For example, in a Chinese factory, guards beat workers, and owners deduct up to 70 percent of workers' pay for food and lodging. In addition, workers are denied overtime payments. At other places, lax safety is usual, and workers are exposed to hazardous chemicals.[4]

For many protesters, a range of images creates a graphic indictment of the human costs of globalization: young children knitting rugs or sewing soccer balls, shantytowns of people drawn to new industrial centers, row on row of workers stitching athletic shoes, export zones surrounded by razor wire. Although such images are compelling, they provide but one snapshot of a complex situation. Some interventions appear to offer promising models. The Rugmark campaign to certify that carpets are made without child labor offers a way to link consumer decisions with labor conditions and increases pressure to reduce the exploitation of children.[5] When accompanied by educational opportunities and support, these programs can make a difference. It is difficult, however, to determine the extent to which such remedial programs compensate for the loss of income for families deep in poverty.

Sometimes intervention results in unintended consequences. Efforts in Pakistan to reduce child labor in the manufacture of soccer balls shifted production from a home-based cottage industry to centralized stitching sites, where labor standards could be monitored. Parents, who previously worked at home, now commute to the central site. The program has reduced the element of child labor, but it may have worsened poverty for the families affected and increased the involvement of their children in the underground economy and sex trade.

Antiglobalists often use emblematic messages that appear to embody fundamental but competing truths about globalization and labor. Those who indict international companies for their labor practices may encapsulate their arguments in statements such as "It is clearly exploitation to pay a worker 10 cents for sewing a sweatshirt that sells for $35."[6]

On the other side of the debate are those who believe that these manufacturing jobs represent valued opportunities and a crucial economic step forward for poor countries. They say that so-called sweatshops are a rung of the ladder of economic development and that long lines of job applicants are testimony that these jobs are the best ones available.

Both of these statements have validity. Their role in the debate on globalization and labor, however, depends on one's theoretical orientation, as well as on a set of empirical assertions. From the perspective of free market economics, external efforts to improve jobs that are already better than the average in a producing country are misplaced. Economists traditionally see nonmarket efforts to improve pay as protectionist and, at best, counterproductive in terms of future economic development. Although this view addresses the overall operation of competitive markets, it offers little guidance on issues of equity and the distribution of economic resources. Theories of justice and traditions of both domestic and international law argue against leaving wage determination solely to market forces and hold that companies have a responsibility for ethical behavior and for the impact of their policies on employees, communities, and the environment.

Empirical questions present a third area of intellectual challenge. There is no clear agreement on answers to fundamental questions, such as whether trade liberalization increases or decreases the standard of living in producing countries. The answer depends on the specific examples selected, definitions, and the time period studied, as well as on the extent to which any change can be explained by other factors. Even straightforward questions, such as those pertaining to the wage level in factories, may be elusive. Official wage rates may not be the same as the wages actually paid. Hidden factors may reduce the wages for workers, and piecework rates can complicate hourly wage standards. On the positive side, incentive pay, bonuses, and in-kind remuneration (in the form of housing, services, and meals) may increase the effective wages of workers.

Assertions underlying positions taken by advocates on both sides of the globalization debate may rest on unproven assumptions. Jobs in export manufacturing are often described as the best jobs available in poor, producing countries. Although this assertion is surely true in many situations, it may not be universally true. Reports of protests by workers in privatized factories in China suggest that conditions and wages in the export sector are not always better than those in other local jobs.

These factors challenge universities to address theoretical and empirical issues in a highly charged environment in which the universities play an operational role. Successfully addressing these challenges will require drawing on the best academic traditions of openness, objectivity, and free debate.

Globalization leads companies to shift manufacturing to other lands, transferring jobs from the home base to distant areas. This statement is true to the extent that globalization as a concept suggests rationalization of operations on a worldwide basis. Thus, a company in a particular industry might decide to manufacture products away from home. But at the same time, companies (whether U.S. or foreign) in other industries might move new jobs into the United States, balancing out the jobs that left. In other words, this argument, especially in the case of the United States, does not hold. As a large market, the United States is likely to attract more jobs from abroad than those lost to foreigners. If Ford and General Motors close their U.S. factories, the loss in domestic jobs is more than compensated for by the jobs created by BMW and Mercedes-Benz in their assembly plants in the United States.

Environmental Issues

Often, NGOs target MNCs for ignoring the natural environment for the sake of commercial benefits. Sometimes these charges are baseless. At other times, MNCs become the scapegoat, because NGOs cannot find anyone else to blame. Unfortunately, the media love confrontations between NGOs and multinational enterprises, which encourage NGOs to grow even more aggressive. Consider the case of the Royal Dutch/Shell Group. In 1990, the company decided to bury one of its platforms at sea. According to company studies, this option was a more environmentally friendly alternative than dragging the platform back to the shore and dismantling it on land. But an environmental group, Greenpeace, was not convinced and launched an offensive media-driven campaign against the company. Shell backed down and accepted Greenpeace's demand to bring the platform back to the shore. In the aftermath, it was found that Shell had been right all along about the environmental impact. Greenpeace eventually issued a public apology.[7]

Occidental Petroleum Corporation faces a different challenge.[8] The Colombian government remains determined to develop its oil reserves in the U'wa region. The local people, the nature-worshipping U'wa community, oppose the development. For them, oil is the "blood of Mother Earth," and they threaten ritual mass suicide if anyone tries to extract it. According to the government, the oil production will bring development for the region and the country, and it will go ahead with the project despite the protest by the locals. Subsequently, Occidental was hired as the contractor for the project. Thanks to the mass media, the company became the victim and has been charged with destroying the region environmentally, ecologically, and culturally. The company claims to be working with community members to design and implement a project that will be the least disruptive to the U'wa as possible. But Occidental is just a contractor. If they pulled out today, the project would not die. There are other companies in the world waiting for this business opportunity. Suppose the Colombian government recruited a Chinese company for the project: Would the protesters such as Greenpeace be as willing to charge the Chinese company by moving their forces in Beijing? Probably not.

Nowhere are the issues more contentious than in investments, such as Occidental's, that extract natural resources from developing nations. Many of these projects have long been marred by corruption, military atrocities, ecological damage, and social upheaval. Sorting out the issues is vastly complex. Developing countries need revenues for growth. But the local people, many of whom still live in the Stone Age, are happy with easy survival and do not aspire to any aspect of modern living. Who is to blame? What can be done? There is no easy answer.

Another issue relative to environment is the concern for global warming. The evolution from fire to fossil fuels to nuclear energy has been a path of improved human health and welfare arising from efficient and effective access to energy. One tradeoff is that energy use by human beings has always produced environmental change. For example, on the one hand, it has resulted in the marking of the landscape by human artifacts, the removal of trees from major areas for wood burning, and regionwide polluting of air from noxious coal burning. On the other hand, the ready availability of energy that produces wealth through the free market system provides ways to remedy or minimize environmental damage from energy use.

With widespread industrialization, human use of coal, oil, and natural gas has become the centerpiece in an international debate over a global environmental impact that is global warming. Fossil fuels provide roughly 84 percent of the energy consumed in the United Sates and 80 percent of the energy produced worldwide. An attempt to address the risk of deleterious global warming from the use of these carbon dioxide–emitting fuels is embodied in the Kyoto Protocol. But on scientific, economic, and political grounds, the Kyoto Protocol as an attempt to control this risk while improving the human condition is flawed for two reasons. First, the risk of global warming is overblown. Second, the Kyoto Protocol is not likely to solve the problem in any significant way.

Projections of future energy use, applied to the most advanced computer simulations of climate, have yielded wide-ranging forecasts of future warming from a continued increase of carbon dioxide concentration in the air.[9] The middle-range forecast in the estimate of the UN Intergovernmental Panel on Climate Change, based on expected growth in fossil fuel use without any curbs, is an increase of 1 degree Celsius over the next half century. A climate simulation including the effects of implementing the Kyoto Protocol—negotiated in 1997 and calling for a worldwide 5 percent cut in carbon dioxide emissions from 1990 levels—reduces that increase to 0.94 degrees Celsius. Thus, the averted temperature increase with the Kyoto Protocol amounts to an insignificant 0.06 degrees Celsius.

To achieve the carbon dioxide emission cuts by 2012 that are required under the Kyoto agreement, the United States would have to slash its projected 2012 energy use by about 25 percent. Why, then, are the temperature forecasts so minimal in terms of averted global warming? The answer is that countries like China, India, and Mexico are exempt from making emission cuts, and China alone will become the world's leading emitter of carbon dioxide in just a few years.

Most economic studies indicate that the cost to the United States of the Kyoto carbon dioxide emission cuts would amount to between $100 billion and $400 billion per year. One major reason these costs are so high is that past U.S. energy policy has been constrained by political influences. For example, substantially expanding the number of U.S. nuclear power plants and reducing the number of coal plants would enable the United States to meet both its future energy needs and Kyoto's mandated carbon dioxide emission reductions. But no nuclear power plants have been built in the United States in over 20 years, owing to nontechnical factors.

Over the same period, renewable energy sources such as wind and solar power have been discussed to the point of distraction. But they are boutique energy sources: they produce relatively minute amounts of energy and do so intermittently. Although they may be cost-effective in limited locales, they are unreliable for large-scale electricity generation.

The Kyoto Protocol also has the potential to worsen international relations. The struggling economies of the world rely on the United States to maintain stability and to provide economic opportunity as a trading partner. Whereas the developing nations are exempt from making carbon dioxide emission cuts, the severe economic impact on the United States would dramatically curtail the country's ability to continue to promote international stability and to help improve those nations' economies. Whereas the economic catastrophe that would occur as a result of implementing the Kyoto Protocol is a certainty, an environmental catastrophe resulting from a failure to implement it is extreme speculation.

Two conclusions can be drawn about global warming and human energy use. First, no catastrophic human-made global warming effects can be found in the best measurements of climate that we presently have. Second, the longevity, health, welfare, and productivity of humans have improved with the use of fossil fuels for energy, and the resulting human wealth has helped produce environmental improvements beneficial to health.

In light of some of the hysterical language surrounding the issue of greenhouse gases, it is also worth noting that carbon dioxide, the primary greenhouse gas produced by burning fossil fuels, is not a toxic pollutant. To the contrary, it is essential to life on Earth. And plants have flourished—agricultural experts estimate a 10 percent increase in crop growth in recent decades—directly because of the fertilization effect of increased carbon dioxide in the air.

To sum up, according to current scientific evidence, the human-made global warming is relatively minor and will be slow to develop, affording us an opportunity to continue to improve observations and computer simulations of climate. These findings will serve to better define the magnitude of human-made warming and allow development of an effective and cost-effective response.

For the next several decades, fossil fuels are key to maintaining global economic integration and improving the human condition. According to the scientific facts as we know them today, there is no environmental reason we should not continue using fossil fuels.

Democratic Deficit

Protesters believe that globalization is destroying democracy. Their principal targets are international institutions. Antiglobalists consider these institutions illegitimate because they are undemocratic. A close examination of international institutions will reveal that they are not as powerful and threatening as the protesters indicate. International institutions emerge out of agreements among nation-states, and thus they have to be highly responsible to their creators. This way, they can claim some real, if indirect, democratic legitimacy. Moreover, they merely facilitate cooperation among member states and derive some authority from their efficacy. Their powers are limited. Most international institutions are weak organizations. Even the much-maligned WTO has only a small budget and staff. Its workings reflect the multilateral agreements of nation-states.

The real problem is that not all member states of international organizations are themselves democratic, so delegates from such governments do not represent the will of their people. As agents of states, international institutions often represent only certain parts of those states. In addition, a strong argument can be made that international institutions represent the viewpoints of the rich and powerful, and thus their accountability is limited to a few nations, mostly Western countries.

The Question of Ethics

Time and again, MNCs have been called unethical for attaching more weight to profits than to human considerations. The point may be illustrated with reference to the recent spotlight on the need to provide drug therapies at reduced prices to African victims of acquired immune deficiency syndrome (AIDS). In 1997, NGOs targeted pharmaceutical companies for suing the South African government for unfair trade practices on this matter. With 20 percent of its population testing positive for the virus that causes AIDS, the South African government passed a law permitting the import and production of cheap generic substitutes for the patented therapies then on the market. Giant drug companies such as Merck charged that the law violates international trade rules governing intellectual properties. The U.S. government backed the firms in this action, threatening to bring the matter to the WTO.[10] But the lawsuit generated a massive amount of negative publicity, partly due to the support of such NGOs as Doctors Without Borders, which had promised to buy and distribute the cheap generic drugs. Subsequently, the U.S. government abandoned its opposition to the South African law. At the same time, Merck and other firms announced that they would sell AIDS-therapy drugs at cost to developing countries, and they also dropped their lawsuit against the South African government.[11] Both the U.S. government and the pharmaceutical companies played an interesting damage-control game.

From the human standpoint, making drugs available to patients who desperately need them, irrespective of their nationality and income status, is a laudable goal. Yet such a policy's possible adverse consequences should be considered. If the giveaway means lower profits for manufacturers, leading to less incentive for innovation, the decision to help the needy may prove expensive for future patients with deadly and debilitating diseases.

This episode raises an interesting question: Who should bear the cost of subsidizing drugs sold to developing countries? Should it be pharmaceutical companies, governments of developing countries, foreign aid agencies, or charitable groups in industrialized nations? NGOs seem to think that only the drug companies should bear these costs. Economically, this position does not make sense. The public health policies of many developing nations are a shameful mess, and industrialized nations put up no more than a pittance to help them. Yet the drug firms are seen as the real culprits.

Linking Hands against Globalization

Undoubtedly, the antiglobalization movement is making headway. Therefore, it makes sense to identify the members of this movement. What do they want? How are they funded? Where are the funds going?

It turns out that antiglobalization activism is a formidable movement. As a matter of fact, it is a movement of movements. It is diverse and inchoate, without a unified agenda or a traditional leadership. It is, however, well coordinated, well informed, and increasingly well funded. What is surprising is that a growing number of people think it has mainstream values and mass appeal.

It would be wrong to dismiss the antiglobalization movement as a traveling circus of anarchists. Most of the participants in the movement are middle-class white individuals in the United States and Europe. The movement is backed by respected economists, businesspeople, and politicians, although there are many members who are clowns, arsonists, Molotov cocktail–throwing thugs, unwashed hippies, Luddite reactionaries, vegan spiritualists, unreconstructed communists, regressive utopians, and smoked-out dreamers.

Basically, the movement presents a mixture of fuzzy thinking and fast-and-loose economic statistics, although its arguments sometimes are supported by sound evidence. There are four characteristics of the antiglobalists that raise questions about their agenda. First, on matters of importance to developing countries, these people behave as self-appointed leaders of these nations. They do not have formal or informal authority to represent developing countries. Second, most of the participants in the movement have little experience of life in developing countries. They do not know what poverty is, yet they speak for the poor. Third, they do not know the basis of the free enterprise system and capitalism. Fourth, their arguments are con-tradictory. To discourage child labor they want MNCs not to buy, for exam-ple, apparel from countries where children work to produce this clothing. But implementing this practice would erect a protectionist wall against imports from developing countries. Above all, although the antiglobalists are unhappy about the current perspectives, their efforts to put together a positive program for change have been fraught and unconvincing. Their bumper-sticker ideology—"Another world is possible"—does not mean much, because they have failed to come up with a vision of what the other world would look like.

The antiglobalization movement does not have a single source. The queasiness about globalization has been fed from many directions: the antiapartheid movement, the campaign against U.S. intervention in Cen-tral America, environmentalism, the emerging protest movements in the Third World, famine relief in Africa, the Asian financial crisis, human rights protection, acid house raves in Europe, road rallies organized by Reclaim the Streets, and hip-hop music in the United States.

Among some, there is a sense of growing inequality, stoked by mass worker layoffs, widespread job insecurity, and disgust at soaring executive pay. There is a discomfort over the commercialism of public space, rein-forced by the idea that Starbucks, McDonald's, and the Gap have overrun everyplace in the industrialized world. Among others, the response is emo-tional, even spiritual. There is an ennui of affluence. The members of the younger generation who have grown up having everything wonder if there is more to life than accumulating wealth. Antiglobalization has given them an opportunity to pursue something worthwhile.

Many antiglobalists are well-heeled people who have a vested interest in supporting the movement.[12] Consider Manu Chao, a Franco-Spanish rock star who has become the bard of the antiglobalization movement. He is the founding member of Attac, Europe's leading antiglobalization group, which seeks to create a just society through raising taxes and restricting financial markets. Although Chao makes his millions through working for an MNC (the company that produces and distributes his music tapes and compact discs), he charges the MNCs with dictating the world economy.

LOOKING AHEAD

On the face of it, the process of globalization is irreversible. Revolution-ary changes in communications and distribution systems, economies of scale, and the obvious benefits of free trade and open borders are too

encouraging to let the process slow down. But the crowds of angry protesters from Seattle to Genoa, Italy, have challenged the political legitimacy of
the process. Will this challenge lead to the failure of globalization? Historically, it has happened, and with grim consequences.

The sixteenth century brought new discoveries, new ideas, new wealth.
But these achievements were followed by a backlash of inflation, large and
brutal armies, new diseases, and intellectual repression. The late nineteenth
century was a period of extraordinary mobility in capital, information,
goods, and people. It was a time of economic stability and great optimism.
War between highly developed industrial states had become unthinkable.
Some of that spirit survived World War I: in the 1920s there remained enormous enthusiasm for internationalism and free trade. But the wave of globalization came crashing down in the Great Depression of the 1930s, a time
of beggar-thy-neighbor policies and militant nationalism.

With the tragedy of September 11, 2001, that struck the United States
and the nation's response in the form of war on terrorism, along with
worldwide economic slowdown, history could repeat itself. Global economic integration is not an ineluctable process, as its enthusiastic advocates believe. Worldwide governments can play a major role in preventing
the process of globalization being stopped.

One obvious difference from the past on the road to globalization is the
significant role of technology as the major driver of the process. The
advances achieved in computing and telecommunications in the West offer
an enormous, indeed an unprecedented, scope of wealth creation, not only
in rich countries but also in the Third World. New technologies promise
not just big improvements in local efficiency but also future and potentially bigger gains that flow from infinitely denser networks of connec-
tions, electronic and otherwise, with the developing world. These gains are
not only the profits of Western and Third World corporations but also the
productive employment and higher income for the world's poor—the
meaning of growth through integration for developing countries. In terms
of relieving want, the adoption of globalization is the difference between
South Korea and North Korea, between Malaysia and Myanmar. It is, in
fact, the difference between North and South. Globalization is a moral
issue, and it is up to nation-states to keep the momentum going. The rabble of exuberant irrationalists on the streets and the mild public skepticism
that is open to persuasion should not become the primary reasons to stop
the process of globalization.

The best way to view globalization is as an ongoing process that is not
new and has not progressed very far. It failed in the past because people and

the institutions that were created could not adequately handle the psycho-logical and institutional consequences of the interconnected world. Institu-tions that were developed to make globalization possible cracked under the strain and became the channels of their own destruction. We face a similar challenge today, but there are steps that the major actors in the globalization game—governments; MNCs; and global institutions such as the IMF, the WTO, and the World Bank—might take to save the movement.

Educational Programs

If globalization is to succeed, governments all over the world will have to undertake a massive educational campaign to seek general support. Pro-grams focused on the virtues of globalization and on recognizing the chal-lenges of this movement will go a long way in this pursuit.

The Role of MNCs

No one will wish to defend corporate irresponsibility or suggest that business should be against globalization. It is little wonder, therefore, that corporate social responsibility is a popular notion. To attack the responsi-bility of MNCs toward society is like assailing motherhood. Yet the stance of social responsibility is not merely undesirable but also potentially quite dangerous.

Hostility to markets is sour old wine. The collapse of Communist nations has destroyed the illusion that abolishing private property would create a paradise. Yet this failure barely touched the enemies of the market. Only their aims have changed. Today's goal is not to eliminate private business but to transform the way it behaves.

One wonders why people in developed countries are hostile to, or highly critical of, multinational enterprises, capitalism, freedom of cross-border trade and capital flows, and the idea of a market economy. After all, their good life, which is the envy of former Communist countries and the devel-oping world, has been the result of this system. One might expect, and indeed hope, that the business community would effectively counter such antibusiness views. Unfortunately, businesses approach the market with apologies, followed by concessions and accommodation.

The point may be illustrated with reference to Nike.[13] In 2001, the com-pany issued its first corporate responsibility report, which claims that it has already done much to address the charges leveled at it by anti-sweatshop campaigners, and yet much more needs to be done in the future.

Nike's experience provides a vivid illustration of the perils facing companies that believe they cannot ignore the efforts of campaigning organizations. The first lesson from Nike's experience is that once campaigners decide to latch onto a company, they can use the Internet to spread the word rapidly.

For example, in 2001 a graduate student at the Massachusetts Institute of Technology responded to Nike's offer to personalize customers' trainers by asking for the word *sweatshop* to be printed on the side. When Nike refused, the student e-mailed the company, saying, "Thank you for the time and energy you have spent on my request. I have decided to order the shoes with a different ID, but I would like to make one small request. Could you please send me a color snapshot of the 10-year-old Vietnamese girl who makes my shoes?" His e-mail exchange with Nike was flashed around the world.

The second Nike lesson is that being accused of malpractice has a damaging effect on employee morale. The company does not own any factories. Its goods are manufactured by subcontractors. Nike's own staff are designers and marketers, and they do not enjoy the campaigns against their company.

Monitoring what is happening in the factories is not easy for Nike, or for other manufacturers of clothing and shoes. The company's products are made in more than seven hundred factories in fifty countries. Malpractices have been documented in several of them.

One notorious example, mentioned in Nike's corporate responsibility report, was in Pakistan, where village children were found to be hand-stitching footballs. Nike describes this as "by far our worst experience and biggest mistake." The company reacted by restricting the manufacturing of the balls to one contractor, which agreed not to hire workers under age 18.

Nike has been dogged by allegations of using child labor elsewhere, too. The company's instructions to its contractors are that workers making clothing or equipment should be at least 16 years old and that no one under 18 should be involved in making shoes. Nike says its policy is that any contractor found employing workers younger than that must remove them from the workplace, send them to school while continuing to pay their wages, and agree to rehire them after they have reached the Nike minimum age.

After a BBC documentary in 2000 accused Nike of using child labor in Cambodia, the company reviewed the records of all 3,800 workers and interviewed the individuals it suspected were under age. Cambodian birth records were never very reliable, and many were erased during the Khmer

Rouge massacres. Nike admits that even its review of the Cambodian factories cannot ensure that the company got it right.

Nike decided to find a partner in the noncorporate world to help it monitor what was happening in its subcontractors' factories. In 1999, it gave a $7.7 million grant to the International Youth Foundation (IYF) to establish an organization called the Global Alliance for Workers and Communities. Gap, the clothing company that also has been heavily criticized by anti-sweatshop campaigners, also has joined the Global Alliance, as has the World Bank.

Despite the fact that it was set up with Nike money, the Global Alliance has not been a soft touch. Last year it published a report on nine Indonesian factories that make Nike products. The Alliance said it had found instances of verbal abuse and sexual harassment in all nine factories. Verbal abuse was the most marked, with 30 percent of the workers having personally experienced, and 56 percent having observed, the problem. An average of 7 percent of workers reported receiving unwelcome sexual comments, and 3 percent reported being physically abused.

Nike admitted that it had no idea of the scale of the problem.

The detractors projected an image of the factories as dark. In fact, they were bright, but what happens underneath is different. The maltreatment of the largely female workforce making Nike products is difficult to deal with. An issue like sexual harassment is highly complex. In the factories, one culture may be managing another. Koreans or Taiwanese may be managing in Vietnam. Despite all Nike's efforts, critics are still unimpressed with the company.

The question is why demonstrations singled out Nike. There are factories all over the world that are truly sweatshops in the classic sense. Protesters chose to target Nike because it had the largest profit margins and could afford to pay more, because it led the push into low-wage countries with poor human rights records, and because it was the market leader. Success many be attractive to shareholders, but it means companies have to be even more alert to the threat of bad publicity.

The idea of corporate social responsibility today is more than a merely defensive one. It is positive and broadly focused, amounting to a transformation of the objectives of the company and so of the market system. In this view, it is not enough for companies to pursue profits within the constraints of law and the principles of honest dealing. They are asked to take a leading role as agents of economic, social, and environmental progress. In other words, business is expected to enthusiastically embrace and adopt the notion of corporate citizenship. This notion takes the form of a triple bottom line corresponding to three facets of economic, social, and environmental consensus for the sake of sustainable development. Implementing the triple bottom line involves a transformation of how businesses operate.

A variety of criticisms can be made of such a radical redefinition of corporate objectives: it accepts a false critique of market economy; it endorses an equally mistaken view of the power of MNCs; it risks spreading costly regulations worldwide; it is more likely to slow the reduction of global poverty than to accelerate it; it requires companies to make highly debatable political judgments; and it supports a form of global neocorporation in which unaccountable power is shared among companies, activist groups, some international organizations, and a few governments.

Critics argue that MNCs should put people before profits. They have a basic hostility toward the profit motive. Unfortunately, it is difficult for them to understand that by seeking out opportunities for profit, business contributes to economic and social development. Competitive businesses are forced to seek new markets and employ underused resources. In so doing, they benefit their customers, their employees, and the country in which they operate. Furthermore, the critics hold the view that governments are impotent before modern MNCs. This point is often underlined by inappropriate comparisons between the revenues of companies and the GDPs of countries. In reality, governments remain potent local monopolists of coercion. At the same time, however, globalization has reduced corporate monopoly power by enhancing competition.

Contrary to what many critics may suppose, the meaning of economic, social, and environmental development is far from self-evident. Frankly, these notions are mush. Judgments on what they mean and how to contribute to each of them are inherently and deeply political. Are MNCs the right institutions to make such judgments? If so, how and by what authority are they to do so?

Lately, some activists have introduced a new notion of civil society. They have wrongly deemed elected governments powerless, and they assert that only concerted action by companies, activist groups, and governments can achieve the global goals on which every right-thinking person is supposed to agree. But this is global neocapitalism. As such, it is as subversive of individual freedom and democratic accountability as the old-fashioned domestic type of capitalism.

MNCs in today's world have a difficult job to do. Shareholders clamor for value. So do the customers. But when MNCs try to deliver, they face the protest from NGOs, which charge that corporations are exploiting workers in poor countries. Many MNCs have responded to this problem by undertaking studies and making the results public. Reebok's endeavors illustrate the effort.

In October 1999, Reebok published a 41-page report on its operations in Asia.[14] The report was put together by an independent local firm, and a senior executive was entrusted with the task of implementing the desired changes in the company's operations in Asia. An interesting difficulty that the company faced was introducing industrial-world values into industrializing-world plants. For example, on the matter of sexual harassment, workers did not even understand its meaning and could not recall any incident of that nature. Thus, before introducing measures for avoiding sexual harassment, workers and managers would need training in gender awareness. Similarly, there would be a thriving local market in empty chemical containers if the firm did not insist on their safe disposal. Many workers in the plants hate wearing protective clothing, so they must be taught that industrial safety measures are for their benefit.

To sum up, people in developed countries need to understand that the role of well-run companies is to make profits, not save the planet. Let them not make the error of confusing the two.

Third World Poverty

Activists who speak on behalf of the poor in developing countries are completely out of touch with reality. What looks like a sweatshop to a comfortable Harvard student or a Manhattan activist can look like the opportunity of a lifetime to a Salvadoran mother of five or a Bangladeshi factory worker.

In the half century before 1914, most capital flows could be traced back to a few thousand wealthy European families. Today, the capital flows are driven by fund managers allocating the savings of hundreds of millions of people in pension funds and mutual funds. Currently, most of the world's retirement assets are in the United States, Great Britain, Switzerland, the Netherlands, and a few other English-speaking countries. But countries as diverse as Chile and Thailand have been promoting pension savings, which should also encourage the growth of their domestic capital markets.[15]

In the past 10 years, free trade has done more to alleviate poverty than any well-intentioned law, regulation, or social policy in history. More people in China and India rose out of poverty between 1990 and 2000 than the

Exhibit 5.3
Globalization Scoreboard

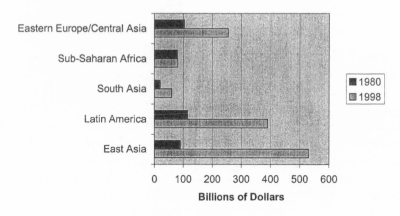

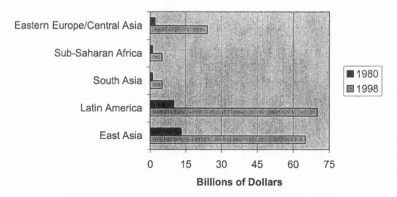

Source: The World Trade Organization and World Bank.

entire population of the United States. China and India alone account for almost 40 percent of the world's population. A number of other countries, such as Brazil and Mexico in Latin America, Poland and Hungary, Thailand, and the Philippines, made huge advances in wealth. As Exhibit 5.3 shows, as a result of globalization, trade has surged everywhere, and foreign investment has expanded.

It is true that not every region or every nation has benefited, and millions still live in appalling poverty. Growth in Africa has remained stubbornly low, and most of the so-called transition economies are still in an economic slump. But even when figures from Africa are included, the annual per capita income grew at an average rate of 3 to 6 percent in the developing nations in the 1990s, which is double the 1.8 percent growth of the advanced economies (U.S. growth averaged 2.7 percent). A recent World Bank study proves that growth helps rich and poor alike. The highlights of this landmark study are summarized in Exhibit 5.4.

Although trade is the single biggest reason for the developing world's growing prosperity, it is not the only one. Earlier, a number of prerequisites for growth were discussed, and in nations where those factors are present there is greater growth. One additional factor for the growing prosperity of the developing world is slower population growth. But because rising income is a precursor of slowing population growth, this factor, too, is at least in part a result of the rising prosperity that accompanies increases in trade.

Why are activists not satisfied with the impact of globalization on Third World countries? It is because most people are unaware of the positive effects of globalization. Thanks to mass media, most people hear only bad news, such as news about disputes between farmers in the United States and Europe, the Asian financial crisis, the Mexican fiasco, and so on. The most potent image of globalization is of the mayhem in Seattle in December 1999, when a meeting of the WTO was disrupted by masked thugs. This happening received wide coverage. Thus, what is needed is an educational program to teach the basics of free trade and how it brings about prosperity to all the players. Governments can take a major role in this endeavor.

Education for the Dissidents in Developing Countries

According to a report issued by a squadron of multilateral agencies, the United Nations, the World Bank, the OECD, and the IMF in June 2000, the number of people who live on less than a dollar a day dropped by 100 million between 1990 and 1998. The number remains astoundingly high, 1.2 billion, but it should be noted that the drop came even as the population of poor nations grew by hundreds of millions. It is generally accepted that the world's poor are getting less poor in both absolute and relative terms. Furthermore, the more globalized that poor nations become, the better their people do in both absolute and relative terms.

Governments in some developing countries may see globalization as a threat to their power. They overstate the dangers. Where governments reflect, democratically or otherwise, the preferences and beliefs of most

Exhibit 5.4
Globalization and the Poor

Critics of globalization often complain that although it leads to growth, it ignores the poor. In other words, under globalization, the rich get richer. As the prosperous become more so, inequalities become wider and the poor is [*sic*] left out. This claim is made about rich and poor countries, and about rich and poor people within any given country. A recent World Bank Study refutes this view.

According to this study, growth really does help the poor; in fact, it raises their incomes by about as much as it raises the income of everyone else.

The authors of this study look at data on growth, incomes and a variety of other variables for a sample of 80 countries extending over four decades. On average, incomes of the poor rise one-for-one with incomes overall. There is relatively little variation around that average. If you plot incomes of the poor against overall incomes, the points all lie close to that one-for-one straight line. For instance the data yield 108 episodes of at least five years in which overall incomes per head grew by 2% or more a year. In all but six of these cases, incomes of the poor also rose. They emphasized that this is not "trickledown"—meaning that the rich get richer and then, after a while, the poor do better as well. The rich, the poor and the country as a whole are all seeing their incomes rise simultaneously at about the same rate.

The study then looks at some other ideas about the course of poverty in development. The oft-cited "Kuznets hypothesis" holds that intra-country inequality increases in the early stages of development and then falls later on. Not so, it now appears. Dividing the sample between rich countries and poor counties, the authors find that the link between incomes overall and incomes of the poor is, as before, roughly one-for-one in each case, and that in this respect the two sets are statistically indistinguishable.

Another myth: in crises, the poor see the biggest falls in income. Again, dividing the sample into crisis and non-crisis episodes, the authors find that the one-for-one link remains intact. (This is not to deny that a 10% fall in income hurts a poor man more than a rich man. But if the claim is that incomes of the poor fall in crisis by proportionately more than the incomes of the rich, it is wrong.) And yet another myth: it is often argued that growth used to benefit the poor, but in the new world economy no longer does so. Dividing the sample into two halves at 1980, the connection between incomes of the poor and incomes overall remains one-for-one in both periods.

Finally, the authors ask whether particular policies and institutions have a systematically different effect on the poor. For instance, does globalization

(continued)

Exhibit 5.4
(continued)

increase intra-country inequality? The answer to that is not. The study looks at the effect of openness to trade (measured by the sum of exports and imports relative to GDP) first on incomes overall, and then on the distribution of income. It finds that openness spurs growth to a statistically significant extent, and has no discernible effect on distribution. In short, globalization raises incomes, and the poor participate in full.

Economists have long argued that the rule of law is crucial in development. The authors confirm this: stronger property rights promote growth. But do stronger property rights skew the benefits of growth away from the poor, as some might suppose? Again, no. The effect on distribution is statistically indistinguishable from zero. What about democracy? The income effects are small and statistically insignificant through both channels. Even primary education, surprisingly, has no perceptible pro-poor bias, although it does, as expected promote growth, and therefore helps the poor to that extent.

Only two policies appear to have a systematically biased effect-that is, they affect the distribution of income as well as growth in incomes overall. One is cutting inflation, and the other is cutting public spending. Both of these raise growth, as can be expected. Interestingly, they also *improve* the distribution of income, benefiting the poor twice over.

Surveys often show that the poor hate inflation more than the rich. This study demonstrates why: the evidence in this study shows that inflation causes a proportionately bigger drain on the incomes of the poor than on the incomes of the rich. The public-spending result seems more surprising. High public spending is often justified as a way to help the poor. So far as their incomes are concerned, it seems to do the opposite: it retards growth, which directly reduces the income of the poor and everybody else, and then on top of that it tilts the distribution of income to the poor's disadvantage. "Social spending," the category of public expenditure most explicitly targeted on the poor, is merely neutral, having almost no effect one way or another on either growth or distribution.

It is hard to believe that this study is going to change many globalization backlashers' minds. After all, the authors are from the World Bank, so their work can be put in the bin unread. But perhaps it is not too much to hope that governments will be a bit less apologetic, a bit less pandering, now that they have been shown so plainly that growth is as good for the poor as it is for everybody else.

Source: Global Economic Prospects and the Developing Countries: Making Trade Work for the World's Poor (Washington, D.C.: World Bank, 2002), pp. 5–8.

citizens, and where those preferences call for cultural distinctness and non-Western values, economic integration does not militate against diversity, least of all against religious beliefs. In the West, globalization has been running at full power for years. Has it mashed the United States, France, Italy, Germany, Sweden, and Japan into a homogeneous cultural putty? It has not, and there is no reason why it ever should.

Psychological Challenges

Globalization brings about change, and change can be frightening, as well as exhilarating. Even individuals who are benefiting the most from globalization are stressed and anxious. Unemployment may be extraordinarily low in the United States, but mergers and layoffs are at record highs, forcing people to live their lives full of uncertainty. Working at Net speed and on Net hours increasingly eats into family time. It is upsetting.

The inrush of cheap communications, powerful computers, and the Internet all demonstrate that change is happening even more rapidly as technological progress accelerates. Moore's Law, the observation that the power of microchips doubles every 18 months, has been tested and found to be correct.[16] It is these rapid changes that give people a sense of the world shifting beneath their feet. Both governments and MNCs have a role to play in quieting people's concerns about the impact of technology in pushing globalization, which in turn requires change.

Globalization's Impact on Labor in Developed Countries

Increased globalization has been viewed with concern in many advanced economies. There is a common belief that globalization harms the interests of workers, especially unskilled workers, either directly by liberalizing immigration or indirectly through trade and capital mobility. These beliefs appear to be at odds with the empirical evidence that globalization has only a modest effect on wages, employment, and income inequality in the advanced economies. (By contrast, changes in technology have led to a pervasive shift toward more skilled workers and fewer less-skilled ones.) Moreover, the belief that globalization threatens wages and jobs is contradicted by the historical evidence that free trade and the mobility of labor and capital improve global welfare and tend to improve national welfare for all countries involved.

Still, despite the overall benefits of globalization for national welfare, there are adjustment costs for particular groups within a nation. The adjustment of workers displaced by import competition occurs slowly and with significant costs, such as the need to obtain information about new opportunities, relocation, and the loss of firm- or industry-specific knowledge. Policy makers must keep in mind potential dislocations and ensure that people who are displaced do not become marginalized.

It is important, however, that any policy actions provide incentives for workers and firms to adjust to, and therefore gain from, changes in the economic environment. The adjustment costs can be minimized by encouraging flexible labor markets and by reducing structural rigidities facing firms, such as onerous work rules, staffing requirements, and hiring and firing costs.[17] Other policies might include gathering and spreading information about labor market conditions, standardizing professional certification procedures across countries, and enhancing training and educational opportunities so that workers in the advanced economies can upgrade their skills to match the demands of the changing global economy.

Unfortunately, policy makers with limited political time horizons may be more concerned with avoiding these short-term adjustment costs than with nurturing the long-term benefits of free trade, increased mobility of labor and capital, and labor market reforms. This view is misguided. The world economy has never been healthier than it is today. A good deal of the credit for this higher standard can be traced to globalization.

Making Globalization Democratic

Many critics of globalization worry that it destroys democracy. This is a genuine concern, and it must be addressed adequately if globalization is to survive. Democracy requires elected officials who are accountable and removable by the majority of people in a jurisdiction, as well as protection for individual and minority rights. How can democracy be instituted at the global level? The concept of one state, one vote is not right, because it would grant a citizen of a small country such as the Maldives a thousand times more power than it would a citizen of China. However, treating the world as a single constituency in which the majority rules would mean that more than 2 billion Chinese and Indians could easily get their way. (Incidentally, such a democratic setup will be very disheartening for NGOs that seek international environmental and labor standards, because both of these two giants are opposed to them.)

Despite these obstacles, there are many ways to make global institutions democratic. The international institutions can be structured so that enough space is preserved for national political processes to operate. For example, the WTO procedures for settling disputes can intrude on domestic sovereignty, but a country can reject a judgment if it pays carefully limited compensation to the trade partners injured by its actions.

Basically, global institutions should be designed so that democratically elected officials of a nation have the final say in accepting or rejecting the institutional decisions. But in the interest of global harmony, a nation that refuses to abide by the decision made by a global institution must be willing to pay some penalty so that nations do not habitually reject all the decisions. Furthermore, a flexible route of political negotiations should be available to each nation so that domestic political choices can be accommodated.

Cost-Benefit Analysis

Globalization has different meanings for different interests. To a businessperson, it means integration of all activities to serve worldwide customers. For technocrats, it means the free flow and free creation of information. To artists, it can mean that the traditional forms of expression find fans overseas to sustain the artists at home: a musician in New Orleans can be influenced by rhythms created in Sydney. For the activists who stormed the WTO meeting in Seattle, however, globalization has darker meanings: it portends exploitation of labor, the destruction of the environment and traditional cultures, and the erosion of national sovereignty in distant regions to meet the needs of people in developed nations for cheaper products and energy.

The single correct meaning of globalization is difficult to find. The crucial point is that the issue of globalization is hardly straightforward, and the differences between economic and social goals must be weighted. Going ahead with globalization will be difficult without a careful cost-benefit analysis of alternatives. But such an analysis is not going to be easy. As far as MNCs are concerned, it will require a balanced reporting that is missing from most media accounts of corporate decision making. NGOs, however, have little incentive to perform such impartial research, because their success lies in asserting their own solutions rather than making compromises. By shouting loudly, they have compelled business executives to reconsider their operations in several important instances. In each of these cases, the corporate about-faces were driven by a combination of NGO activism and bad publicity.

Government reports on controversial issues are colored by political considerations and thus lack objectivity. Thus, only the multilateral institutions and universities are left to engage in empirical studies that show the true impact of globalization on different sections in a region or nation. An example of academic study on globalization is Ann Harrison's work on the role of MNCs in economic development.[18] Her four studies on the multinationals operating in the Ivory Coast, Mexico, Morocco, and Venezuela made the following conclusions:

- More foreign investment at the enterprise level is associated with improved performance and higher productivity. Clearly, joint ventures benefit from foreign partnerships.

- Joint ventures and foreign subsidiaries, however, do not transfer technology to domestic enterprises. Domestic competitors, in fact, appear to be harmed by foreign entry.

- Multinational enterprises (MNEs) act as export catalysts, helping domestic firms break into export markets.

- MNEs pay much higher wages than domestic firms, which suggests that incoming foreign investment may provide one way to raise living standards for at least a part of the population.

- There is almost no evidence that MNEs are drawn to industrial sectors, where pollution emissions or pollution abatement costs are high. This finding provides evidence against the pollution haven hypothesis.

- MNEs are much more energy efficient than domestic firms and also use cleaner types of energy.

The impact of globalization on wages and export jobs has been the subject of a study by IMF researchers.[19] The study showed that in terms of import prices or import volumes, the effect of international trade on wages and income inequality has been modest. This conclusion might seem puzzling in light of the presumption that the advanced economies have become more open to international trade since the 1970s, and the study advances two explanations for this conclusion. First, it is possible that, on balance, the advanced economies have not become substantially more open to trade because, although tariffs have fallen, they have been replaced by nontariff barriers (for example, voluntary export restraints in automobiles and steel). Second, firms have upgraded their product mix, producing high-value-added goods in the face of low-wage foreign competition. If this explanation is true, foreign competition has been blunted and need not lead to large changes in relative product prices.

These studies are useful but have two drawbacks. First, they are not commonly shared with the general public and therefore do not generate widespread information. Second, many studies are too technical to make sense to most people. There is a need for an institutional setup for locating studies on globalization, summarizing their findings in nontechnical language, and disseminating the information widely.

An alternative way to consider the cost-benefit of any global project is to have all concerned parties work together. MNCs and host governments can jointly consider all the pros and cons of a project before launching it. An international agency, such as the World Bank, would provide technical assistance, whereas an NGO would force consideration of issues such as the environment. Such cooperation can be highly effective if all the parties work as a team and have built a trusting relationship among themselves.

The point may be illustrated with reference to the Chad pipeline project.[20] The villages, farms, and scrub-covered fields of southern Chad do not offer visions of great wealth. The villagers, mostly farmers, live in small one-room huts with brown thatched roofs and walls of yellow sun-baked brick. The tallest objects in the landscape are the mango trees, standing like church steeples over clearings that serve as village squares. It's a preindustrial economy with few cars, telephones, electric lights, televisions, or refrigerators. Only a few Chadians can afford a metal pushcart or a cow to pull the plow through their fields of corn, millet, and manioc. Indeed, with an annual per capita income of $230, Chad is one of the poorest countries on Earth. On the UN human development index, which includes measures of health, education, and income, Chad is 167th of 174 countries. Babies born in Chad have a life expectancy of 47.5 years, a little more than half that of babies born in the United States. In the capital city, N'Djamena, many drivers buy their gas from roadside entrepreneurs who set up wooden tables and sell it in cast-off one- and two-liter bottles.

Now, however, Chad is about to enter the twenty-first century. Roughly a mile below the farmers' fields lie at least 1 million barrels of what people in the oil industry say is sweet heavy crude—viscous, low-sulfur oil worth more than $30 billion at today's prices. In October 2000, Exxon-Mobil launched an ambitious plan to construct a 650-mile pipeline that will carry some 225,000 barrels of oil per day from landlocked Chad, near the geographic center of Africa, across Cameroon to an offshore export terminal. The $3.5 billion project could bring Chad about $200 million per year for the next 25 years, roughly doubling the government's annual budget. If used wisely, this income could help rescue Chadians from their crushing poverty.

Because of political instability in Chad and Cameroon, ExxonMobil set up the project in an unusual way: It invited the World Bank to participate. The bank wants to show that projects can both make money for corporate investors and improve the lot of the poor. It also wants to defuse criticism from Western activists, who have made the pipeline a centerpiece of their war against globalization. ExxonMobil wants the World Bank to help guarantee the cooperation of the governments of Chad and Cameroon. If the project is not able to repay those loans because the operations are nationalized or there is a major civil war, ExxonMobil will be excused from repayment.

The World Bank has gone to unprecedented lengths to make sure the project succeeds. It insisted on many changes in the pipeline's route in Cameroon to minimize damage to virgin rain forests and endangered wildlife. The bank also insisted on equitable sharing of the oil revenues. Under a law passed by Chad's parliament two years ago, 10 percent of the revenues will be held in trust for future generations. Eighty percent of the funds are to be used for education, health, and rural developments. Many at the World Bank saw participation in this project as an obligation. When one of the poorest countries in the world gets a windfall like this, an institution like the World Bank must be willing to help in any way it can.

Some critics say the World Bank's agreements are not strong enough to insure the project's success. For example, what can prevent the government from using the money for arms and bombs? Unfortunately, there is not much that an international institution or a multinational firm can do if the leadership in a nation is corrupt or there is political instability.

Some Chadians would like to see stiffer environmental and revenue-sharing commitments, fearing the government will renege. But whether or not that happens, this experiment in global capitalism is now under way. In September 2000, factories in Germany and France began fabricating pipe for the project. In 2002, work began on a 10,000-foot airstrip near the oil fields to accommodate a steady stream of cargo planes hauling machinery and supplies. ExxonMobil hoped to be pumping its first oil by the end of 2003 and thus cause revenues to begin flowing into the treasuries of Chad and Cameroon. Then the project's backers, as well as its critics, will find out whether the people of Chad and Cameroon will truly benefit—and whether multinationals can change their way of doing business in the developing world.

If the project succeeds, other MNCs might decide that they, too, can turn a profit from incorporating humanitarian goals into their plans. (ExxonMobil's original partners in the project, ElfTotalFina and the Royal Dutch/Shell Group, pulled out in 1999, citing other commitments, and they were replaced by Chevron and Petronas, Malaysia's state-owned oil company.)

Transparency

Rather than rejecting the poorly formulated arguments of protesters, leaders of international institutions should experiment with ways to improve transparency. They can provide more access to their deliberations, even if that is done after the fact. NGOs could be welcomed as observers (as the World Bank has done in the past) or be allowed to file friend-of-the-court briefs in WTO dispute-settlement cases.

It is also possible to experiment with direct voting for board members of international organizations, which may be fruitful. Of course, such a step carries the danger of the boards being taken over by well-organized interest groups. Hybrid network organizations that combine government, intergovernment, and NGO representatives, such as the World Commission on Dams or the UN Global Compact, are other avenues to explore. Assemblies of parliamentarians can also be associated with some organizations to hold hearings and receive information, even if not to vote.

There is a genuine need to make global institutions more transparent and no easy answers as to how to do it. But only when they are more transparent can these institutions become legitimate. Neither denying the problem nor yielding to demagogues in the streets will accomplish anything.

Accountability

Three institutions play a dominant role in the globalization process: multilateral institutions (the World Bank, the IMF, and the WTO), MNCs, and nation-states. NGOs accuse the first two of operating independently, without any control or accountability. Critics question whether the third of a trillion dollars lent since 1946 by the World Bank has helped the poor of the world. According to Catherine Caufield, the answer is tragic.[21] The poor have benefited but have paid dearly for such investments. Caufield goes on to say that the ones who profit from the World Bank are its bureaucracy, the heads of governments, well-connected contractors, exporters, and consultants in rich countries. The donors to the World Bank, the taxpayers of the rich nations, are the middle class or poor, who pay taxes for distribution to the rich in poor countries.

Similar concerns have been raised about MNCs. These organizations have evolved from a nation-based hierarchical firm to a network organization, ushering in an era of alliance capitalism and ascendancy of finance capital. MNCs now have the power to shape the direction, location, and rate of growth of a country; its technological evolution, and its peoples' well-being. They wield power and are accountable to no one.

Better accountability should start at home. If the people believe that World Bank meetings do not adequately account for environmental standards, they can press their governments to include environmental officials or ministers in their World Bank delegations. Legislators can hold hearings before or after meetings and themselves become delegates to various organizations. It must be recognized that democratic accountability can be indirect. Often, it is ensured through means other than voting. In the United States, the Supreme Court and the Federal Reserve Board respond to elections indirectly through a long chain of delegation, and judges and government bankers are kept accountable by professional norms and standards as well. International institutions can be subjected to similar indirect accountability.

For MNCs, in the last few years a host of external standards, certificates, and auditing procedures such as triple-bottom-line or sustainability accounting have emerged, which go beyond the financial statements. Although these accountability measures serve a useful purpose, they are onerous, expensive, and time-consuming reporting requirements, even for large companies. Such an investment, however, is justified if it serves the interests of so-called socially responsible investors, consumers, and NGOs, as well as those of mainstream shareholders.

In addition, firms can seek recognition from industry groups, accounting bodies, or NGO organizations for their social and environmental performance. A number of bodies, such as the European Chemical Industry Council and the International Organization for Standardization, with its 14,000 series of standards, operate worldwide and measure the nonfinancial performance of MNCs. The problem with such auditing and certification is that they carry a high price, particularly from the viewpoint of small companies. The Gap, for example, spends $10,000 a year to hire independent monitors for just one of its factories in El Salvador, an expense that would be beyond the means of a small firm. Further, there are a variety of other problems associated with these auditing and certification procedures. External certification produces ambiguous effects on local labor. A firm may improve working conditions in the factory to satisfy certification requirements, but the wages do not increase. Might not the workers have opted for wage increase instead, if they had been given the choice? However, if they do not improve working conditions, MNCs become a target of ethical crusaders who—at the instigation of U.S. unions—force them to stop doing business with factories with poor working environments. One wonders whether labor in developing countries is better off as a result of such agitation.

Besides, improving environmental and working conditions costs money, which must affect some other area of business. Corporate ethicists must be careful to balance their demands for standardization. These demands should not stifle other badly needed programs, such as innovation.

Finally, corporations should be defended against ignorant, ideological, or strategic assaults. Corporations generally do good, not harm. However, the question has to be, Can they do even more good? According to purists, it is stockholders, not corporations, that should be the ones to do the social good. But that argument makes little sense. A number of nonprofit corporations aid underprivileged people in the society. Similarly, Microsoft, Ford, and IBM assist the communities in which they operate. More corporations need to do just that, each in its own way. Pluralism is of the essence here: No NGO or government has the wisdom or the right to lay down what corporations must do. Social good is multidimensional, and different corporations may and must define social responsibility, quite legitimately, in different ways in the global economy. As Jagdish Bhagwati notes: "A hundred flowers must be allowed to bloom, creating a rich garden of social action to lend more color to globalization's human face."[22]

Working with Developing Countries

In a multitude of ways, bodies like the World Bank and the OECD tackle labor rights, corruption, and environmental concerns. Even some of the same groups that have led protests play a direct role in proposing rules and monitoring corporate compliance. But for the labor and environmental standards to take root, the world's developing nations must also be at the table. Poor nations view Western attempts to inject social issues into trade regimes as cloaked protectionism, and as a result the West and developing countries have been deadlocked in negotiations over many trade issues. An Indian bureaucrat made this relevant remark: "Now that you have exploited your own resources, you say we should not cut our own trees or you won't trade with us."[23]

The West should heed such complaints. The Third World rightly views trade negotiations over the past decade as a one-way street, with rich nations pressing for intellectual-property rights and lower tariffs but not increasing the access of the developing world to Western markets for food and apparel.

Developing nations also learned a harsh lesson in the 1990s, when they agreed to let foreign capital gush in and then saw their economies collapse when it poured out. They perceive that social demands undercut what little competitive edge they have.

For globalization to progress, the West should listen carefully and involve Third World nations in matters that concern them. It is not that these nations are proud of sweatshops and oil spills. Indeed, they face plenty of pressure at home to address these problems. Most nations have signed agreements barring trade in endangered species, counterfeits, and prison goods. They have also signed a new workers' rights initiative pushed by the International Labor Organization. But Third World nations are struggling to balance these issues with the need to create jobs for huge populations and to maintain social stability. Thus, they want to see the tangible benefits of labor rights and environmental reforms. One way to address the problem is to give them access to Western markets. Further, developing nations want clear rules instead of having Western companies cave in to pressure groups back home without regard for the economic impact.

Briefly, developed and developing countries should reach a consensus on rules and regulations to guide the globalization process. Without cooperation by all sides, rules are useless. Everyone prospers when rules have been established by mutual consent. Simply wielding the blunt weapon of sanctions does not work. Developing countries must be fully convinced that they are not being shortchanged.

Efforts of the European Union in this matter are noteworthy.[24] It is pushing for adoption of the so-called everything-but-arms initiative, which will ensure that the 48 poorest countries can export to the European Union free of quotas or tariffs on all goods except arms. The European Union wants an interdisciplinary approach, including trade, on access to medicines to tackle the critical health problems facing Africa. It wants to prove that trade policy has to do more than show that it is not a malign force. It must make a positive, material difference to the poorest people on the planet. Now the challenge is for the United States to take steps to alleviate the concerns of developing countries. At the same time, governments in Third World countries should accept responsibility rather than denying it, and they should create conditions for globalization to flourish. Corrupt governments in developing nations deny responsibility when they blame the IMF or the World Bank for troubles chiefly created by their own policies.

Immigration Policies

While the world's population has doubled during the past several decades, to more than 6 billion persons, birthrates in many countries have fallen to unprecedented low levels. The result is a demographic divide between nations with high and low rates of population growth that has enormous economic and political significance. Virtually all high-income countries, and a few poor ones, especially China and Russia, have fertility rates that are too low to fully replace their populations. The average is only a little above one child per woman. Even in the United States, which has the highest fertility rate among rich nations, women give birth to only about two children on average. The picture is different in most of Latin America, Africa, and South Asia, because the much higher birthrates cause their populations to grow rapidly.

An efficient remedy for this population divide would be for many men and women in countries with low incomes and growing populations to move to countries with high incomes and stable or declining populations. The biggest constraint on the spread of globalization in developed nations will not be commodity inflation or product shortages. Rather, the main problem will be finding enough high-skilled and computer-literate workers. The problem can be solved by drawing on the enormous supply of college-educated workers in countries such as India and China. Asia accounted for two-thirds of the global increase in college and other postsecondary school enrollments in the 1990s. Indian universities turn out 122,000 engineers every year, compared with 63,000 in the United States. And engineers account for some 40 percent of China's enormous number of annual graduates.[25]

The growth of the U.S. high-tech industry has been fueled by a steady flow of highly educated immigrants. Thus, the future of globalization depends on advanced nations opening their doors to foreign workers. Changes in immigration rules and regulations permitting entry to skilled people from developing countries are a prerequisite for the success of globalization.

Attitudinal Change

For globalization to progress, it is important that it be presented as a process that is mutually beneficial to both developed and developing countries. Often one gets the impression that globalization is a way for MNCs to take advantage of the emerging opportunities in developing countries.[26] Markets for many staple products in Western societies are saturated. To be viable, MNCs must grow, and globalization provides unsaturated Third World markets for them. Inasmuch as all owners of MNC stock live in developed countries, the increased markets in developing nations ultimately make the rich countries' stockholders richer. Although there is nothing wrong with the MNCs expanding their business to developing countries, the advantages must be emphasized. In the absence of such a perspective, globalization would appear to be a new form of colonization.

Furthermore, MNCs need an attitudinal change to become truly global. This change requires leaving home country affiliation aside and behaving and acting as a worldwide corporation belonging to world stockholders, serving global customers using global resources and labor. For example, senior managers should represent a much greater cultural and ethnic mix. At present, however, with a few exceptions, managerial ranks are filled with nationals of the company's home country. How many MNCs are prepared to have 30 to 40 percent of their top management teams of two hundred coming from China, India, and Brazil? Such a cultural infusion, of course, affects the company's decision making, risk taking, and team building. As C.K. Prahalad and K. Lieberthal have said:

> The challenge will be intensified by the power. The new perspective suggests more than a new relationship between the developed and the emerging economies. It also suggests an end to the era of centralized corporate power—embodied in the attitude that "headquarters know best"—and a shift to a much more dispersed power and influence.[27]

Globalization influences life in emerging markets, but it also presents dramatic new challenges to MNCs. The future of globalization would be affected greatly by the willingness and ability of MNCs to cope with these challenges.

Erosion of Cultural and Moral Values

Antiglobalists blame globalization for its intrusion into cultural norms of different societies worldwide. There cannot be a greater fallacy than the power attributed to globalization to change values that people share and have cherished for ages. Globalization is a simple economic phenomenon in which liberal policies unite the world into a large global market, creating enormous wealth for everyone to share. International economic integration widens choices, because it makes resources go further.

Globalization accepts the social-cultural diversity of human society. Undoubtedly, these human communities are real, natural, and produced by historical evolution. They are necessary for the physical, social, moral, and spiritual development of human beings. They shape peoples' perceptions of reality and experience, and they provide a moral vision that liberates individuals to rise above their narrow self-concern and self-interest.

This sociodiversity needs to be sustained and safeguarded, as well as enriched.

Cultural uniqueness aside, all people want to live comfortably. Over time, Western societies have proved that free markets enrich economic life. The virtue of the free market is neither American nor British. But these nations have been the first ones to adopt the free market policy. Socialism, after the unfortunate experience of the post–World War II period, has failed. Nations that aspire to provide a good economic life for their people are encouraged to try the free market recipe. Japan did it and emerged into the second largest industrial power in the world. Did Japan give up its cultural traits? No, although it has a large number of U.S. fast-food restaurants, and its youth like U.S. pop music and clothes.

Critics blame U.S. companies for imposing the U.S. lifestyle on people worldwide. They are naive, however, to think that people will give up their long-held values blindly. Consider India: Even though it is a democratic nation, it has been slow to adopt liberal economic policies. The U.S. Domino's and Pizza Hut chains entered the nation's market with single restaurants in the mid-1990s. What they brought to India is not an American-style pizza but a way of serving food in a nice, clean, bright place at a price an ordinary family can afford. But the food they serve is what Indians like.[28] In many cities in India, Domino's offers a 100 percent vegetarian pizza, cooked in a separate kitchen where no meat items are allowed. Even cooking utensils for vegetarian fare are kept separate so as not to touch utensils used in cooking meat. Added to that, to cater to the Jains, the company serves Jain pizza, a vegetarian pizza without forbidden vegetables such as onions, garlic, and potatoes.

Pizza may be of Italian or Greek origin, or even a U.S. invention, but the Indian cultural values are intact when Indians eat it. Such customization of food by multinationals in different markets is routine. An interesting side effect of MNCs' entering non-Western markets is the challenge and opportunity the MNCs pose to the local fast-food vendors. The vendors learn the concept of fast food and get into the act on their own. Imagine 50 years from now: Different Indian meals and snacks will be sold in small shops all over the country in big and small cities, towns, and villages. These shops will be owned or franchised by a few Indian companies, will employ thousands of people, and will serve food under healthy conditions. Meanwhile, there will be plenty of McDonald's and Pizza Huts offering alternative menus. It will be up to individuals to decide if they want to eat a hamburger (vegetarian or nonvegetarian), a pizza, or one of the traditional Indian dishes. If after the initial fascination with pizza, Indians don't like it, Pizza Hut will wind up its operations. If there is no market, and if there is no opportunity to make money, it will be foolhardy for Pizza Hut to remain in India.

Globalization introduces a new concept to India. The Indian people have the right to eat the food they prefer. They eat what they like and simultaneously keep intact their cultural habits, likes and dislikes, and preferences.

Take another industry, U.S. pop culture, which some have predicted will conquer the world.[29] Initially, U.S. companies transmitted the hippest U.S. television sitcoms to different nations. The critics soon blamed the U.S. entertainment industry for spreading U.S. values worldwide. That was perhaps stage one. Now the same companies are producing different shows relevant to different societies, and they transfer them to U.S. and other global markets according to how well they are initially accepted.

In the emerging markets of Asia and Latin America, where the big U.S. media conglomerates own channels, the companies have started developing local shows, besides selling U.S. programs. And according to experts, the trend toward local programs is going to accelerate. For example, 70 percent of compact disc sales outside the United States come from local artists.[30] In other words, people enjoy shows and music that appeal to their cultural orientation. A media company will go along with what sells. If some customers enjoy watching U.S. shows, they will have the choice. Further, it is not necessary that U.S. companies win in all markets. In many cases, other Western companies have done better. In some instances, multinationals could not compete with the local rivals. Foreign entertainment companies had rough going in India, where start-up costs are enormous, the regulatory environment is unpredictable, and the advertising market is underdeveloped. Added to that situation is the fact that the Indian movie industry, unorganized and mismanaged as it is, has been surviving well for years. But Sony Entertainment Television in India is willing to challenge the monopoly of the traditional players using its managerial talents and vast financial resources.

Who will benefit ultimately? The consumers and the economy of India will be the winners. Business will run more efficiently, and the consumers will be provided better entertainment. No matter how one looks at it, there is no threat to Indian culture. The antiglobalists' main intellectual problem is their aversion to capitalism—that is, to economic freedom. Culture is not hurt under globalization, as skeptics allege. Indeed, globalization is indispensable if the people in developing countries are ever to be raised out of poverty. If globalization is to advance further, its virtues must be communicated, targeted especially toward intellectuals and activists in developed countries.

Government's Role

The gains from globalization include not only to the profits of Western and Third World corporations but also productive employment and higher incomes for the world's poor. That is what growth through integration has meant for all the developing countries that have achieved it so far. Yet this message has not been properly communicated to the anticapitalist protesters, who continue to wreck meetings of international institutions and groups.

Unfortunately, Western governments have failed miserably in meeting the resistance against globalization, both intellectually and politically. It is surprising that governments are apologizing for globalization and promising to civilize it, whatever that means. If these governments had any regard for the plight of the poor, they would instead be accelerating globalization, celebrating it, and exulting in it; and they would at least be trying to explain it. But they are not doing these things.

It would be naive to think that governments could let globalization proceed mainly under its own steam, trusting to technological progress and economic freedom, desirable as such a course would be. Politicians will not permit a smooth progression of globalization. However, they certainly can defend globalization on its merits as a truly moral cause against a mere rabble of exuberant irrationalists on the streets and the mild public skepticism that is open to persuasion.

It is a pity that Western governments do not support globalization enthusiastically, while fully understanding its far-reaching benefits. They almost seem to be saying that now that the poor countries have decided they would like to reduce poverty as quickly as possible, they cannot be allowed to, because such a gain would inconvenience the West. But what inconvenience are we talking about? The governments of rich countries know that the alleged adjustment problems of expanded trade are greatly exaggerated. It would be grossly unconvincing to blame accelerating globalization for the migration of jobs from the North to the South, when the United States, before the tragedy of September 11, 2001, had an unemployment rate of less than 4 percent and real wages that had been growing right across the spectrum.[31] Yet even under these wonderful circumstances, politicians in Europe and the United States wring their hands about the perils of globalization, abdicating their duty to explain facts to voters and equipping the anticapitalists with weapons to use in the next fight. To a very large extent, then, the future of globalization depends on governments in Western countries.

Currently, the champions of globalization, governments and big business, are giving a deeply unimpressive account of themselves. Intellectually, their defense of globalization under the banner of its being good for our exporters and helpful in creating jobs is a disgrace. Governments deserve fierce criticism for many of their policies, not least in the areas of particular concern to antiglobalists. Furthermore, governments of the rich countries, and not only the U.S. government, often use the IMF, the World Bank, and the WTO—institutions that in practice could never defy their wishes—as scapegoats to deflect blame. Worst of all, governments take advantage of globalization as an excuse for broken promises, failures of will, and capitulations to special interests. That is no harmless evasion, and it must stop. Samuel Huntington points out:

> The West is attempting and will continue to attempt to sustain its preeminent position and defend its interests by defining those interests as the interests of the "world community." That phrase has become the euphemistic collective noun (replacing the "Free World") to give global legitimacy to actions reflecting the interests of the United States and other Western powers. The West is, for instance, attempting to integrate the economies of non-Western societies into a global economic system, which it dominates. Through the IMF and other international economic institutions, the West promotes its economic interests and imposes on other nations the economic policies it thinks appropriate. In any poll of non-Western peoples, however, the IMF undoubtedly would win the support of finance ministers and a few others but get an overwhelmingly unfavorable rating from almost everyone else, who describe IMF officials as "neo-Bolsheviks who love expropriating other people's money, imposing undemocratic and alien rules of economic and political conduct and stifling economic freedom."[32]

More specifically, governments in developed countries should take the following steps to enable globalization to move ahead:[33]

1. *Open markets for poor countries.*

    Industrialized countries have consistently promised to open their markets to developing countries. During the Group of Seven (G7) meeting in Halifax in 1995, the rich countries clearly agreed that they would implement the Uruguay Round agreement fully, and they reaffirmed their commitment to resist protectionism in all its forms.

    Improved access to Northern markets would help to create employment opportunities in developing countries and achieve a fairer distribution of global wealth. Trade is far more important than aid in this respect. Every 0.7 percent increase in the exports of developing countries generates as much income as these countries receive each year in aid. But increased market share requires improved access to markets.

Since the mid-1980s, South Asia, Latin America, East Asia, and sub-Saharan Africa have all halved their average tariffs. Industrialized countries have used their control of the IMF and World Bank to reinforce trade liberalization through loan conditions. One recent IMF review of 23 of its programs found that they included 186 loan conditions related to trade.

While developing countries have been setting the pace in liberalization, rich countries have responded by maintaining exceptionally high trade barriers. These barriers cost developing countries approximately $100 billion each year—twice the amount they receive in aid. Far from supporting poor countries, industrialized countries are actively discriminating against them. For example, for manufactured goods, tariffs facing exports of developing countries to high-income countries are on average four times higher than tariffs facing exports by industrialized countries. Further, high tariffs and nontariff barriers are concentrated in areas of special interest to developing countries, such as agriculture and labor-intensive goods. Tariffs on leather and footwear imports are double the average tariff rates in the United States and Canada. In addition, the United States and the European Union have launched 234 antidumping cases against developing countries since the end of the Uruguay Round trade talks in 1994.

One of the reasons why trade reforms in poor countries have failed to deliver the anticipated benefits is that they have not been matched by reforms in rich countries. Unbalanced liberalization is denying poor countries an opportunity to share in the benefits of globalization.

2. *Eliminate agricultural protectionism.*

The Uruguay Round Agreement on Agriculture was heralded as a triumph for resolve and political will—as the start of a new era in which the withdrawal of subsidies in rich countries would open up new opportunities for poor countries. The new era has yet to start.

Agricultural trade has a major bearing on poverty reduction efforts. Approximately three-quarters of the poorest people in developing countries live in rural areas. Their livelihoods are affected both by export opportunities and by competition from imports. Subsidies in rich countries exclude poor countries from world markets. They also result in unfair competition in local markets, because small farmers cannot compete with subsidized European and U.S. export prices. As an example, in Mexico, livelihoods of the maize farmers have been ruined by cheap subsidized imports from the United States. Women rice farmers in Haiti are facing similar problems. EU export subsidies are having similar effects in sub-Saharan Africa.

The Uruguay Round Agreement on Agriculture committed industrialized countries to cutting agricultural subsidies by 36 percent and tariffs by a similar amount. But rich nations have been able to avoid meaningful action in this matter. There has been no real reduction in agricultural protection.

Although headline figures point to a cut in subsidization, it has been achieved through a reclassification exercise. Income transfers have continued but are now classified as support payment rather than subsidies. Annual emergency payments to U.S. farmers, permissible under the WTO, have grown rapidly. The net effect has been to create the appearance of subsidy cuts while allowing past practices to continue. At the end of the 1990s, subsidies accounted for almost 40 percent of the value of OECD farm output, the same as in 1986–88. The average tariff imposed by industrialized countries on agricultural goods from developing countries is close to 20 percent, almost five times higher than the average tariff on all goods. Tariff peaks for commodities such as groundnuts in the United States, and meat and dairy products in the European Union, exceed 100 percent. Processed food products attract tariffs at least twice as high as tariffs on unprocessed products.

These barriers represent a major obstacle for developing countries seeking to break into export markets and are estimated to cost these countries approximately $20 billion yearly.

The continuation of export subsidization has been equally damaging. Agriculture is the only area in the WTO rules in which the practice of dumping, or the sale of exports at prices below the cost of production, is institutionalized as an acceptable practice. Of the 25 countries that reserved the right to use export subsidies under the agreement, 23 were developed countries.

The verdict on the Uruguay Round Agreement on Agriculture is that it was designed to let industrialized countries continue with essentially the same policies; it has introduced minimal restraints. Imbalances in the agreement highlight the way in which the WTO framework has been subordinated by rich countries to the vested interests of large farmers and powerful lobbies in the farm-business sector.

3. *Provide market access for textiles and garments.*

During the Uruguay Round, industrialized countries agreed to phase out the Multi-Fibre Agreement (MFA) in four stages by 2005, per the Agreement on Textile and Clothing. The MFA is widely regarded by developing countries as one of the most pernicious features of the trade policies of industrialized countries; the new agreement was seen as a step in the right direction. But industrialized countries have found various ways to comply with the letter of the agreement while comprehensively violating its spirit.

Despite the commitments made in the Uruguay Round, developing countries continue to face excessive trade barriers in textiles and garments. To make the point, the European Union and the United States should already have phased out around half of their MFA restrictions, but developing countries still face quota restrictions on 80 percent of their exports. The average industrial country tariff on textiles and clothing imports from developing countries is 11 percent—three times higher than the average industrial tariff. Bangladesh, one of the world's poorest countries, faces tariffs as high as 20 percent on its key exports to the United States and Canada.

These measures are having a devastating effect on many developing countries. Textiles and clothing are one of the most important areas of export activity for developing countries, accounting for around 10 percent of total exports. South Asia alone is estimated to lose around $2 billion a year because of trade barriers in rich countries.

Lost markets mean lower wages and fewer jobs in textile and garment industries, which employ millions of vulnerable people. Women account for the vast majority of workers in this sector. Social groups are working to improve labor and social welfare rights for women garments workers, but their efforts are being undermined by restrictions on market access.

4. *Create global patent rules that safeguard public health in poor countries.*

The application of the Trade-Related Aspects of Intellectual Property Rights (TRIPS) agreement to pharmaceutical products was one of the most controversial parts of the Uruguay Round. The governments of developing countries raised concerns about the potential effect of more stringent patent protection on the affordability of vital medicines to the poor, and on development more generally. Therefore, the agreement acknowledged these concerns by allowing governments to adopt measures necessary to protect public health. However, this apparent safeguard was substantially weakened by the caveats provided by the agreement.

But the provisions under the agreement have been blatantly ignored, and TRIPS was roundly abused by rich nations and their MNCs. The agreement has been used to subordinate poor people's health to the pursuit of corporate profits.

The TRIPS agreement, which provides a minimum 20-year period of patent protection, has figured in two high-profile disputes. In South Africa, 39 drugs companies began a court action to prevent the South African government from importing cheap generic copies of patented drugs to treat human immunodeficiency virus (HIV) infections and AIDS. This case was followed by the U.S. decision to take Brazil to a WTO dispute panel. Once again, the aim of the complaint, subsequently withdrawn in the face of public protest, was to prevent Brazil from producing generic copies of vital drugs.

These two cases are part of a broader problem. This year, 14 million people in developing countries will die from infectious diseases. Many factors contribute to this distressing figure, including poverty, weak health infrastructure, inadequate access to water and sanitation, and bad policies. But many of these deaths could be prevented if people could afford basic medicines. The TRIPS agreement poses such an acute threat because it will raise the cost of medicines. Patented medicines frequently cost more than 10 times the price of generic equivalents. And for poor people, price differences of this scale can be a matter of life and death.

Rich nations have supported the efforts of pharmaceutical MNCs to enforce the most stringent interpretation of the TRIPS agreement. The United States has also used the threat of bilateral trade sanctions to demand that the patent claims of U.S. companies be enforced. Countries such as India, Argentina, the Dominican Republic, Brazil, Vietnam, and Thailand all have been threatened under the Special 301 provision of U.S. trade law.

Industrialized countries are guilty not just of threatening the health of vulnerable communities in developing countries but also of having extreme double standards. The U.S. and Canadian governments have shown themselves willing to threaten to override patents at home when faced with bioterrorist threats (for example, from anthrax) to their own citizens. Although no compulsory licenses for patented antibiotics were eventually issued, the threat of purchasing low-cost generic drugs was successfully used to bargain down prices.

The application of one set of rules when North American public health is threatened and another set of rules when there is a health crisis in poor countries is unacceptable. Whatever the future threat posed by anthrax, the number of casualties that prompted the change in approach to patents pales into insignificance against the number of deaths associated with HIV/AIDS alone, which claims 2 million lives each year in Africa alone. Moreover, the budget constraints of Northern governments are far less severe than those of developing countries.

5. *Help the least developed countries (LDCs).*

Time and again, rich nations have agreed to a plan of action, including provision for duty-free access aimed at improving the overall capacity of LDCs to respond to opportunities provided by the international trading system. But as in other areas, there has been no real progress toward policies that might help the poorest countries capture a bigger share of the benefits from trade.

The 49 countries classified by the United Nations as LDCs are among the poorest in the world. Around half of their population—some 300 million people—live below the poverty line. Collectively, they account for less than 1 percent of world trade. Yet six years after the end of the Uruguay Round, their exports continued to face stringent protectionist barriers in rich countries. For example, in the United States and Canada, only around one-tenth of all tariffs are pitched at levels above 5 percent. Yet in both countries, approximately half of LDC exports face tariffs higher than this level. Imports into industrialized countries from LDCs are twice as likely to face tariffs in excess of 15 percent as imports from other industrialized countries. Trade barriers are highest in sectors where LDCs have a potential comparative advantage. Restrictions are particularly high for sugar exports to the European Union and for clothing and footwear exports to the United States and Canada.

Eliminating duties and quotas on LDC exports would generate $2.5 billion in additional export earnings. This figure would translate into hundreds of thousands of new jobs and increased incomes—opportunities denied by existing policies. In some countries, such as Canada and the United States, trade barriers against LDC imports cost more than is given in aid, demonstrating how bad trade policies can seriously undermine development assistance.

To its credit, the European Commission attempted to act on the commitment to improve LDC market access. Its Everything but Arms proposal called for the removal of all tariffs and quotas on LDC imports. But following intensive lobbying by powerful farmer and agribusiness lobbies, liberalization was postponed for key products such as rice and sugar—the very products that offered the largest foreign exchange gains for LDCs by the European governments.

6. *Provide aid and technical assistance for developing countries.*

At the end of the Uruguay Round, industrialized countries promised technical assistance to developing countries to help them meet the costs of implementing the Uruguay Round agreement and to enhance their ability to participate in the WTO. The LDCs were promised special treatment, but there is a huge gap between this promise and the actual disbursement of funds.

For many developing countries, the cost of implementing the Uruguay Round agreements is prohibitive and places a huge burden on limited human resource capacities. It will cost Tanzania $10 million to meet WTO customs evaluation standards, for example. The cost of drafting and enforcing new laws on intellectual property in Bangladesh is estimated at more than $1 million yearly. Despite this situation, at the end of the 1990s, the WTO budget for technical assistance was only $550,000, sufficient to meet less than one-fifth of the requests made for technical assistance.

The integrated framework to provide technical assistance to the poorest countries (the LDCs), launched in 1996, has an even more abysmal record. By the end of the 1990s it had failed, and it was re-launched in 2003. To date, industrialized countries have provided $7 million to undertake a needs assessment in a small group of pilot countries. There are no concrete funding commitments for the future to address the priorities that emerge.

Failure to provide adequate technical assistance is reflected in the huge imbalances in negotiating strength and institutional capacity at the WTO. The average developing country trade mission at the WTO has three people, compared with seven for developed countries. Even a large country like Bangladesh has only one representative. Of the 38 African countries in the WTO, 15 have no resident delegate; 4 countries maintain only 1-person offices.

On average, there are 46 delegate meetings per week in the WTO. There are complex negotiations across large areas of industrial, agricultural, investment, and services policy that have profound implications for human development. Yet many of the world's poorest countries lack the capacity to monitor, let alone influence, the direction of these negotiations.

Rich countries also promised action to help developing countries acquire a greater share of the benefits of international trade. Financial and technical assistance are crucial to help developing countries take advantage of new market opportunities. In particular, they need support to address the constraints in producing goods for export, such as inadequate infrastructure (e.g., roads, electricity), limited technical facilities, and limited skills needed to add value to domestic produce and ensure that goods meet quality and other export standards.

Increased aid, targeted to promote trade in developing countries as part of their national poverty reduction strategies, could help to overcome these constraints. Yet between 1990 and 2000, aid flows from the rich G7 countries fell from 0.3 percent to 0.19 percent of their national incomes, far below the UN target of 0.7 percent. Aid flows have fallen in every G7 country except the United Kingdom over the past decade.

STAGES OF GLOBALIZATION

As we look to the future of globalization, we should remember that all nations, all industries, and all companies in an industry will not become global at the same time. There are conditions that must be fulfilled before a nation, an industry, or a company can go global. The purpose of this section is to discuss the elements that drive globalization. As in the previous chapter, globalization is looked at as the process of interdependence over vast distances. It is a huge concept that may be difficult to capture by today's limited information on various globalization drivers. This limitation, however, should not be a deterrent to gaining a deeper understanding of globalization, although it cannot be totally accurate.

Country Globalization

Measurement of country globalization has been attempted by A.T. Kearney in the magazine *Foreign Policy*.[34] The index ranks countries using four variables: *goods and services* (convergence of domestic prices with international prices, and international trade as a share of GDP), *finance* (inward and outward—direct foreign investment, portfolio capital flows, and income payments and receipts as shares of GDP), *personal contact* (cross-border remittance and other transfers as a share of GDP, and minutes of international telephone calls per capita), and *technology* (percentage of a population on-line, number of Internet hosts per capita, and number of secure servers per capita). Using the hard data supplied by these four factors, the top 20 global economies are those of Singapore, the Netherlands, Sweden, Switzerland, Finland, Ireland, Austria, the United Kingdom, Norway, Canada, Denmark, the United States, Italy, Germany, Portugal, France, Hungary, Spain, Israel, and Malaysia.

Singapore leads the rankings as the most global nation in the index, due in large part to its high trade levels, its heavy international telephone traffic, and its steady stream of international travelers. The others in the top five countries are European nations. Despite high levels of integration on various technological measures, the United States remains less integrated in economic terms, putting it 12th in the index. Some nations have pursued integration with the rest of the world more aggressively than others. The most globalized countries are small nations for whom openness allows access to goods, services, and capital that cannot be produced at home. In some cases, geography has played an important role in sustaining integrated markets. The Netherlands, for instance, benefits from (among many other factors) its position at the head of the Rhine, which knits together countries that account for almost three-quarters of Dutch trade. In other cases, such as Sweden and Switzerland, relatively small domestic markets and highly educated workers have given rise to truly global companies capable of competing anywhere in the world. And a host of other factors have contributed to the globalization of other small states. Austria, for example, benefits from heavy travel and tourism, whereas remittances of large populations living abroad contribute to Ireland's integration with the outside world.

One of the most heated debates about globalization today is whether competition among countries forces them to cut taxation—as well as social spending—in order to attract foreign investors and other international business interests. In this way, according to critics, globalization generates a race to the bottom in which local populations lose out as their governments curtail spending on the jobs, education, and social safety nets that higher taxation levels might support.

However, comparison of the globalization index scores discussed above with each country's level of taxation and government expenditures on public goods does not show any relationship. As a matter of fact, some of the highest levels of taxation are in countries that are also highly globalized, and levels of spending vary across the board. Israel and the Czech Republic, for example, rank among the most global of emerging markets, yet they collect taxes totaling more than 40 percent of national economic output. Those levels are far above tax collection rates in such countries as Colombia, Indonesia, and Pakistan, which rank much lower on the globalization index. By the same token, Sweden and Finland, which rank among the world's most global countries, boast levels of social spending that are among the most generous in the world—all supported by relatively high tax rates. And with Scandinavian countries attracting record levels of FDI in recent years, there is little evidence that high tax rates are driving away investors, who appear more concerned about economic prospects, available infrastructure, education levels, and other fundamentals.

An interesting question is, Are people in highly globalized nations happier? Since 1995, an international network of social scientists has collaborated on a global investigation of sociocultural and political change known as the World Values Survey. These researchers conduct national surveys in more than 65 societies, accounting for almost 80 percent of the world population. Each survey features hundreds of questions, ranging from assessments of personal satisfaction and financial security to views on whether local governments are capable of coping with environmental decay or runaway crime.

Simultaneous examination of happiness scores along with the index of globalization failed to prove that globalization brings happiness. But it was clear that people in highly globalized countries tend to have higher levels of perceived well-being than do people in societies that are not as well connected to the outside world.

Although most of the highly globalized countries tend also to be wealthy, the correlations among globalization, wealth, and happiness are fuzzy at best. This conclusion may be explained by the finding of the World Values Survey that per capita income correlates well with happiness levels up to a certain level of economic development, beyond which happiness becomes a much more subjective phenomenon.

Although 2000 saw an unprecedented surge in global integration, a closer look at the data reveals a more mixed picture for the developing world. For instance, although emerging markets have seen Internet access grow at remarkable rates (on average, twice the rate in the developed world in recent years), those same markets are still dwarfed by the industrialized countries. The OECD estimates that 95.6 percent of the world's Internet hosts in 2000 were located in its member countries. Hong Kong, Singapore, and Taiwan accounted for more than half of the remainder, leaving little for the rest of the world. By the end of 2003, OECD countries were likely to have had more than 100 Internet hosts for every 1,000 inhabitants, whereas the rest of the world might have been lucky to average 1 host for every 1,000 people. This digital abyss made it only more difficult for many emerging markets to expand their integration with the rest of the world.

Moreover, evidence suggests that some regions are becoming relatively less integrated within the world economy. The African countries, for example, saw their average level of economic integration fall, then rise, then fall again over the past six years. This activity was a reflection of variable economic performance and the rise and fall of prices for oil and commodity exports, these countries' main connection to global economic markets.

Industry Globalization

Industries may be broadly broken into three categories: local, national, and global. Exhibit 5.5 shows which industries belong in which category. At present, roughly one-third of the world's economic activity takes place in locally defined industries, one-third in nationally defined industries, and the remaining one-third in global industries.[35]

Many factors affect the speed at which markets aggregate into global structures, including the specific geographic barriers in operation, the risks involved, the evolution of global standards and protocols, the opportunity to leverage specialization and scale effects, and the actions of individual participants. High-end segments such as luxury goods globalize faster than down-market segments. Some parts of the value chain go global before other parts do, creating new opportunities to specialize globally. Take the case of the automotive industry. The luxury brand segment, which includes brands such as Mercedes, is global, whereas the middle-class segment that includes the Buick brand is not. Whereas there is intense global competition in the sale of new cars, the businesses involved in repairing and maintaining cars and in selling used cars are still largely local.

Industry globalization can be measured by four factors: *cost drivers* (global-scale economies, favorable logistics, and differences in country costs), *market drivers* (common customer needs, global customers, global

Exhibit 5.5
Stages of Globalization of Different Industries

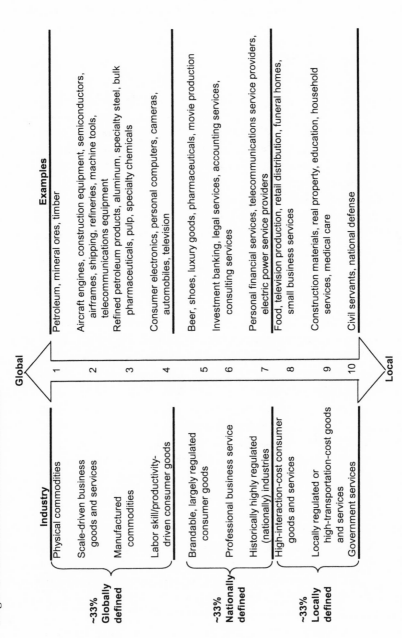

		Industry	Examples
~33% Globally defined	1	Physical commodities	Petroleum, mineral ores, timber
	2	Scale-driven business goods and services	Aircraft engines, construction equipment, semiconductors, airframes, shipping, refineries, machine tools, telecommunications equipment
	3	Manufactured commodities	Refined petroleum products, aluminum, specialty steel, bulk pharmaceuticals, pulp, specialty chemicals
	4	Labor skill/productivity-driven consumer goods	Consumer electronics, personal computers, cameras, automobiles, television
~33% Nationally defined	5	Brandable, largely regulated consumer goods	Beer, shoes, luxury goods, pharmaceuticals, movie production
	6	Professional business service	Investment banking, legal services, accounting services, consulting services
	7	Historically highly regulated (nationally) industries	Personal financial services, telecommunications service providers, electric power service providers
~33% Locally defined	8	High-interaction-cost consumer goods and services	Food, television production, retail distribution, funeral homes, small business services
	9	Locally regulated or high-transportation-cost goods and services	Construction materials, real property, education, household services, medical care
	10	Government services	Civil servants, national defense

Global ← → Local

Source: Based on World Bank data.

channels, and transferable marketing), *government drivers* (favorable trade policies, compatible technical standards, and common marketing regulations), and *competitive drivers* (globalized competitors and competitors using global strategy). Further, industry globalization has five dimensions: *market participation* (selecting and investing in countries on the basis of global strategic importance), *products and services* (designing and producing products and services with global needs in mind instead of designing them for individual countries), *location of value-adding activities* (creating one global network of activities on the value chain instead of reproducing the value chain in many countries), *marketing* (using the common marketing mix across all markets), and *competitive moves* (integrating actions against competitors into a worldwide plan rather than fighting separate country battles).

Using this framework, it is feasible to analyze the globalization status of an industry and to see which parts of the value chain are globally integrated. This ability should permit companies to identify the right opportunities for globalization and implement them effectively.

Corporate Globalization

For a company, four stages of doing business across borders can be identified:[36] *local* (using foreign outposts to distribute goods made at home, or a sort of corporate colonialism), *international* (integrating manufacturing along global lines), *multinational* (using subsidiaries for ideas, as well as production), and *global* (becoming multicultural and multinational, acquiring the state of mind where the nationality of a state ceases to matter).

Few attempts have been made to measure the global status of different companies. Mainly, companies have been ranked for globalization based on the proportion of sales from foreign markets. Other factors, such as the number of nationalities represented on the board of directors or R&D expenditures abroad, may be considered, but companies do not reveal such data in their annual reports.[37]

Exhibit 5.6 ranks 100 worldwide corporations on the basis of globalization using three factors: foreign sales, foreign assets, and foreign employees. Forty-nine companies with a ratio of over 50 percent on two of the three factors were considered global. Among the top 10 companies, 8 were European and 2 were Canadian. Only 8 U.S. companies were considered global according to this framework; they are ExxonMobil, Coca-Cola, Crown Cork & Seal, McDonald's, Dow Chemical, IBM, Hewlett-Packard, and Johnson & Johnson.[38]

Evolution of Global Corporation: Some Examples

Companies evolve globally based on market opportunity and the long-term cost-benefit impact of going global. A variety of external factors may assist or inhibit global expansion. For example, in consumer electronics, better methods of packaging helped globalization, because it meant delicate products could be shipped long distances without breaking. Illustrated here are the globalization efforts of two companies, one European and one U.S. company.

Nokia—A Success Story of Globalization[39]

Nokia, a Finnish company, traditionally manufactured such products as toilet paper and rubber boats. It became a global corporation and the industry leader with a high-tech product, mobile phones. In 2000, this company sold 60 million of the 200 million telephones sold around the world. How did this happen?

Finnish people have a great fascination with telephones. The telephone business in the country was scattered among a large number of small companies. Nokia entered the telephone business in the 1970s, buying a couple of telephone companies as a way of diversifying. In the 1980s, the new head of the company, Jorma Ollila, set two goals: to aggressively pursue the mobile phone business and to go global. The result was astonishing. In the early 1990s, telephone business constituted about 10 percent of the company's sales, of which about one-third came from Finland. Ten years later, telephone business accounted for over 90 percent of the company's business, with only 4 percent coming from Finland. Today, the company does business in about 140 countries.

Nokia's exceptional success is attributed to three factors: the emergence of the mobile phone market, management's commitment to globalization, and the continued pursuit of new technological breakthroughs. In addition, Nokia's roots in a country where 63 percent of the population have mobile phones, the highest percentage in the world, helped keep the company on the cutting edge of fashion. On advice from its advertising agency (a British firm), the company has divided its market into four segments: poseurs, trendsetters, social contact seekers, and high fliers. The company reasons that once these customers are captured, telephones spread inexorably to the rest of the population.

Another factor in Nokia's success has been its willingness to use consumer-goods marketing principles in its business: it introduces several

Exhibit 5.6
Globalization Rankings of the World's Largest MNCs.*

Rank	Company Name	Country	Industry	Foreign to Total Assets	Foreign to Total Sales	Foreign to Total Employment	Trans Index
1	Seagram Company	Canada	Beverages	97.85%	96.83%	NA	97.34%
2	Asea Brown Boveri (ABB)	Switzerland/Sweden	Electrical equipment	NA	97.45%	94.72%	96.09%
3	Nestle SA	Switzerland	Food	90.88%	98.13%	96.91%	95.31
4	Thomson Corporation	Canada	Printing and publishing	97.17%	94.07%	93.47%	94.90%
5	Solvay SA	Belgium	Chemicals/ pharmaceuticals	NA	95.60%	88.74%	92.17%
6	Holderbank Financiere	Switzerland	Construction materials	92.02%	86.28%	91.04%	89.78%
7	Electrolux AB	Sweden	Electrical appliances	85.79%	92.46%	87.59%	88.61%
8	Unilever	Netherlands/United Kingdom	Food	85.16%	86.35%	89.80%	87.10%
9	Grand Metropolitan	United Kingdom	Food/beverages	NA	90.46%	83.72%	87.09%
10	Roche Holding AG	Switzerland	Pharmaceuticals	83.15%	98.17%	79.79%	87.04%
11	Philips Electronics N.V.	Netherlands	Electronics	77.29%	95.11%	82.29%	84.89%
12	Kvaerner ASA	Norway	Shipbuilding/engineering	NA	76.92%	86.41%	81.67%
13	Northern Telecom	Canada	Telecommunication	72.46%	88.93%	NA	80.69%
14	Bayer AG	Germany	Chemicals	90.98%	82.20%	66.37%	79.85%
15	Cable And Wireless Plc	United Kingdom	Telecommunication	83.62%	71.61%	79.08%	78.10%
16	Glaxo Wellcome Plc	United Kingdom	Pharmaceuticals	66.82%	92.11%	75.21%	78.05%
17	Eridania Beghin-Say SA	France	Food	74.78%	78.66%	75.58%	76.34%
18	Novartis	Switzerland	Pharmaceuticals/ chemicals	49.31%	97.95%	78.49%	75.25%
19	Ericsson LM	Sweden	Electronics	NA	93.25%	53.28%	73.26%
20	Akzo Nobel N.V.	Netherlands	Chemicals	70.77%	73.65%	74.82%	73.08%
21	Exxon Corporation	United States	Petroleum exploration/refining/ distribution	58.20%	87.18%	NA	72.69%
22	Petrofina SA	Belgium	Petroleum exploration/refining/ distribution	67.17%	80.13%	67.83%	71.71%
23	Hanson Plc	United Kingdom	Building material	57.84%	94.25%	62.50%	71.53%
24	BTR Plc	United Kingdom	Plastics and foam	66.53%	75.47%	NA	71.00%
25	News Corporation	Australia	Media	59.85%	87.03%	64.92%	70.60%

146

Exhibit 5.6
(continued)

26	BASF AG	Germany	Chemicals	63.38%	73.41%	40.94%	68.39%
27	Ferruzzi/Montedison	Italy	Chemicals/agri-business	NA	76.23%	59.43%	67.83%
28	Coca-Cola	United States	Beverages	68.38%	67.60%	66.67%	67.55%
29	Rhone-Poulenc SA	France	Chemicals/pharmaceuticals	NA	79.13%	55.57%	67.35%
30	B.A.T. Industries Plc	United Kingdom	Food/tobacco	29.77%	80.73%	91.07%	67.19%
31	Shell, Royal Dutch	United Kingdom/Netherlands	Petroleum exploration/refining/distribution	66.16%	55.42%	78.22%	66.60%
32	Pharmacy & Upjohn	United States	Pharmaceuticals	65.34%	67.70%	NA	66.52%
33	Hoechst AG	Germany	Chemicals	78.98%	54.48%	63.38%	65.61%
34	British Petroleum (BP)	United Kingdom	Petroleum exploration/refining/distribution	65.09%	56.13%	70.30%	63.84%
35	Alcatel Alsthom Cie	France	Electronics	48.52%	77.64%	62.34%	62.83%
36	Mobil Corporation	United States	Petroleum exploration/refining/distribution	67.45%	66.04%	53.26%	62.25%
37	Saint-Gobain SA	France	Industrial material	53.23%	65.00%	66.67%	61.63%
38	Sony Corporation	Japan	Electronics	51.30%	71.91%	58.28%	60.50%
39	Crown Cork & Seal	United States	Packaging	60.37%	60.07%	NA	60.22%
40	McDonald's Corporation	United States	Restaurants	55.22%	57.04%	64.56%	58.94%
41	Honda Motor Co., Ltd.	Japan	Automotive	53.13%	62.41%	NA	57.77%
42	Elf Aquitaine SA	France	Petroleum exploration/refining/distribution	61.63%	59.32%	48.71%	56.55%
43	Dow Chemical	United States	Chemicals	58.36%	56.17%	52.21%	55.58%
44	Danone Groupe SA	France	Food	40.13%	56.27%	68.63%	55.01%
45	IBM	United States	Computers	51.03%	61.30%	50.56%	54.29%
46	Bridgestone	Japan	Rubber and plastics	51.32%	55.67%	NA	53.49%
47	Canon Electronics Inc.	Japan	Electronics	36.77%	67.60%	50.51%	51.63%
48	Hewlett-Packard	United States	Electronics	54.88%	55.65%	39.51%	50.01%
49	Johnson & Johnson	United States	Chemicals/pharmaceuticals	45.98%	49.54%	53.30%	49.61%
50	Michelin	France	Rubber and plastics	NA	84.91%	NA	84.91%

Exhibit 5.6
(continued)

51	Total SA	France	Petroleum exploration/refining distribution	NA	75.83%	NA	75.83%
52	Robert Bosch GmbH	Germany	Automotive	NA	62.42%	NA	62.42%
53	BMW AG	Germany	Automotive	NA	73.44%	44.70%	59.07%
54	Volvo AB	Sweden	Automotive	49.66%	88.83%	36.76%	58.42%
55	Volkswagen Group	Germany	Automotive	NA	63.63%	47.18%	55.40%
56	Daewoo Corporation	Korea, Republic of	Diversified	45.84%	38.82%	78.77%	54.48%
57	RTZ CRAg	United Kingdom/Australia	Mining	46.26%	49.96%	61.40%	52.54%
58	Nissan Motor Co., Ltd.	Japan	Automotive	46.49%	54.29%	NA	50.39%
59	Siemens AG	Germany	Electronics	43.35%	61.34%	46.44%	50.38%
60	Societe au Bon Marche	France	Beverages/luxury products	31.58%	64.38%	NA	47.98%
61	Xerox Corporation	United States	Photo equipment	45.12%	50.61%	NA	47.86%
62	Philip Morris	United States	Food/tobacco	37.54%	44.41%	61.47%	47.81%
63	Motorola, Inc.	United States	Electronics	35.72%	60.35%	45.85%	47.31%
64	BCE Inc.	Canada	Telecommunication	38.21%	64.56%	38.02%	46.93%
65	Petroleos de Venezuela	Venezuela	Diversified/trading	19.60%	93.51%	21.50%	44.87%
66	Texaco Incorporated	United States	Petroleum exploration/refining distribution	47.10%	47.67%	39.10%	44.62%
67	Procter & Gamble	United States	Chemicals/cosmetics	38.85%	48.81%	NA	43.83%
68	Du Pont (E.I.)	United States	Chemicals	48.44%	47.57%	35.05%	43.69%
69	Renault SA	France	Automotive	45.07%	53.92%	30.79%	43.26%
70	Daimler-Benz AG	Germany	Automotive	NA	62.85%	23.17%	43.01%
71	Mitsubishi Corporation	Japan	Diversified	NA	39.43%	43.43%	41.43%
72	American Home Products	United States	Pharmaceuticals	34.16%	40.84%	47.37%	40.79%
73	Mannesmann AG	Germany	Engineering/telecommunication	47.18%	35.58%	34.80%	39.20%
74	FIAT Spa	Italy	Automotive	38.08%	38.65%	38.00%	38.24%
75	Ford Motor Company	United States	Automotive	30.66%	44.77%	NA	37.72%
76	Broken Hill (BHP)	Australia	Metal	40.55%	36.80%	33.94%	37.10%
77	Mitsui & Co., Ltd.	Japan	Diversified	27.95%	42.84%	NA	35.40%
78	Chevron Corporation	United States	Petroleum exploration/refining distribution	41.32%	34.74%	29.63%	36.23%
79	Toyota	Japan	Automotive	34.57%	47.30%	23.11%	34.99%
80	International Paper	United States	Paper	36.81%	29.95%	35.63%	34.13%

148

Exhibit 5.6
(continued)

81	ENI Group	Italy	Petroleum exploration/refining/distribution	NA	33.47%	NA	33.47%
82	Nissho Iwai Corporation	Japan	Trading	NA	32.36%	29.88%	31.12%
83	General Electric	United States	Electronics	30.40%	25.61%	35.15%	30.72%
84	Pepsico, Inc.	United States	Beverages/food	31.82%	29.06%	NA	30.44%
85	General Motors	United States	Automotive	24.94%	31.67%	34.21%	30.27%
86	Marubeni Corporation	Japan	Trading	21.55%	38.81%	NA	30.18%
87	Sumitomo Corporation	Japan	Trading/machinery	26.19%	27.56%	31.47%	28.41%
88	Fujitsu Limited	Japan	Electronics	23.34%	29.80%	31.74%	28.29%
89	Matsushita Electric	Japan	Electronics	18.15%	38.36%	NA	28.26%
90	Mitsubishi Motors	Japan	Automotive	30.71%	28.69%	25.30%	28.23%
91	AMOCO Corporation	United States	Petroleum exploration/refining/distribution	32.09%	22.16%	22.27%	25.50%
92	Generale des Eaux	France	Diversified/utility	18.53%	30.84%	26.43%	25.27%
93	Itochu Corporation	Japan	Trading	22.99%	26.16%	26.46%	25.20%
94	Toshiba Corporation	Japan	Electronics	16.22%	31.84%	NA	24.03%
95	Atlantic Richfield	United States	Petroleum exploration/refining/distribution	28.78%	18.11%	NA	23.44%
96	Nippon Steel	Japan	Metal	NA	23.40%	NA	23.40%
97	Hitachi, Ltd.	Japan	Electronics.	14.18%	28.82%	17.09%	20.03%
98	AT&T Corp.	United States	Telecommunication/electronics	NA	16.92%	NA	16.92%
99	Chrysler Corporation	United States	Motor vehicles	14.77%	13.40%	20.63%	16.27%
100	GTE Corporation	United States	Telecommunication	18.48%	13.11%	NA	15.70%

*Of the 100 largest MNCs that we examined, only 49 were identified as global (i.e., companies that had a ratio of 50 percent or more on at least two of the three factors from their operations outside the home country; the three factors considered were assets, sales, and employment).

Source data: UN Conference on Trade and Development; *analysis:* GE Global Learning Center.

new models every year, changes colors according to fashion, encourages consumers to customize their telephones with clip-on covers, and adapts features to meet unique traits of a nation (e.g., Chinese customers need to have long-lasting batteries, and Japanese customers are fascinated with dialing by voice).

Although half of the company's 44,000 employees come from Finland, the company has a global mindset. The official language of the company is English, the meeting rooms have been named after the world's greatest cities, the senior management spends some time working abroad, and over half of the company's R&D is done outside the home country.

Citigroup's Global Push

Citigroup was the result of the merger of Citibank and Travelers. Travelers was a strictly domestic financial company serving the middle and lower classes. Citibank was content to grow its well-established franchise abroad but had no ambition to be a global player. Now, the company has decided to go global by buying various businesses abroad.[40]

Since 2001, Citigroup has bought credit card portfolios in Great Britain and Canada; Bank Handlowg, a Polish retail bank; a stake in Fubon Group, a Taiwanese financial services group; Associates First Capital Corporation, a U.S. consumer financial company with a big Japanese presence; and Grupo Financiero Banamex-Accival, the holding company of Mexico's largest independent bank and brokerage house. Thus, Citigroup has established a broader footprint in Latin America. At present, it is considering Brazil, Turkey, Korea, and other markets abroad. The company's ultimate objective is to spread the full array of U.S.-style financial services around the globe.

CONCLUSION

The war against terrorism has brought home forcefully that we share a common planet; that we are interdependent; and that if we are to address the world's central problems, we will have to work together. If ever there was a compelling argument for globalization, that is it. Yet the events of 9/11 have also greatly increased the incentive for the United States to think harder about globalization and the policies and practices needed to make it work.

Even before 9/11, globalization had lost some of its sheen. Its advocates had oversold it. It was supposed to bring unprecedented prosperity to all nations that subscribed to its tenets, which included opening markets not only for trade in goods and services but also for investment and speculation.

The financial crisis that began in East Asia in 1997 and spread around the world revealed a darker side. Hot money fueled a speculative real estate boom, giving the appearance of economic prosperity. But when the bubble burst, the speculators fled, leaving devastation. And before the hardest-hit economies could fully recover, the world began moving into the global slowdown as we stepped into the new century.

The United States, meanwhile, had taken a most peculiar position on globalization. There was a huge gap between what the United States and its European allies preached and what they practiced. They told developing countries to eliminate subsidies and trust free markets, yet they continued to subsidize their own agriculture massively. The United States used antidumping laws to keep out foreign goods that undersold U.S. products and tried to set up global cartels to protect aluminum and steel. While the United States and Europe worked to force developing countries to open their markets, they kept their own markets closed to many imports from developing countries, such as agriculture and textiles. The United States and Europe—quite rightly—were accused of hypocrisy.

Matters were made worse by the U.S. turn toward unilateralism, most evident in the stand on global warming. Until 9/11, the U.S. Treasury also resisted OECD efforts to fight money laundering and global efforts to increase transparency at offshore banking centers that doubled as tax havens. Evidently, preserving those offshore banking centers served the Treasury's clientele on Wall Street. Now that situation has changed.

The events of 9/11 will affect globalization in myriad ways, small and large. The image of the United States has changed. While television pictures nightly depict anti-U.S. protests in a few parts of the world, the attacks have brought enormous sympathy for the United States elsewhere, enormous respect for how we as a country have conducted ourselves in the aftermath of the attack, and enormous curiosity about how we are coping.

There is also great concern for what is happening to the U.S. economy, which may have the longest-lasting effects on globalization. The United States was on the brink of recession before 9/11; 2001–2002 data, including data on GDP, unemployment, and industrial production, showed that the attack pushed the nation over the edge.

The United States will inevitably export its downturn, as cutbacks in spending by consumers and businesses hurt demand for foreign-made goods. The great danger is that whereas the United States can weather a downturn, the developing countries cannot. Poverty, especially outside

China, has been increasing; the growth that marked the first part of the 1990s has turned into stagnation and recession; and what growth has occurred has largely accrued to the wealthy. The current downturn will fuel the growing backlash in the developing world against globalization and free market policies.

To make matters worse, the United States is sending contradictory signals. In the United States there is now a broad consensus behind expansionary monetary and fiscal policies, but in developing countries the IMF continues to insist on contractionary policies. But the United States refuses to resort to expansionary monetary and fiscal policy. There is no good solution, but this inconsistency breeds anti-U.S. and antiglobalization sentiment.[41]

The war on terrorism has brought a new dimension to globalization: a common response to a global threat. But globalization can, and should, be used not only to fight against evil but also to fight for good. We have already seen some of the fruits: globalized civil society successfully pushed for the antipersonnel-mines treaty over the objections of the Pentagon and successfully pushed for debt forgiveness, overcoming years of foot dragging at the IMF. Just as there is an alliance against terrorism, there needs to be an alliance against global poverty and an alliance for a global environment. By forcing us to recognize our common interests, perhaps the events of 9/11 will help forge these new alliances.

NOTES

1. Rob Norton, "Not So Fast: Anti-Trade/Pro-Poverty," *Fortune,* 10 January 2000, p. 40.

2. Robert Wright, "Will Globalization Make You Happy," *Foreign Policy,* September/October 2000, pp. 55–64.

3. "Global Capitalism," *Business Week,* 6 November 2000, p. 80.

4. " 'Santa' and Sweatshops," *Wall Street Journal,* 21 September 2000, p. 16.

5. Ethan B. Kapstein, "The Corporate Ethics Crusade," *Foreign Affairs,* September/October 2001, pp. 105–11.

6. Lawrence S. Root, "Globalization's Challenge," *Journal of International Institute,* Spring/Summer 2001, p. 2.

7. Joseph S. Nye Jr., "Globalization's Democratic Deficit," *Foreign Affairs,* July/August 2001, pp. 2–6.

8. "Global Capitalism," p. 88.

9. "The Environment: Defending Science," *Economist,* 2 February 2002, p. 15.

10. "The Anxiety behind Globalization," *Business Week,* 20 December 1999, p. 188.

11. David Pilling, "Merck Offers to Slash AIDS Drug Prices," *Financial Times,* 8 March 2001, p. 4.

12. Yaroslav Trofimov, "Manu Chao, the Bard of Anti-Globalization Sings for a Major Label," *Wall Street Journal,* 10 September 2001, p. 1.

13. Michael Skapinker, "Why Nike Has Broken into a Sweat," *Financial Times,* 7 March 2002, p. 12.

14. "Best Foot Forward at Reebok," *Economist,* 23 October 1999, p. 74.

15. David Hale, "A Second Chance," *Fortune,* 22 November 1999, p. 190.

16. "The New Economy," *Business Week,* 31 January 2000, p. 77; also see Gary S. Becker, "How Rich Nations Can Defuse the Population Bomb," *Business Week,* 28 May 2001, p. 28.

17. "A Semi-Integrated World," 20th Century Survey, *Economist,* 11 September 1999, p. 41.

18. Ann Harrison, "The Role of Multinationals in Economic Development," *Columbia Journal of World Business,* Winter 1994, pp. 6–11.

19. Mathew J. Slaughter and Phillip Swagel, "Does Globalization Lower Wages and Export Jobs?" *International Monetary Fund Issues,* 1997, no. 11, pp. 6–8.

20. "Global Capitalism," p. 94.

21. Catherine Caufield, *Masters of Illusion: The World Bank and the Poverty of Nations* (New York: Henry Holt, 1996).

22. Jagdish Bhagwati, "Coping with Antiglobalization," *Foreign Affairs,* January/February 2001, p. 7.

23. "Growth Is Good," *Economist,* 27 May 2000, p. 82.

24. Pascal Lamy, "Trade Is Changing—So Must Europe," *Financial Times,* 5 December 2000, p. 19.

25. "Semi-Integrated World," p. 44.

26. Frank Rose, "Think Globally, Script Locally," *Fortune,* 8 November 1999, p. 156.

27. C.K. Prahalad and K. Lieberthal, "The End of Corporate Imperialism," *Harvard Business Review,* July/August 1998, pp. 69–70.

28. Ninad D. Sheth, "Time to Say Cheese," *India Today,* 18 September 2000, pp. 30–31.

29. "Is Globalization Doomed?" *Economist,* 29 September 2001, p. 14 (special section on globalization).

30. "Meet Free Traders' Worst Nightmare," *Business Week,* 20 March 2000, p. 113.

31. "Is Globalism Doomed?" p. 82.

32. Samuel P. Huntington, *The Clash of Civilizations and the Remaking of World Order* (New York: Simon and Schuster, 1996), p. 184.

33. World Bank, *Global Economic Prospects and the Developing Countries: Making Trade Work for the World's Poor* (Washington, D.C.: World Bank, 2002); also see Xavier Sala-I-Martin, "The World Distribution of Income," unpublished study, Columbia University, New York, 2002.

34. "Measuring Globalization," *Foreign Policy,* January/February 2001, pp. 56–65.

35. Lowell Bryan et al., *Race for the World: Strategies to Build a Great Global Firm* (Boston: Harvard Business School Press, 1999), chap. 1.

36. Subhash C. Jain, *International Marketing,* 6th ed. (Cinncinati: South-Western College Publishing, 2001), pp. 12–13.

37. D. Sullivan, "Measuring the Degree of Internationalization of a Firm," *Journal of International Business Studies* 25, no. 2 (1994): 325–42.

38. Subhash C. Jain and Piotr Chelminski, "True Globalization Has a Long Way to Go," *Journal of Commerce,* 16 August 1999, pp. 4–6.

39. John Micklethwait and Adrian Wooldbrige, *A Future Perfect* (New York: Crown Publishers, 2000), pp. 129–32.

40. "Sandy Weill Wants the World," *Business Week,* 4 June 2001, p. 88.

41. *Fortune,* 26 November 2001, p. 74.

Chapter 6

A GLOBAL BUSINESS CONFEDERATION

Developing countries represent unsaturated markets with billions of potential consumers. Thanks to the advances in telecommunications and the Internet, these consumers are aware of living standards in developed societies, which they want to copy. MNCs need new markets to grow, because their traditional markets in Western nations are fast reaching the saturation point. Thus, it is mutually beneficial to a company and to a developing nation when MNCs go global: the company finds new markets to serve that help it grow and increase its stockholders' wealth; the developing countries enjoy a boost in economic activity that generates employment and enhances material well-being. Briefly, MNCs are the most significant force for worldwide material prosperity in this century. The future shape of the global economic system will be sculpted by MNCs, which will lift billions of people around the globe out of centuries of darkness by means of increasing economic activity.

Traditionally, national economies have remained predominantly local. In a globalizing economy, the local perspectives do not apply. Because MNCs operate globally, the rules and regulations of a single nation-state (say, the United States) or of a regional authority (say, the European Union) do not suffice. Therefore, new rules must be created. Who should create these rules and monitor their adherence? No global institution yet exists that can do this activity. This chapter advances a conceptual framework for such an institution.

PANGS OF GLOBALIZATION

We are living in a confused world. Architects of unbridled international trade and investment promise growth and development, but for many people life has not improved, and in fact it has worsened. Consider the tens of millions of people for whom the reality of life is struggle for existence: Americans displaced by jobs that have moved overseas, Russians overcome by gangsterism instead of capitalism, children enslaved in Asian sweatshops.

According to the World Bank, the 200 richest people in the world have more assets than the 2 billion poorest; the ranks of the most impoverished people increased by 200 million in the decade of the 1990s. Although foreign investment increased sevenfold in the 1990s, 70 percent of it is going from one rich country to another, with another 20 percent going to only 8 developing countries, which are more likely to be dictatorships than democracies. The remaining investment is being divided among 100 nations, many of them the poorest.[1]

As nations struggle under the debt from which the rich profit, countries around the world react by shedding their social safety nets, waiving environmental laws, ignoring food safety and public health regulations, and outlawing workers organizing for a better life—all to meet the demands of global investment. Then, as poor nations try to export their way out of trouble, thousands of high-wage manufacturing jobs in developed countries disappear. Each day in developing nations, an estimated 250 million children focus on going to work instead of going to school, making goods that profit global corporations. This kind of global economy is bound to be challenged.

Trade accords will face opposition if workplace and environmental standards are not included. Companies will face embarrassment for trampling on basic rights, and countries eventually will be challenged for allowing it.

The future of globalization should not be about ad hoc solutions to these problems but about embracing a new internationalism, one based on understanding that trade is an economic tool to meet the ends of development, democracy, and a better deal for working people and their families around the globe.

A great change is on the horizon that will rearrange the politics and economics of the world. There will be no national products or technologies, no national corporations, no national industries. As a matter of fact, there will no longer be national economies. All that will remain rooted within national borders will be the people who populate a nation. Each nation's primary assets will be its citizens' skills and insights.

This transformation can result in global prosperity. However, a fundamental prerequisite for that result is egalitarianism in trading and investment relationships. Fairness is a way to conduct business with another person, a reason to trust another person. Fairness promotes cooperation among people, based on reciprocity and comity. Unfortunately, the world does not yet practice reciprocity, because nations take from one another but find it hard to give in return. Globalizing corporations reflect the attitude of their nations. There is much value in designing trading and investment rules that respect the mutual need of all peoples for fairness. Life will be a lot better with such rules, and trust will become justified.

Reciprocity is only feasible when nations have common standards, which they do not now have. MNCs play by rules that are very different from one country to another. MNCs in Japan and Europe follow different trade and investment rules from those of the United States. Thus, for all the talk about globalization, the foundation for an integrated world business does not exist. Essentially, we have a series of nations and regional markets linked in precarious ways. Therefore, global business transactions are held hostage to diverse standards, rules, and technologies. Obviously, there is a critical need for a new global business architecture.

Consider the case of cross-country mergers. The existence of over sixty different antitrust systems forces global companies to consider many regulatory hurdles, yet companies must merge to restructure and position themselves to face the future. The evolving world economy presents several thorny questions for which no single national system has all the right answers. How should antitrust policy deal with the bundling of services and products, an issue that arose in the failed General Electric–Honeywell merger? What should officials think about the tendency for monopolies to arise so quickly in technology industries? When national antitrust authorities think about their jurisdiction, what is their legitimate geographic scope?

In the case of labor, environment, and human rights issues, the WTO had been expected to take care of conflicting approaches of different nations. But the WTO is deadlocked, because it has no ultimate authority. As a short-term measure, more than 240 companies or industry associations have agreed to abide by a patchwork of new rules. More than 25 of these efforts involve independent monitoring. Exhibit 6.1 illustrates corporate self-regulating standards to respond to globalization concerns.

Currently, there are 6 billion people in the world, of which 1 billion enjoy a decent standard of living. However, there are enough resources (i.e., technology, materials, capital, and talent) in the world to meet at least the basic needs (food, clothing, shelter, education, and health care) of the

Exhibit 6.1
Corporate Self-Regulating Standards for Globalization: Selected Examples

INDUSTRY GROUPS

▶ Three human rights groups have linked with industry players, mostly in garments and shoes, to inspect members' factories: Britain-based Ethical Trading Initiative; Fair Labor Association in the United States; and U.S./European Social Accountability International.

▶ U.S.-based Workers Rights Consortium monitors factories that make clothes with university logos; under pressure from Europe's Clean Clothes Campaign, garment companies are improving factory conditions.

COUNTRIES

BANGLADESH International Labor Organization (ILO) monitoring of child labor in the garment industry is expanding to include other labor standards.
CAMBODIA ILO inspects garment factories under a trade pact giving participating companies higher U.S. quotas.
PHILIPPINES Monitors are policing 1,000-odd garment factories, a program now widening to other industries.

COMMODITIES

Western companies in bananas, chocolate, coffee, and timber have agreed to external inspections of farms and other operations around the globe.

Source: *Business Week*, 19 November 2001, p. 76

remaining 5 billion people. The majority of these people might not achieve the standards of Western living, but if economic activity is fairly distributed, they will not lead subhuman lives.

The MNC is the principal institution capable of bringing about improvement for the 5 billion people living in poverty. MNCs can produce and market products and services, as well as provide employment. They require, however, a mechanism of laws, regulations, incentives, and support from nation-states to be able to deliver these benefits. The challenge is for MNCs and nation-states to work together for the welfare of the human race.[2] They should create partnerships with special interest groups representing labor, the environment, and human rights so that their concerns are addressed simultaneously. Establishing a global business confederation (GBC) would encourage the MNCs to bring about global economic prosperity in a manner responsive to cultural, social, and human issues. The GBC comprising MNCs, nation-states, and special interest groups would help MNCs act in accordance with internationally accepted principles of human rights, labor standards, and environmental protection. The existing international institutions (the United Nations, IMF, WTO, and World Bank, among others) would be duly aligned with the GBC so that they would be able to pursue their own vital tasks. For example, the WTO would continue to work in extending the benefits of free trade fully to both developed and developing countries.

K. Moore and D. Davis have identified four types of capitalism: Assyrian (temple-princely capitalism with a high state involvement in business in concert with religion), Phoenician-Carthaginian (temple-naval capitalism with medium state involvement in business), Greek (entrepreneurial capitalism with a relatively low state involvement in business), and Roman (legionary-family capitalism with a medium state and religious involvement).[3] The proposed framework for a GBC offers a new type of capitalism that could be called *globally shared capitalism;* it seeks to include the entire world, and state involvement is low, yet in full concert with other special interest groups. A GBC would combine dialogic idealism with deontological and teleological elements to generate acceptable norms of dialogue and action among the multiple parties with their various concerns. The opportunity for open dialogue among different institutions from different cultures should improve mutual understanding and might help leaders make decisions that would be not only universally valid but also acceptable to all parties' vested interests.

Multinational business clearly enhances economic opportunities by creating and expanding markets for goods and services. It offers consumer benefits by increasing choice and lowering prices. At the same time, the existence of more open business regimes has real consequences on the flow of goods and services around the world. Trade and foreign investment policies affect labor conditions, distribution channels, and production plans. And any changes in global production and consumption have environmental consequences. Global business raises many difficult issues. Therefore, multilateral approaches must be found to address different concerns that arise in doing business across national boundaries. Only then can globalization proceed smoothly.

THE GBC: A CONCEPTUAL MODEL

The GBC would be a unique, treaty-based, institutional framework that would define and encourage the activities of MNCs around the globe in the greater interest of worldwide economic and social prosperity. Worldwide treaties (e.g., on labor practices) agreed to by nation-states, MNCs, and special interest groups would create communities of shared sovereignty in matters that would enhance the MNCs' effectiveness in generating global economic well-being while being responsive to social needs.

The GBC will operate on the principle of subsidiarity. That is, it will be granted jurisdiction over only those policies that cannot be handled effectively at the level of the nation-state. For example, GBC rules will apply against pornography in advertising; but closeness between males and females in advertisements may be left to nation-states, because some countries have a relatively free attitude toward sex, whereas other nations completely reject open displays.

Exhibit 6.2 depicts the initial GBC structure. Ultimately, the structure will be inherently evolutionary. It will be designed to grow gradually over the years before emerging in its final form. The GBC commission will be

Exhibit 6.2
Structure of the Global Business Confederation

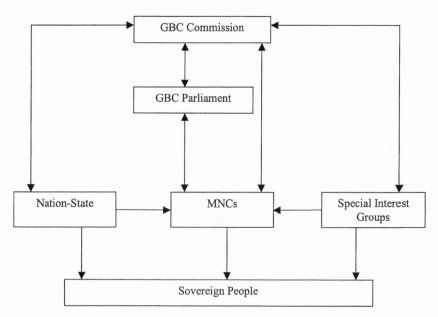

the central nerve of the entire structure. It will have 36 commissioners representing different entities: 14 from nation-states (1 commissioner each from the 14 largest economies, i.e., the United States, Japan, Indonesia, China, India, Germany, South Korea, Thailand, France, Great Britain, Brazil, Italy, Russia, and Mexico); 14 from MNCs (4 commissioners each from the United States, Japan, and Western Europe; and 2 commissioners from developing countries); and 7 from special interest groups (1 commissioner each from the United Nations, the WTO, the World Bank, the IMF, and the International Labor Organization; and 1 person each representing the environment and human rights). The 36th member will be the head of the commission, who might be called the managing director or president of the commission. Rules and procedures will have to be developed to choose the commission's head. He or she should be a proven leader in either business (e.g., Jack Welch, the former CEO of General Electric) or government (e.g., former president Bill Clinton), irrespective of nationality.

The commission will deal with issues such as the following:

- Registration of MNCs.
- Transparency and accountability of MNCs.
- Anticorruption measures.
- Capital- and tax-related investment incentives.
- Labor policies, including subsidies and training.
- State procurement policies.
- Technology policies.
- Small-firm policies.
- Policies to encourage industrial restructuring.
- Policies to promote investment.
- State ownership of production assets.
- Merger and competition policies (including antitrust policies).
- Company legislation.
- Taxation policies.
- Labor regulation (labor union legislation and immigration rules).
- Technical and product standards.
- Environmental regulations.

The commission will propose legislation relative to these issues, and the legislation will be sent to the GBC parliament for examination. The parliament will consist of elected members from different nations, MNCs, and special interest groups. Initially, all WTO members would be invited to join the GBC.

The total strength of the parliament will be about five hundred, each country being assigned a membership quota based on a formula that includes population and GDP. Similarly, MNCs and special interest groups will be able to choose a few parliamentarians. The parliament will be headed by a speaker, who will be chosen based on mutually agreed upon criteria. The legislation proposed by the commission will be debated by the parliament, which will give the commission its recommendations. After examining the recommendations, the commission will finalize the legislation and submit it to the national governments.

Each national government will consider the commission's legislation in its own way. Only after the legislation has been passed by the national legislative body (i.e., congress, diet, or parliament) it will become the law in the country. Multinationals in that country will be required to abide by such laws. These laws will be duly sensitive to the needs of labor, environmentalists, and other interest groups, such as minorities and disabled people. Even the needs of religious organizations will be addressed. After all, religion is a major aspect of life for many people in the world, and it offers important moral underpinnings for various economic and social issues. The role of religious institutions in endorsing contracts and underwriting commercial exchanges should be considered a transaction cost–reduction element because of religion's role in encouraging forbearance and mutual trust.

The GBC will be a supranational organization. The nation-states will relinquish part of their national sovereignty to the GBC institutions so they can work together with the MNCs and special interest groups for their mutual interest through joint administration of some of these sovereign powers. In other words, although nothing will be applicable until the national parliaments accept the rulings of the GBC institutions, the national parliaments will be required to approach issues from a global perspective. Although a country may not have legally agreed to adopt measures against global warming, for example, it should do so in the interest of the planet as a whole. Likewise, in some areas nation-states will relinquish powers altogether in favor of the GBC, again in the interest of global economic advancement and harmony. Thus, the GBC may require all MNCs to prepare their annual reports in English and translate the financial information into U.S. dollars for easy comparison.

Briefly, the proposed model suggests an alliance of different institutions that influence society. To achieve their respective economic and social objectives and to meet the dictations of the international marketplace, the main stockholders in the wealth-creating process need to cooperate actively and purposefully with one another. The GBC model proposes nothing less than the grand intention of speaking authoritatively on a worldwide level of analysis. It represents an expansive, multidisciplinary, and inquisitive view of the MNC. It is designed to provide a platform to all those who have a stake in the societies affected by MNCs. The underlying rationale is that as globalization increasingly touches the lives of all peoples, trade and investment agreements should no longer be treated as the sole province of nation-states.

The final few years of the twentieth century were an astonishingly positive period, far more positive than the 1980s and certainly more so than the gloomy 1970s. Liberty—political, economic, and personal—has become a widespread reality for the first time. Ignoring the U.S. war against terrorism in the aftermath of the September 11, 2001, tragedy, which is a special case, the threat of war casts its dark shadow over a smaller proportion of the world's population, and fewer people live in constant fear of arbitrary arrest or torture, or worse. Stated differently, there are four freedoms that humans cherish: freedom from fear, freedom from want, freedom of belief, and freedom of expression. Today, three of these freedoms—freedom from fear, freedom of belief, and freedom of expression—are possessed by more people, more securely, than ever before. The current challenge of the twenty-first century is to create conditions to make it feasible for more and more individuals to have freedom from want. Philosophically, human progress is inevitable, all problems are solvable by reason, and humankind is forever conquering new frontiers. Using this philosophical base, it is within reach in the next two decades or so to secure freedom from want for the billions who still do not have it. The MNC represents the force that can make it happen, if only other forces (e.g., the nation-states) are willing to work within the noble pursuit of eradicating global poverty. The framework presented in the next section suggests organizational arrangements for this purpose.

GBC INSTITUTIONS

The world lacks well-developed institutions for dealing with global economic, social, environmental, and labor issues. For this reason, international cooperation among nation-states, MNCs, and special interest groups is required to establish GBC institutions and to generate structural and policy changes that will encourage economic growth and ensure protection of the environment, moral standards, and labor rights. At the least, the institutions described in this section should be established initially.

The Registry Office

All companies making direct investments outside the home country should register with the registry office. A company may have been registered initially in a U.S. state. The moment it decides to cross borders, though, it must register with this international entity. The registration process may comprise completion and submission of a simple one-page form for smaller companies, whereas a lengthy process may be required for large companies. For example, a company active in at least 10 countries or doing at least $1 billion worth of business abroad will have to furnish more information than a small firm with annual sales amounting to $10 million.

Currently, most MNCs, despite the adjectives used to describe them (e.g., *transnational, international, interterritorial, global, worldwide, mega,* and *cosmocorp*), are national firms with international operations. In other words, in today's world, in legal terminology, there is no such thing as a multinational or global company. There is no international law under which a transnational or supranational company can be incorporated and have legal existence in several nation-states. The entity proposed here would solve this problem. By registering with such an international entity, MNCs would be able to pursue global business interests without being unduly influenced by a particular nation-state. Registration with a global institution would prevent associating MNCs with specific countries in terms of their critical functions; they would essentially be stateless.

Office of Standards

MNCs may attempt to be fair to all stakeholders, but the lack of international standards leaves them wondering what is right and what is wrong. The office of standards will be responsible for setting standards of behavior and responsibility in all areas in which MNCs are involved.

Once standards are set, companies are willing to make a positive response to meet a standard. The standards can be grouped into financial reporting standards, social responsibility standards, and others.

Financial Reporting Standards

Global capital markets cannot work without uniform, high-quality financial reporting standards; and without these standards, lasting value cannot be built, and capital will dry up. Today, investors, public companies, accounting firms, stock markets, and regulators around the world face one of the great challenges for the future of the global financial system: how to fashion an enabling system that will provide reporting that is accepted worldwide.

The explosive growth of markets and economies makes developing such a system imperative. There is simply no other way to ensure the efficient allocation of capital on a long-term and global basis.

Companies around the world clamor to sell their stock to U.S. investors. But all along, regulators have insisted that to do so, these companies must make their financial statements conform to U.S. GAAP. The U.S. financial reporting system is far from perfect, but it has more transparent and comprehensive disclosure rules than do others. This conclusion is supported by the fact that the U.S. system has inspired systemic confidence in capital markets.[4]

Regulators around the world continue developing a set of international accounting standards, and they want the United States to embrace them. The United States refuses to abide by the international standards because they are less rigorous than the U.S. standards.

Globalization of business brings an urgent need for worldwide standards accepted by all parties. The standards must be unambiguous and comprehensive. They must avoid or minimize alternative accounting procedures to alleviate inconsistencies. And they must be capable of strict interpretation. The proposed entity will undertake to set such standards with excellence in quality, comparability, and verifiability.

Social Responsibility Standards

Often companies are charged with unethical labor practices simply because of accusations by one group. If adequate standards are set, companies will know what must be done.

In 1999, 18 U.S. retailers and clothes manufacturers were charged with unethical labor practices. Although they admitted no liability, Nordstrom, Gymboree, Cutler & Buck, and J.Crew nevertheless paid millions of dollars to a fund to support independent monitoring of their suppliers. Even some companies that were not specifically charged, such as Donna Karan, Ralph Lauren, Phillips–Van Heusen, and Chadwick's, agreed to support the monitoring.[5] The office of standards will recommend standards for making companies global responsible citizens relative to labor and other areas of social concern.

The natural environment surrounding us must be protected for human survival and progress. Therefore, standards relating to various aspects of the environment must be set. An example is the Kyoto Protocol approved by 178 countries in July 2001. It calls for industrial nations to reduce their carbon dioxide emissions to 5.2 percent below 1999 levels during an accounting period that runs from 2008 to 2012.[6]

Because the United States rejected the Kyoto Protocol, U.S. companies have an advantage over their foreign rivals, who as signers of the agreement are forced to reduce greenhouse gas. Nonetheless, U.S. MNCs need to conform to the Kyoto rules for their operations abroad, which creates a confusing situation for them.

The office of standards proposed here will set standards in consultation with MNCs and nations-states. This way, the will of the nation-states alone will not be the determining factor in setting the standards.

Office of Business-Related Issues

There are business issues with worldwide impact for which global rules and regulations are necessary. As companies undertake massive restructuring of global markets by megamergers, coordinating antitrust policy across borders becomes essential. Antitrust issues are taking center stage in the shaping of global industries and in the delicate balancing of public and private interests in the world economy.

Antitrust issues, as well as other matters of similar impact, will come under the jurisdiction of the office of business-related issues. This way, regulations among countries will be harmonized. A broader multilateral effort geared to streamlining the issue process, reducing administrative burdens on companies, and focusing on more transparent investigations should result.

Audit Office

The audit office will be responsible for an annual examination of the performance of different offices. All the entities that constitute the confederation must be held accountable for what they do. This office will develop measures of performance in terms of goal realization and the efforts devoted to achieve the goals.

The confederation entities will not behave as superstructures with worldwide impact without being responsible to some entity. The audit office will make sure they are fully transparent and conduct themselves well.

Information Office

All MNCs should be transparent in sharing their perspectives with the world community. Of course, it is necessary to protect proprietary information relative to trade secrets of commercial value and other intellectual properties, but abundant facts and figures pertaining to MNCs still should be available to the sovereign people. Just as the World Bank compiles information on nation-states, this GBC entity will collect, analyze, and disseminate information on MNCs on a yearly basis. Such information will be broader and deeper in scope than the annual report information.

One of the most troublesome features of MNC operations is the ignorance among the public concerning them. The torrents of data about both the domestic and foreign business of MNCs are often incomprehensible and rarely comparable. The result is confusion for all the stakeholders. This problem has two causes. First, the headquarters of MNCs receive huge amounts of information from subsidiaries in a raw form, which is impossible to present in a concise fashion. Second, despite this onslaught of data, many important items are missing. Sometimes no attempt is made to obtain important information. Tax authorities would rather not have additional information, because auditing would be beyond their means.

It is important to open up the operations of MNCs to more thorough public scrutiny. Very little relevant information currently is available on MNCs. Even overseas sales, revenues, and employment information is not shared by many corporations. Openness is the hallmark of democratic regimes, and MNCs should be willing to be transparent in all areas except proprietary information. Any organization needs to be truthful to survive; MNCs are no exception. A policy of openness would enhance the effectiveness of MNCs, besides having a positive impact on world commerce.

The proposed information office will develop measures of cross-border information that all MNCs must share. Take the case of the U.S. apparel and footwear industries, which have subcontracted production in Asia for decades. For the most part, consumers have been glad to buy inexpensive garments and have been relatively unconcerned about the low-paid, sometimes underage workers who make them. Occasionally, though, consumers spurred by human rights and labor activists and the media become more sensitive to ethics than to prices. If they become sufficiently aroused, consumers may turn on a once-loved brand name. As a consequence, companies may suddenly find their manufacturing decisions being subject to the force of public opinion. A company like Nike, with its carefully crafted high-profile image, could become vulnerable to bad publicity this way. But if information on MNCs is openly shared, people will be able to determine for themselves whether a company indeed has been consistently unethical or whether there has been just an occasional slip.

Many critics maintain a biased view of MNCs, and any bad news relative to their operations spreads quickly. Consider the pharmaceutical industry. Most large firms in the industry recognize that proactive environmental practices allow them to operate more efficiently and enhance wealth creation.[7] Furthermore, such practices give them greater operational freedom than they would have if they had to scurry to respond to changes in government regulations. Indeed, proactive firms that set high standards can influence regulatory requirements. But the public is unaware of this fact. Criticism of MNCs often is based on an unsystematically evolved and haphazard collection of ideas consisting mostly of selective, personal impressions and opinions. This problem can be solved if there is an authority that regularly collects and disseminates information on different facets of MNCs' operations.

Office of Dispute Settlement

Many times MNCs are questioned for their business decisions. Companies defend their positions, of course, but the public criticism does not go away. There is a need for a global entity to settle such disputes for mutual understanding.

Take the case of the pharmaceutical industry. The industry claims that its high prices are necessary for drug research, but Public Citizen, a consumer advocacy group, disputes the statistics put out by the industry and says drug companies spend as little as 10 percent on research for each new medicine.[8] The drug companies' position is that it costs, on average, $500 million to research and develop each new drug, given that they have to spend money studying hundreds of molecules that turn out to have no therapeutic value. This high cost of R&D leads firms to charge high prices for prescription drugs. The firms argue that without adequate returns, new medicines would dry up, because investors would be loath to invest in a high-risk industry without the chance of good profits.

The consumer groups, based on their analysis, claim that typically the R&D is about $50 million to $60 million for each new drug. According to these groups, R&D expenditures are tax deductible, allowing companies to reduce reportable profits.[9] Besides, they argue, companies use unrealistic scenarios of risks to justify their point and spend a greater proportion of their revenues on marketing than on research.

There is a need for an international office of dispute settlements to mediate in such situations. It will create a congenial environment where all parties can devote their energies to substantial issues rather than to charging and countercharging.

Summary

In establishing the GBC institutions, two aspects must be addressed. First, the institutions should be made accountable for their actions and decisions. Second, in structuring these institutions, the multiple veto points that make them less effective in policy realms should be avoided.

The proposed GBC framework preserves the autonomy of the nation-state, the MNCs, and the special interest groups. As a matter of fact, the framework is a way to contain the autonomy of the MNCs over and beyond national sovereignty, while at the same time restoring the unity of the worldwide polity. The framework is designed with the assumption that each GBC institution will focus on a narrow and specific function that gives it the capacity, as well as the willingness and ability, to work with political authority for the common good.

The MNC is the central actor, with an objective agenda of creating wealth through the transfer of technology, market making, and global managerialism. The government's role in the emerging era is generally supporting, supplemental, and secondary to the needs of the firm. To avoid a materialistic bias, corporate leadership should make an effort to consider the power of ideas, spirituality, and other nonmaterial sources of human motives. These aspects of culture are important. The special interest groups serve to draw attention to them.

Every institution has its heyday. During the fifteenth and sixteenth centuries, the church held sway. Since then, it has been the nation-state. The twenty-first century may well belong to the corporation, which is the most representative institution of society today.

The GBC is not intended to be a single, supranational government of the world. It is to be an institutional framework on an international basis within which MNCs can better deliver economic prosperity worldwide. National sovereignty will remain intact; global action will be taken only where national treatment is not likely to work. Take the case of environmental problems such as global warming, which unavoidably cross national borders. A nation-state would tend to neglect the cost of these externalities when setting domestic regulations. A global authority is therefore needed to protect all nations. Consider fishing: Individual countries may fail to limit overfishing, even though all suffer as a result. Even if some nations impose limits, they might not achieve any benefits if other countries continue to overfish. So there is a strong case for international agreement in this regard as well. The framework introduced here provides the means for this type of international control. It depicts the MNC as a complementary institution on a par with the nation-state.

JUSTIFICATION OF THE FRAMEWORK

MNCs do a lot of things right, but their record in certain areas, such as the environment, labor rights, and human rights, leaves much to be desired. New multilateral approaches must be found to address these lapses. Some attempts in this direction have already been made. For example, the Montreal Protocol on ozone depletion and the Kyoto Protocol on global warming address environmental concerns. In labor rights there is the International Telecommunications Union, which regulates international communications via radio, telephone, and telegraph; the Universal Postal Union, which facilitates postal communication; the International Standards Organization, which promotes standardization of different products and processes; the International Labor Organization, which addresses workers' welfare and rights; and the International Telecommunications Satellite Consortium, which deals with new satellite technology.

There have even been attempts to develop multilateral rules for MNC activities, such as the proposal by the OECD for a multilateral agreement on investment to design a set of global rules for investment by MNCs. In fact, a long history exists of attempts to introduce an international framework relating to MNC operations. Examples include the OECD Guidelines for Multinational Enterprises (first introduced in 1976), the International Labor Organization Tripartite Declaration of Principles Concerning Multinational Enterprises and Social Policy (1977), and the UN Code of Conduct for Transnational Corporations (initiated in 1982). Despite all these initiatives, relatively little progress has been made in creating an international regulatory framework for direct investment and other aspect of MNC operations (see Exhibit 6.3). The paradigm presented here approaches all the concerns in an integrated fashion. There is no need to establish the principles, processes, and rules for each concern separately when common practices are involved.

Practicality of the Framework

If the experience of GATT is any guide, the GBC paradigm introduced above should work. Since its creation, the multilateral system under the auspices of GATT has helped trade expand more than twice as fast as production, and the system itself has expanded along with it. GATT's original

Exhibit 6.3
Globalization of Capital Markets: How Investors Get Lost in Regulatory Limbo

For all the talk about globalization, the foundation for an integrated world financial system does not yet exist. What we now have is a series of national and regional markets linked in precarious ways. The following episode illustrates the point.

In 1996, a Dublin, Ireland couple, on the advice of a broker from the International Asset Management (IAM) in Brussels, invested $17,000 in "red-hot" U.S. stocks. A year later, the couple called the broker to sell the stock. Meanwhile, the broker had moved to Barcelona, Spain. He agreed to sell their stock, if they were willing to plow the proceeds and $10,000 more into shares of a tiny California company called Zia Sun Technologies Inc.

The couple complained to Spanish regulators. They were of no help. They had no jurisdiction because IAM did not sell to Spaniards. Frustrated by the Spanish regulators' decision, the couple was able to sell some shares through another broker, but failed to unload their biggest holding, a stake in a troubled startup that they had bought for $6,000 and now was worth only $90. Since then, they lost contact with the IAM broker and were stuck with worthless stock.

This is not a single incidence, since buying stock overseas is not as easy as globalization would have us believe.

In recent years, investors from Athens to Australia have purchased millions of dollars of stock in U.S. companies from IAM and its affiliates. Many, like the Irish couple, have found themselves unable to sell their shares or even get stock certificates, and nearly all are unable to get help from regulators. One investor even called the U.S. Securities and Exchange Commission. The agency, he says, told him that it couldn't help because the shares were issued under Regulation S.

These Regulation S stock sales are allowed under a 10-year-old provision of U.S. securities law that is intended to allow American public companies to raise capital from foreign investors without the onerous registration process required to sell stock in the U.S. Once sold abroad, Regulation S shares cannot legally be resold to U.S. investors for at least a year; they can, however, be sold to other foreigners during that period.

(continued)

Exhibit 6.3
(continued)

While hundreds of perfectly legal and legitimate S-share transactions occur each year, unscrupulous operators have found a way to exploit Regulation S to their advantage. The way it often works, a promoter that is at least nominally based outside the U.S. buys large blocks of S shares from American issuers at deep discounts and then sells them at huge markups to neophyte investors abroad.

The SEC doesn't comment on specific cases and won't comment on the current state of Regulation S. Non-U.S. regulators aren't much help either, though they periodically warn citizens to avoid boiler-room brokers operating outside of their home country. British stock regulators recently noted a sharp rise in the number of boiler rooms in continental Europe that target English residents. The firms are not registered in the U.K.; it is up to governments in other nations to regulate them, which is very frustrating.

Consider a startup company, Zia Sun. It has operated under various names since it was founded and went public in 1996, and it has engaged in business ranging from motorcycles to soda dispensers. In news releases, it now bills itself as "a leading Internet technology holding company focused on international investor education and e-commerce." About 85% of Zia Sun's 1999 revenue came from a business that operates traveling seminars on Internet stock trading for $2,995 a person. More than half of Zia Sun's own 27 million shares outstanding have been sold to foreigners under Regulation S, according to the company's SEC filings. In two transactions in 1997, Zia Sun sold 15 million shares at 10 cents a share under Regulation S to foreign investors, whose identities didn't have to be disclosed in public records. At about the same time, investors in Europe and Asia say they received calls from salesmen from IAM and related brokerage offering Zia Sun stock at $4.50 or more a share. In the U.S. during the same period, Zia Sun, under previous corporate names, was trading on the Nasdaq Bulletin Board at between $1.25 and $5.50 a share on average daily volume of several thousand shares.

Vladimir Kaplan, a Zurich doctor, bought some of those Zia Sun shares. His Barcelona-based IAM broker offered Zia Sun at $4.50 a share on Oct. 7, 1998—when the stock was trading in the U.S. for between $2.50 and $4.00 a share. Unable at the time to independently determine Zia Sun's

Exhibit 6.3
(continued)

stock price, Dr. Kaplan bought nearly 8,000 shares to start, and more over the ensuing weeks. Dr. Kaplan knew his broker as a senior portfolio manager at IAM and trusted his judgment, especially after he flew to Zurich to make a personal sales call. The doctor didn't know that the broker also was one of Zia Sun's founders per the SEC filings.

The story goes on with many disgruntled investors. Laws pertaining to buying and selling stock differ form nation to nation, so that crooks can take advantage of loopholes and cheat innocent people who are willing to invest their hard-earned savings. They have no recourse if things go sour.

Source: Adapted from John R. Emshwiller and Christopher Cooper, "Hot for U.S. Stocks, Foreigners Get Burned in Regulatory Limbo," *The Wall Street Journal*, 16 August 2000, p. 1.

23 contracting parties have increased to more than 132, and there are 31 candidates for membership, an impressive vote of confidence. And all the candidates are developing or transition economies, as are 80 percent of the members.

By lowering barriers to trade, GATT has also helped lower barriers between nations and peoples, contributing to the growing interdependence that is an important feature of the modern world. The collective wisdom of governments and traders under GATT has taught us that trade and international economic ties promote and reinforce stability and peace and that the only conflict worth pursuing is competition in an open market. In addition, GATT has helped bind nations and peoples together on a nonpolitical basis. There is every reason to believe that the GBC would further boost economic prosperity and bring the people of the world closer to one another.

The practicality of the proposed GBC framework is supported by the WTO experience as well. Consider that the WTO enforces intellectual property standards, not only in rich countries but also in many developing ones. For example, if Thailand fails to stamp out counterfeit Louis Vuitton handbags and pirated Viagra, France and the United States can seek WTO approval to retaliate by imposing trade sanctions against Thailand. Now consider this: if an institutional framework can be successfully developed and implemented for reducing trade barriers and protecting intellectual property rights worldwide, standards could be set and enforced in other areas as well, such as labor, executive compensation, taxes, and disclosure of information.

Many scholars are concerned that putting MNCs at center stage amounts to announcing the demise of the nation-state. This book does not advance the idea that the nation-state is finished. It simply argues that MNCs should be supported, guided, and controlled on an international basis rather than by the laws and rules of a single nation, the reason being that an MNC operates in many nations at the same time, whereas the perspectives of a country are individualistic and self-serving. But this book does not pursue the concept of world federalism or a one-world government. The proposed paradigm leaves the nation-state as the ultimate arbitrator.

The world is rapidly changing and seemingly getting smaller. The internationalization of domestic economies, the interdependence of issues and nations, the linked interests of business and government, and the opportunity to think and act globally have forced us all to note that a new political-economic regime is at hand. Technology has created abilities for the movement of information, goods, services, and techniques as never before. All that is needed is the development of a worldwide institutional framework to create a stable environment so that trade and investment can be free to grow and distribute wealth in unprecedented ways. An opportunity to create a true world economy is at hand. To fight these changes is both folly and fantasy.

For the people of the world to get the most out of this new world order, free market institutions and practices must be supported while government is simultaneously limited to the important role of protecting and guaranteeing free market activity. Barriers to exchange, trade, and investment should be lowered so that all may benefit from the increased access to markets and resources. Even though these steps will create some dislocations and costs, in the end the ever-rising tide of prosperity will make everyone better off. In this new world, the dynamic of competition, through the agency of the corporate form of enterprise, will be the objective determinant of rank and success. Only the firms and governments that create lean, efficient, and responsive operations will survive and thrive. The proposed framework enhances the efficiency and fosters the responsibility of all parties.

A paradox must be resolved: on the one hand, people harbor suspicion toward multinationals, but on the other hand, they seem to want the jobs and status those companies provide, and they are eager to buy their products and services. It could be that people are hostile to groups of any type. Groups demand conformity and impose uncomfortable obligations. Joining groups may confer benefits, but most people are disinclined to embrace them.

Another cause of public hostility is the sheer size of an MNC. Large companies seem to be getting bigger, and their size overwhelms individuals. Further, the onrush of cheap communications, powerful computers, and Internet-related events creates a sense of rapid change that makes many people anxious about adjusting to the effects of technological progress. They feel the world is shifting beneath their feet, and they wonder if they can keep their balance. The GBC addresses these fears of the general public, not by attacking MNCs for neglecting human concerns but by engaging their leaders in a dialogue that can bring about amicable resolutions.

Church, Nation-State, and MNCs

Western civilization has always recognized two centers of authority: church and state. But people in both realms have believed that there should be boundaries that define authority. Religious institutions, whatever their lust for civil control, have acknowledged that there were forms of political power that they should not exercise. Similarly, the nation-state, whatever its drive to dominate, has acknowledged that there were areas of human life that were beyond its reach.

In the twentieth century, the concern for economic advancement gave rise to a new institution, the company: a gathering together of large numbers of people in a voluntary collaborative effort to share their skills, knowledge, and energy for a common purpose. Although it has been supremely successful, the company has been viewed with great suspicion. Such suspicion did make sense at the turn of the last century, when the modern company was being invented. Until then, businesses had been run by their owners and for their owners, a breed known in the United States as robber barons: Andrew Carnegie, Cornelius Vanderbilt, John Rockefeller, and others. But technological change made it desirable and possible for these businesses to grow much bigger. At the same time, a managerial class developed that took over the running of companies from their owners. Furthermore, with shareholders becoming more fragmented and distant and with the parallel development of mass education, a much greater sense of equal opportunity was established. The company was no longer the creation of one hugely wealthy individual or family.

Another noteworthy change has been the development of company funds that seek to provide for workers' retirement through broad, diversified investment in equities and bonds. These funds give employees a direct interest in corporate profits and economic growth, as well as some long-term security.

In the post–War II era, the company as an institution has proved its significance in raising the level of economic well-being of individuals and societies. If given the economic freedom, the company has the capacity to bring prosperity worldwide. At the threshold of the twenty-first century, then, three institutions are dominant: church, nation-state, and company. So far, however, companies have been subsidiary to the nation-state. But with the expansion of their activities beyond national boundaries, they cannot operate following only national laws and regulations. There is need for global principles, processes, and rules for companies that are active globally.

Danger of Interventionism

The United States has become great and rich under an economic system that sets no limit on the free pursuit of individual wealth, and it has thereby made room for the development of the country's productive power. The free market system has been credited for the economic hegemony of the United States. After the breakdown of the Soviet Union, the failure of the socialist system was fully acknowledged. Thus, in the process of globalization, it is important that the free market system be fully preserved.

It should be stated that the economic system the United States follows is not strictly a free market model. It has been replaced by interventionism. Indeed, interventionism is the predominant economic system in the world today. Nearly all writers on economic policy and nearly all statesmen and party leaders are seeking an ideal system, which in their belief is neither purely capitalistic nor purely socialistic and is based on neither unrestricted private property in the means of production nor public property. These individuals seek a system of private property that is restricted, regulated, and directed through government intervention and social forces such as labor unions. This system can be called *interventionism* or the *hampered market order*.

A genuine free market economy exists when (1) all means of production are privately owned; (2) use of the means of production is controlled by private owners, who may be individuals or corporate entities; (3) consumer demands determine how the means of production will be used; (4) competitive forces of supply and demand determine prices for consumer goods and various factors of production, such as labor; (5) the success or failure of individual and corporate enterprises is determined by the profits or losses these enterprises earn, based on their greater or lesser ability to satisfy consumer demand in competition with their rivals in the marketplace.; (6) the market is not confined to domestic transactions and includes freedom of international trade; (7) the monetary system is based on a market-determined commodity (e.g., gold or silver) and the banking system is private and competitive, neither controlled nor regulated by government; and (8) government activity is limited to the enforcement of laws that protect life, liberty, and property.

When it comes to identifying the role of governments in the market order, even most conservative economists assume that the government must be responsible for an economic safety net that includes social security and unemployment compensation, must have discretionary monetary and fiscal powers to support desired levels of employment and output, must regulate industry to ensure competitive conditions in the market and fair labor conditions for workers, and must directly supply certain goods and services that the market allegedly does not provide. Indeed, thousands of individuals who claim to be on the right believe that government should institute some or all of these public policies. However, the term *public policy,* as it is almost always used, implies government intervention in the market in ways that are simply inconsistent with a genuine free market economy.

The interventionist economy exists when (1) private ownership of the means of production is restricted or abridged; (2) use of the means of production by private owners is prohibited, limited, or regulated; (3) users of the means of production are prevented from being guided by consumer demand; (4) the government influences or controls the formation of prices for consumer goods, the factors of production, or both; (5) the government reduces the impact of market supply and demand on the success or failure of various enterprises, while it increases the impact of its own influence and control through such artificial means as price and production regulation, limits on freedom of entry into segments of the market, and direct or indirect subsidies; (6) free entry into the domestic market by potential foreign rivals is discouraged or outlawed through import prohibitions, quotas, or tariffs; (7) the monetary system is regulated by government for the purpose of influencing what is used as money, the value of money, and the rate at which the quantity of money is increased or decreased, and all these measures are used as tools for affecting employment, output, and growth in the economy; and (8) the government's role is not limited to the protection of life, liberty, and property.

It is important to note that the so-called public policies that most governments pursue are built around the points discussed above. In other words, interventionism is the order of the day. The framework of the GBC depoliticizes policies nationally and presents them in a globally relevant form. The framework rejects any protection for inferiority and uncompetitiveness over efficiency and competitiveness. It presents no new dangers of interventionism.

Keeping MNCs at Bay

Big companies have disproportionate clout in national legislation. The scandalously porous laws for campaign contributions in the United States, for example, leave little doubt that megacompanies exercise great power over politicians when it comes to such issues as environmental standards, tax policy, Social Security, and health care. Furthermore, megacompanies are almost beyond law, because their deep pockets allow them to stymie prosecutors in ways smaller defendants cannot. If they lose in court, they can pay large fines without much damage to their operations.[10]

Corporate giants also exert massive pressure on a nation's international behavior. In the United States, defense contractors such as Lockheed Martin have successfully pushed for expansion of the North Atlantic Treaty Organization (NATO) and for related military sales to Poland, the Czech Republic, and other countries. Entities such as Boeing have a formidable grip on U.S. trade policy. Companies such as ExxonMobil deal with oil-producing countries almost as equals, conducting the most powerful private diplomacy since the British East India Company wielded near-sovereign clout throughout Asia.

The structure of the GBC and its institutions prevents any company or industry from pursuing selfish interest. The rules and regulations must accommodate the needs of a diverse group of companies, countries, and special interest groups. The confederation policies must find the right balance between markets and the public frameworks of different nations in which the MNCs might operate. MNCs by themselves will not be able to tip the balance in their favor.

WORKING UP EXISTING INSTITUTIONS

A number of existing multinational institutions deal with global economic issues; they include the IMF, the World Bank, the WTO, the International Labor Organization, and others. Most of these organizations have sprung up in the post–World War II period. Why not reorganize one of these institutions into a GBC? A variety of reasons deter such action.

All existing institutions have been created by nation-states, and therefore politics is their lifeblood. Further, these institutions have been in business for over half a century and over time have developed a culture of their own. It would be difficult for them to adopt a new perspective.

The policies of these institutions are largely dictated by rich countries. Consider the IMF. Most IMF funding is not directly aimed at poverty reduction per se, but rather at helping countries achieve the macroeconomic and financial stability that are the foundations of prosperity. Thus, working on a theoretical model, countries that receive IMF bailouts are expected to implement a number of harsh steps with dire effect on poor people in the country. Indonesia, for example, was asked to fulfill 140 conditions before receiving financial support. These conditions can be relaxed at times if rich countries—particularly the United States, the biggest shareholder in the IMF—agree. By the same token, the United States can use similar leverage to stop IMF support in order to pursue its own foreign policy goals.

Many existing institutions are facing midlife crises relative to their goals, methods of operations, and measurement of performance. In 2000, a commission sponsored by the U.S. Congress clearly concluded that both the IMF and the World Bank have been trying to do too much. The IMF, first considered as a provider of liquidity in emergencies, has become a development institution, advising and requiring borrowers not merely to repay but to reform the deep microstructure of their economies. The IMF has little expertise in this area; such policies, when forced on governments in circumstances like these, tend not to stick; and in any case, so wide a mandate overlaps with that of the World Bank. The World Bank, however, although it has not broadened its operations, has failed to narrow them with changing conditions, such as the development of global financial markets. Most of the loans go to countries with access to private international capital. The countries that could make best use of World Bank resources receive a comparatively small share. To be more effective, both the IMF and the World Bank need to do less. They should sharpen their focus, shed lots of people from their payrolls, and shrink their operating budgets (see Exhibit 6.4).

Briefly, existing international institutions suffer from multiple goals, fragmentation, and deep confusion. They have little idea how to achieve their goals and form a coalition that can make progress on vital issues such as global warming, AIDS, and genetically modified organisms.

Consider trade talks. The rifts between developing and developed countries, the European Union and the United States, technology-based and agricultural economies, and capital-importing and capital-exporting countries are becoming more pronounced each year. The search for consensus

Exhibit 6.4
Problems with the Existing International Institutions: The Case of the World Bank

If the World Bank were a private company, the 1990s should have been a decade of record profits and the institution a growth stock. With the decline of communism, governments worldwide became disillusioned with the public sector as an engine of growth and embraced market-based capitalism. From Latin America to Eastern Europe, political leaders slashed barriers to trade, privatized state-owned enterprises and deregulated markets. Governments beat a path to the World Bank's door, seeking out its unequalled expertise in the field of development and its money. The bank's potential for influencing global events appeared to be on the verge of an unprecedented expansion.

It did not happen. Instead the World Bank has found itself in crisis, its power severely diminished and its global role under attack from across the political spectrum. Critics now speak freely of closing the institution altogether, or at least of radically shrinking it. Poised for spectacular growth 10 years ago, the World Bank is now groping for relevance precisely when profound change in the global economy should have placed it centre stage.

Under these conditions, what would a private company do? Easy: fire the chief executive officer. But not the World Bank. Its president, James D. Wolfensohn, was reappointed for a second, five-year term, to June 2005.

Yet critics inside and outside the bank accuse Mr. Wolfensohn of presiding over a tragic deterioration of the world's premier development institution, which they describe as rudderless and lacking strategic direction. They blame Mr. Wolfensohn's personal failings: a phenomenal temper, a constant need for approval, and an inability to resist the latest development fad. They allege that Mr. Wolfensohn's attempts to make the bank friendlier to myriad outside constituencies—in particular, to non-governmental organizations—have made the institution soft-headed, less analytical, and so less relevant. They also say that Mr. Wolfensohn's poor stewardship and lack of focus have weakened the bank's internal organization.

A former senior economist of the bank points out that high volume of private capital flowing to developing nations has seriously diminished the importance of the institution. But, he says, Mr. Wolfensohn's actions have accelerated the trend.

In the last six years since his appointment, Mr. Wolfensohn has completely overhauled the bank. He has appointed 36 of 38 vice-presidents, while three out of his five managing directors were brought in from outside.

(continued)

Exhibit 6.4
(continued)

Bank documents show that about a quarter of its 10,000 employees have joined in the past three years.

But many are critical of the internal changes. It is said that he has been unwilling or unable to set up a management structure beneath him to compensate for the fact that he can't run the institution on a day to day basis.

Critics charge that, under pressure from NGOs and other interest groups, the World Bank has surrendered its intellectual integrity, rushing to embrace the latest fashions in development thinking. No initiative embodies this trend better than Mr. Wolfensohn's "Comprehensive Development Framework," launched in January 1999—a "holistic, long-term and country-owned approach that focuses on building stronger participation and partnerships to reduce poverty."

According to critics, the CDF represents a capitulation to NGOs. Many borrowing governments complain that it is inappropriate for the World Bank to anoint non-elected, self-styled representatives of civil society to interfere in bank programs. "I am deeply troubled by the distance the bank has gone in democratic countries toward engagement with groups other than governments in designing projects," lamented Larry Summers, the former US Treasury secretary. According to him, there was little evidence that giving weight to local communities resulted in improved decision-making. The move toward empowerment rather than an economic approach is standing in some ways for a reduced emphasis of the analytic element in the bank's work, and it is a troubling development.

Many think that Mr. Wolfensohn's positioning of the bank has accentuated a lack of focus at the institution, leaving staff unsure about priorities. His ad hoc initiatives create a big confusion.

These initiatives include: the World Faiths and Development Dialogue, which brings together leaders of various religious denominations from around the world with the bank and other development institutions; support for cultural projects in the Balkans; and the Global Development Gateway, a new attempt to encourage "new economy" ideas in developing countries.

Ultimately, a good part of the responsibility for the World Bank's growing agenda and apparent lack of focus lies with its shareholders in rich countries. "As its own bilateral aid program has shrunk, the US has found the World Bank an especially useful instrument for projecting its influence in developing countries. The bank is a source of funds to be offered to US

Exhibit 6.4
(continued)

friends or denied to US enemies," argues Robert Wade of the Institute for Advanced Study in Berlin.

Although no other member states come close to matching US power over the bank, all its influential owners—Britain, France, Germany and others—have borrowing governments whose interests they purport to sponsor, as well as key issues (such as the environment) that are viewed as important by their electorates. Otherwise, accountability and scrutiny from donor governments are uneven at best and non-existent at worst. Meanwhile, the few powerful borrowing nations that could exert some influence are afraid to voice their concerns lest they lose access to bank finance.

This pressure on the bank is overlaid on what some consider another source of confusion: the idea that neither the World Bank nor others have the right recipe for development. The marked oriented economic reforms introduced over the past decade throughout the developing world have brought some recovery of economic growth but nowhere near what was expected. This frustration reaches right inside the bank. The International Monetary Fund and World Bank have over the past decade given 10 or more loans each, with conditions attached, to 36 poor countries. But the growth rate of income per person of the typical member of this group during the past two decades was zero.

Source: Adapted from *Financial Times*, 28 August 2001, p. 13.

among countries often is placed in the hands of multilateral organizations such as the WTO or the World Bank. These institutions do not have the authority, capabilities, or resources to handle such responsibility. As the *Economist* has noted: "It is hard to imagine that a single, understaffed and underfunded multilateral institution such as the WTO will ever be capable of providing the unifying framework, needed to break the stalemate over the rules of international trade."[11]

Lately, the United Nations has been in the news for its efforts to create conditions to ensure that globalization emerges in a socially responsible manner. The secretary-general of the United Nations has formed a new unit, entitled the Global Compact, to deal with issues of a globalized world. It is intended to provide a platform for all government and nongovernment organizations and the MNCs to work together to sort out problems and find solutions to them. Although it is too early to say how far the Global Compact will go, the members of the United Nations are already concerned about extending its charge. To them, the United Nations is abdicating its role in terms of social improvement and poverty alleviation, but adding new responsibilities with such a compact.[12]

Globalization continues to exert its disorganizing and often unequalizing effects, making the job of the countries that must agree on common worldwide business rules even more difficult. None of the existing multinational organizations can provide the leadership needed to create the coalitions necessary to break deadlocks.

GETTING IT OFF THE GROUND

Membership in the GBC will be open to MNCs, countries, multilateral institutions, and special interest groups. The United States, working closely with the International Chamber of Commerce, should take the lead in forming the GBC. Initially, the 500 largest MNCs should be invited to join the confederation. The International Chamber of Commerce will elect 14 confederation commissioners from these companies for a three-year period. (It is assumed all 500 companies are members of the chamber of commerce.) Of the 14 commissioners, 4 each should represent MNCs from the United States, Western Europe, and Japan, and 2 should represent developing countries.

The six multilateral institutions—that is, the United Nations, the WTO, the World Bank, the IMF, the International Labor Organization, and the WHO—each should name one person as a commissioner in the GBC. A separate meeting of NGOs representing environmentalists and human rights interests should be organized, with each group naming one person to serve as a GBC commissioner.

For nations, membership in the GBC will require meeting at least three of the following four conditions: (1) liberal trading policies, with average tariff rates below 10 percent; (2) encouragement of domestic and foreign investment; (3) protection of private property with a court system that enforces contracts; and (4) a balanced regulatory burden on businesses. Assuming that all 14 large economies qualify for membership, each of these nations will name a GBC commissioner to serve for a three-year period. If a nation does not qualify for membership, then the next largest economy (i.e., the 15th largest economy) will be invited to name a GBC commissioner. Later on, as the larger economy that was disqualified for GBC membership becomes eligible, the commissioner's position will revert back to it. As has been mentioned, a world figure such as former president Bill Clinton or Jack Welch should be invited to serve as the president of the GBC. Overall, the GBC will have 36 commissioners, including the president.

The GBC will be different from most existing global institutions in the sense that the MNCs will play a dominant role. Initially, the U.S. government will work with the International Chamber of Commerce to get the confederation established and commissioners named. Thereafter, MNCs will be responsible for operations of the confederation, including finances. All MNC members of the GBC will pay membership dues to defray the expenses of the confederation's secretariat. Nation-states, multinational institutions, and NGOs will be responsible for the salaries and related expenses of their commissioners and their offices and staff.

CONCLUSION

The framework presented in this chapter is based on the intellectual tradition that actively challenges, sharply questions, and diligently refines the understanding of the concepts and theory of the MNC. MNC scholars come from a variety of fields. The views they present are colored by their backgrounds. They do not represent a formal school of thought, but instead are self-selected researchers who have a common interest in the MNC. They are quick to take the MNCs to task without understanding their problems and dilemmas.

As a matter of fact, it is hard to be a well-meaning multinational these days. The shareholders clamor for value, and so do the customers. But when MNCs try to deliver, NGOs protest that they are exploiting workers in poor countries and depleting the environment. New governmental rules and regulations follow accordingly. MNCs, governments, and special interest groups need to hammer out mutually acceptable laws governing international commerce. The proposed GBC framework serves this purpose.

To be fully effective, MNCs must be free from control by their home countries, which often have poorly conceived policies that force MNCs into complex and hard-to-understand arrangements involving subsidiary corporations, alliances, and joint ventures. Only multilateral rules and regulations can offer a proper environment for efficient operation.

Futurists have pondered the question of who will rule in the twenty-first century. According to Lester Thurow, Europe will be the leader.[13] John Naisbitt declares that Asia will become the dominant power of the world. The high performance of the U.S. economy in the latter half of the 1990s has led many to believe that the United States will continue to be the leader in the twenty-first century.[14] This book suggests that the new century will belong not to Asia, the United States, Europe, or any other single geographic entity but to the MNC, which will work to increase worldwide prosperity in a progressively more interdependent economy. The evolution of the MNC has not ended; it has only begun. The defining event of the twenty-first century—the dethroning of the nation-state—has already started.

NOTES

1. John J. Sweeney, "Not a Backlash but Birth Pangs of a New Internationalism," *International Herald Tribune,* 27–28 January 2001, p. 12.

2. George Soros, "Toward a Global Open Society," *Atlantic,* 20 January 1998, p. 20.

3. K. Moore and D. Davis, *Birth of Multinational Enterprise: 2000 Years of Ancient Business History* (Copenhagen: Copenhagen Business School Press, 1999).

4. Arthur Levitt, "The World According to GAAP," *Financial Times,* 2 May 2001, p. 15.

5. A.H. Nill and G. Schultz II, "Marketing Ethics across Cultures and the Emergence of Dialogue Idealism," *CIBER Working Papers* (Thunderbird, American Graduate School of International Management, Phoenix, AZ, 1997).

6. "Kyoto Spurned as Mixed Bag for U.S. Firms," *Wall Street Journal,* 25 July 2001, p. A2.

7. P. Christman, "Environmental Strategies of Multinational Chemical Companies: Global Integration of National Responsiveness," *CIBER Working Paper Services* (Los Angeles: Anderson School at UCLA, 1998).

8. Adrian Michaels, "Consumer Group Queries Drug Companies Price Justification," *Financial Times,* 24 July 2001, p. 8.

9. Ibid.

10. Jeffrey E. Garten, "Megamergers Are a Clear and Present Danger," *Business Week,* 25 January 1999, p. 28.

11. "Reforming the Sisters," *Economist,* 17 February 2001, p. 23; see also Enzo Grilli, "A More Modest World Bank," *Financial Times,* 12 April 2001, p. 18.

12. "No Tear Gas, but No Cheers for Globalization," *New York Times,* 6 September 2000, p. 26.

13. Lester Thurow, *Head to Head* (New York: William Morrow, 1992).

14. John Naisbitt, *Megatrends Asia* (New York: Simon and Schuster, 1996).

Chapter 7

THE NATION-STATE

Since its emergence in the mid-seventeenth century, the nation-state has been regarded as the dominant actor in international economic relations. In recent years, however, interdependence and interconnection in the world marketplace have increased dramatically, calling into question the nation-state's control on international economic relations. According to Kenichi Ohmae, in a borderless economy the nation-state does not make sense: "that artifact of the eighteenth century has begun to crumble, battered by a pent-up storm of political resentments, ethnic prejudice, tribal hatred, and religious animosity."[1]

In 1914 there were 62 nations; in 1946, 74; and today, 194. For more than three hundred years, nation-states have served geopolitical purposes on the planet. The question is, Will they continue to play a significant part on the world's stage in the twenty-first century? Stated differently, the question is, What is it that makes a group of a few million people think of themselves as *us* and as different from all those other groups of people out there, *them?* And are those factors that create the sense of identity of *we* changing more radically than anything that has been seen in the past few centuries? The last question is fundamental. If the answer to it is yes, then the geographic lines that separate these groups from one another—the state frontiers—will grow blurrier and eventually may disappear.[2] The rationale behind this scenario is that nation-states are getting more and more like one another, so they have no need to fight one another. This is similar to saying that no two nations that both have McDonald's will ever go to war with each other.

THE BIRTH OF THE NATION-STATE

Until about 1530, the church was the highest institutional power. Its authority could not be challenged. But then, beginning with Henry VIII, clerical centers that had stood for centuries began to be smashed. The dissolution of the church signified worsening poverty for some people (especially people who received free food from monasteries) and upheaval for many (especially nuns, who were put back into the world but forbidden to marry). (In contrast, some men who left the monasteries got a pension.) The Treaty of Westphalia in 1648 laid the foundation of the nation-state, a new institution that replaced the church in its secular authority.[3]

A nation consists of people who share common customs and history, as well as a common currency. These individuals also share economic goals and values, although there may be internal divisions. An underlying characteristic of the nation-state is its territorial basis. The state's sovereign power over its territory is enshrined in international law. The use of that power varies, depending on the political system of the state. However, it is a maxim of international law that how a state organizes its internal affairs is entirely its own business so long as the state does not extend its territorial influence over other states.

THE NATION-STATE AND BUSINESS

In the context of business, the nation-state performs two important roles: containing distinctive business practices and regulating economic activities within and across its borders.

Distinctive Business Culture

Economic activity is embedded in broader cultural structures and practices. Culture is a learned, shared, compelling, interrelated set of symbols whose meanings provide orientations for the members of a society. These orientations offer solutions to problems that the societies must solve to remain viable. One of the primary containers of such structures and practices is the nation-state. Over time, the national homeland becomes a cultural container wherein national ideals are being reproduced through schooling, the mass media, and all manner of other social institutions. The fact that nation-states act as containers of distinctive cultures means that ways of doing things tend to vary across national boundaries. Of course, such containers are not rigid; cultural flexibility is common and is accelerated by technological developments. Nevertheless, there is enough evidence to support the notion of the persistence of national distinctiveness, which Richard Whitley has defined as

> distinctive configurations of hierarchy-market relations, which become institutionalized as relatively successful ways of organizing economic activities in different institutional environments. Certain kinds of activities are coordinated through particular sorts of authority structures and interconnected in different ways through various quasi-contractual arrangements in each business system. They develop and change in relation to dominant social institutions, especially those important during processes of industrialization. The coherence and stability of these institutions, together with their dissimilarity between nation-states, determine the extent to which business systems are distinctive, integrated and nationally differentiated.[4]

The major social-institutional variables that influence business systems are summarized in Exhibit 7.1. They can be divided into two classes: background and proximate variables. Their assemblage differs considerably in

Exhibit 7.1
The Social-Institutional Variables of Business Systems

Background social institutions

- The degree, and basis, of trust between non-kin
- The extent of commitment and loyalty to non-family collectives
- The importance of individual identities, rights, and commitments
- The extent of the depersonalization and formalization of authority relations
- The degree of differentiation of authority roles
- The reciprocity, distance, and scope of authority relations

Proximate social institutions

- Business dependence on a strong and cohesive state
- State commitment to industrial development and risk sharing
- A capital market or credit-based financial system
- A unitary or dual education and training system
- The strength of still-based labor unions
- The significance of publicly certified skills and professional expertise

Source: Richard D. Whitley, *Business Systems in East Asia: Firms, Markets, and Societies* (London: Sage Publications, 1992), pp. 20–27

different national contexts. In other words, the distinctiveness of business systems depends on the integrated and separate nature of the contexts in which they developed. The more the political and financial systems and the organization of the labor markets and educational institutions of societies form distinctive and cohesive configurations, the more the business systems in those societies will be different and separate.

Although there may not be a straightforward one-to-one relationship between a particular kind of business system and a particular nation-state, there are always national cultural tendencies that differentiate individual countries and groups of countries. If we recognize that countries differ as containers and regulators of distinctive structures and practices, it becomes obvious that we do not live in a homogenized world.

Regulation of Economic Activity

The regulation of economic activity within a state is determined by its cultural, social, and political structures, institutions, and practices.[5] Specifically, the following factors play a crucial role:

> The political and cultural complexion and the strength of institutions and interest groups: Conceptually, conservative governments pursue less interventionist policies than liberal or socialist governments. However, the power of institutions and interest groups within the national economy such as business and financial interests, labor unions, and environmental groups will influence the extent to which the economy is regulated. The degree of consensus or conflict among institutions and interest groups is embedded in the nation's history and culture. The nature of the political structure, centralized or federal, will be another determining factor.
>
> The size of the national economy: This is especially relevant in the context of trade policies. The larger the domestic market, the less important external trade. Thus, regulation of foreign trade will not be significant where the domestic market is large.[6]
>
> The resource endowment of the nation: A weak natural resource endowment will necessitate importing essential materials that must be paid for through exports. Foreign trade regulations, therefore, become more important. Regulations pertaining to economic activity are also influenced by the size, composition, and skills of a nation's potential labor force.
>
> The nation's relative position in the world economy: A nation's freedom in the matter of regulating economic activity depends very much on its position in the global economy and its dependence on external trade and investment. The policy emphasis of an industrialized nation will be different from that of a developing country.

Exhibit 7.2
Different Types of National Economic-Political Systems

Market-ideological state	Plan-ideological state
Driven by the "new right" economic and social policies of the 1980s. Based on a reversion to the state-civil society relations of the epoch of competitive capitalism. Policy choices based on ideological dogma.	The state owns and controls most or all economic units. Resource allocation/investment decisions are primarily a state function. State controls redistribution of wealth/income. Policy choices based on ideological dogma.
Market-rational/regulatory state	Plan-rational/developmental state
The state regulates the parameters within which private companies operate. The state regulates the economy in general, but investment, production and distributive decisions are the preserve of private companies, whose actions are disciplined by the market. The state does not concern itself with whether specific industries should exist and does not have an explicit industry policy.	The state regulation of economic activity is supplemented by state direction of the economy. The economy itself is largely in private ownership and firms are in competition, but the state intervenes in the context of an explicit set of goals. High priority placed on industry policy and on promoting a structure that enhances the nation's economic competitiveness.

Source: Peter Dicken, *Global Shift,* 3d ed. (New York: Guilford Press, 1998), p. 89.

Exhibit 7.2 identifies four different types of national economic-political systems. These four constructs should be considered as ideal types, because, in practice, nations combine them in various historically contingent ways. Currently, the market-rational/regulatory state quadrant and the plan-rational/developmental state quadrant reflect the perspectives of most nations.

Exhibit 7.3 summarizes the role of government in regulating economic activity under these two constructs. R.P. Appelbaum and J. Henderson describe the difference:

A regulatory, or market-rational, state concerns itself with forms and procedures—the rules, if you will—of economic competition, but it does not concern itself with substantive matters. For example, the United States government has many regulations concerning the antitrust implications of the size of firms, but it does not concern itself with what industries ought to

Exhibit 7.3
Role of Government in Regulating Economic Activity

Market-rational perspective

- To maintain economic stability
- To provide physical infrastructure, especially those with high fixed costs (e.g., harbors, railways, airports)
- To supply "public good" (e.g., defense and national security, education and legal system)
- To contribute to the development of institutions for improving markets for labor, finance, technology
- To offset or eliminate price distortions in cases of demonstrable market failure
- To redistribute income to the poorest sufficient to meet basic needs

Plan-rational perspective

- To place a priority on economic development (defined in terms of growth, productivity, competitiveness, rather than in terms of welfare)
- To sustain private property and the market
- To guide the market with instruments formulated by an elite bureaucracy, led by a pilot agency or "economic general staff"
- To create institutions to facilitate extensive consultation and coordination with the private sector. Such consultations constitute an essential part of the process of policy formulation and implementation
- To maintain separation between a "ruling" bureaucracy and "reigning" politicians in order to sustain the autonomy of the state within a stable political environment. Associated with a "soft authoritarianism," often linked with virtual monopoly of political power in a single political party or institution over a long period of time

Source: Richard Wade, *Governing the Market: Economic Theory and the Role of Government in East Industrialization* (Princeton, N.J.: Princeton University Press, 1990), pp. 11, 26.

exist and what industries are no longer needed. The developmental, or plan-rational, state, by contrast has as its dominant features precisely the setting of such substantive social and economic goals.

The [plan-rational state] will give greatest precedence to industrial policy, that is, to a concern with the structure of domestic industry and with promoting the structure that enhances the nation's international competitiveness. The very existence of an individual policy implies a strategic, or goal-oriented, approach to the economy. On the other hand, the market-rational state usually will not even have an industrial policy (or, at any rate, will not recognize it as such). Instead, both its domestic and foreign economic policies, including its trade policy, will stress rules and reciprocal concessions (although perhaps influenced by some goals that are not industrially specific, goals such as price stability or full employment).[7]

The above discussion asserts the continuing significance of the nation-state as a major influence in the domestic economy and in the negotiation of regional and global deals. It must be noted, however, that the role and functions of the state continue to change. For example, the position of the state is being redefined in the context of polycentric political-economic systems in which national boundaries are more permeable than in the past. In any event, the nation-state continues to contribute significantly toward the shaping and reshaping of the global economic map.

THE NATION-STATE IN RETREAT

Public policy discussions these days often debate whether the nation-state is in retreat. At the start of the twenty-first century, governments are being challenged by two strong forces: technology and ideology. A new industrial revolution is under way. Advances in computing and telecommunications shrink distance, eroding natural boundaries and enlarging the domain of the global economy. Increasingly, international markets are becoming supreme.[8]

The technological shift has been reinforced by a transformation in the realm of ideas, starting toward the end of 1970s and reaching a climax 10 years later with the collapse of communism. That failure destroyed the system not only in the form practiced in communist countries but also for westerners, who never experienced it directly as a sustaining utopian myth. Judged as propaganda, the events of 1989 did for big governments what the events of 1929 did for laissez-faire. Accordingly, it is argued that the nations-state is indeed in retreat. Globalization will play the decisive role in determining the future of the state, and any infringement of the power of the state must be counted as a cost against corresponding bene-fits. This section aims to sort through these ideas and to come to some con-clusions about the future of the state.

Size of Governments

Considering the size of today's governments, their role is not eroded by globalization.[9] At the beginning of the twentieth century, government spend-ing in today's industrial countries accounted for less than one-tenth of national income. In the year 2000, the government's share of output was slightly above half. Decade by decade, the change in government's share of the economy moved in one direction only: up. During war it went up; during peace it went up. Between 1920 and the mid-1930s, years of greatly dimin-ished trade and international economic activity, it went up. Between 1906 and 1980, as global trade and finance expanded, it went up. Between 1980 and 1990, as the intensity of globalization increased, it went up again. During the 1990s, as globalization spread over the world, it went up some more.

Among the rich industrial countries, the United States and Japan have the smallest governments. In 2000, their public spending was 33 percent and 36 percent of their GDP, respectively. Even so, both countries have shared in the consistently upward trend of state spending. In the United States, government spending in 1913 accounted for less than 2 percent of the economy; by 1937, it was still only 9 percent. Since 1960, the U.S. government has grown by about one-fifth, a comparatively modest rise. Internationally, the average increase over that period was more then three-fifths, whereas public spending in Japan more than doubled. Government everywhere has grown and has kept on growing, even in those countries where, by today's standards, government is small. Big government, far from being dead, is flourishing mightily.

The trend toward bigger government in the industrial countries has been almost universal. Total government spending falls into four broad cate-gories: (1) public consumption, measured by what the state, as a supplier of services, spends on wages and other inputs; (2) public investment; (3) transfers and subsidies; and (4) interest on the national debt. For the industrial countries as a group, between 1960 and 2000, public spending as a proportion of national income fell in only one of these categories: public investment, down from an average of 3 percent of GDP to 2 percent. Of the other categories, debt interest has grown most quickly. The category that grew the next fastest, and by far the biggest category, was transfers and sub-sidies, followed by public consumption.

The growth of public spending faithfully reflects the wide acceptance of an expanding list of essential goods and services that the government should provide. In other words, governments are giving their constituents what they want. As citizens demand more, the scope of government functions increases, which is quite acceptable in a democratic society.

State's Performance

Citizens demand new goods and services from the government, and it obliges by collecting more in taxes and expanding the offerings. The question is whether heavy-spending governments do better than governments that spend much less in providing social goods such as education and better health.

In the analysis of this issue, countries are divided into three groups: big-government countries, where public spending in 2000 was more than 50 percent of the output; small-government countries, where public spending in 2000 was less than 35 percent of the output; and the rest of the countries, which are disregarded for this analysis.[10] The big-government group includes Belgium, Italy, the Netherlands, Norway, and Sweden; the small-government group comprises Australia, Japan, Switzerland, the United States, Hong Kong, and Singapore. How do these groups compare on broad measures of public offerings? The best single such measure is output per capita, adjusted for international differences in purchasing power. By this test, the small-government countries are ahead. Their adjusted per capita output in 1999 was $24,600; the corresponding figure for the big-government countries was $21,300. The growth rates of the small-government economies were higher, too: an average rise of nearly 4 percent a year in per capita income between 1960 and 2000, compared with 2.5 percent for the others. In the area of health, spending varies greatly, but the outcomes are not so different. The average life expectancy in big-government and small-government countries is very similar, at 78.0 years and 77.8 years, respectively. Rates of infant mortality also are much the same in the two groups: 6.0 per 1,000 births in the big-government economies and 5.5 per 1,000 in the small-government ones.

As with health, spending on education varies a good deal; again, however, the results are much closer. The UN Development Programme calculates a composite school enrollment ratio, weighing together the proportion of children attending school at different ages. The higher the percentage, the better a country is doing. In the big-government countries, the index is 85 percent; in the small-government countries, it is 78 percent. The estimated level of adult illiteracy is very low in all the countries in both groups. In a recent international survey of children's skills in mathematics and science, the small-government countries, on average, did markedly better, particularly in math, than the big-government countries.

Today's fastest-growing emerging market economies have much smaller governments than many of the Western nations had at comparable stages of their development. When Western analysts reflect on the role of government in East Asia, they concentrate on trade and industrial policies. They attribute the rapid growth in East Asia more to clever industrial intervention than to a policy of letting markets have their say. This debate seems to have blinded analysts to an equally important fact: in the world's fastest-growing economies, government has stayed small in terms of the extent of its spending in the economy. This fact raises an interesting question: In years to come, will the Asian Tigers build transfer states of their own—and if so, will they be able to maintain their faster rates of growth?

In the meantime, a puzzle presents itself. Government in the West has grown to a point where some liberty is being limited. Yet this enormous expansion of the state appears to continue and to yield below-average returns. Why, then, do people want government to expand its role? Further analysis is needed to determine who benefits most from government spending. In most Western countries today, many of the expensive government programs are the middle-class entitlement programs—programs intended not to provide safety nets for the poor but to deliver elaborate and expensive services to all. These services include pensions, health care, education (up to and including university education), public transportation, and housing subsidies. The poor get some benefits from these programs, but it is plain that these policies are no longer aimed principally at helping the least well off, if that was ever the goal.[11] What this implies is a kind of democratic failure, akin to the market failures that government intervention is supposed to remedy. Collectively, citizens may understand that big government is producing ever-more-disappointing results, but individually they and their political leaders keep demanding more from government.

But now there is an intriguing new possibility. Technology has greatly strengthened market forces at the expense of government. Perhaps thinking has reflected this change and has shifted in the same direction—that is, if big government is really desirable. But even if thinking has not moved that much, an age-old skepticism about government has now gained an extremely powerful new ally. In either case, a new question is raised: Will globalization tame the Leviathan state?

The Crisis of Confidence

After the collapse of communism, the world saw a surge in the number of new democracies. At the same time, however, citizens of mature democracies were losing confidence in their political institutions. In the United States, the high opinion that the people had of their government has declined steadily over the past four decades. Similar disillusionment with politicians is noticeable in other mature democracies. One study concluded that out of 14 countries, confidence in parliament has declined in 11, with sharp falls in Canada, Germany, Great Britain, Sweden, and the United States.[12]

Such findings are alarming if taken at their face value, but they should be interpreted with care. Democracy may just be a victim of its own success. It could just be that people nowadays expect more from government, impose new demands on the state, and are therefore more likely to be disappointed. After all, the idea that governments ought to do such things as protect and improve the environment, maintain high employment, arbitrate moral issues, or ensure the equal treatment of women or minorities is relatively modern and still controversial. Besides, disillusionment is a healthy product of rising educational standards and the accompanying skepticism. In addition, disillusionment is caused by the media's highlighting failures of government that previously were kept in the dark. Perhaps the most serious threat that the government faces comes from the increasing professional pressure groups and lobbying organizations that work behind the scenes to influence government policy and defend social interests, often at the expense of the electorate as a whole.

The crisis of confidence that governments in mature democracies face provides these governments an opportunity for democratic renewal. Already there are signs that countries as different as Italy, Japan, Great Britain, and New Zealand have introduced changes in their electoral systems. It would be a positive step if more governments critically examined their political institutions and made appropriate changes to instill and revive people's confidence. Although in retreat, the nation-state as such is in no danger of being wiped out.

THREATS OF GLOBALIZATION

National governments have at their disposal a variety of ways to control and stimulate economic activity within their own borders and to shape the composition and flow of trade and investment at the international level.

Invariably, regulations pertaining to international commerce are designed to promote national interests. When the scope of foreign involvement is limited, this arrangement more or less works, although at times there are conflicts with foreign trading partners. Before World War II, it became a common practice among nations to pursue highly protective deals and investment policies to further individual interests. Immediately after the war, Western leadership realized the importance of boosting worldwide economic activity to prevent nations from going to war again.

This determination called for reducing trade barriers and stabilizing currencies. In addition, there was a desperate need to provide economic assistance to newly independent poor countries. Subsequently, the IMF, the World Bank, and the GATT (now the WTO) came into being.

Traditionally, foreign business amounted to trading, exporting, and importing manufactured goods. In the 1960s, a new form of foreign commercial involvement became popular: foreign direct investment. Most nations enacted their individual policies toward foreign investment. Unfortunately, in the case of foreign direct investment, there is no international body comparable to the WTO that can provide a set of rules for international trade.

The absence of a global framework is a big hindrance for the MNCs, the institutions that are in the forefront of foreign direct investment. Conflicting national laws create problems in conducting foreign business. The following cases illustrate how the lack of international rules makes MNCs susceptible to national rules and regulations. In the interest of their business, the MNCs are forced to seek alternative routes to avoid these rules.

Royal Dutch/Shell Group's Bid to Develop Oil Fields in Iran

The Royal Dutch/Shell Group is one of the world's largest privately held oil companies. Although its home base is the Netherlands and the United Kingdom, its huge presence in the United States accounts for more than a fifth of the group's assets. According to U.S. law, no national company doing business in the United States can do business with Iran.

In 2001, the company agreed to a deal with Iran to invest about $1 billion to develop two oil fields there.[13] Because of its substantial business in the United States, the company's agreement with Iran is subject to U.S. sanctions. The company must reckon on a U.S. waiver if it signs up the Iranian projects. Such waivers put U.S. MNCs at a disadvantage, because they must abide by the U.S. sanctions.

In the global market, Iran is attractive as an oil region, and MNCs from all over are interested in opportunities there. Most of the time U.S. sanctions against Iran do not work, because under political pressure the U.S. government ends up granting waivers to foreign companies. This situation shows the ineffectiveness of U.S. sanctions against Iran, which to all intents and purposes affect only U.S. multinationals. The non-U.S. multinationals can get away with doing business in Iran, although they must go through a long-drawn-out bureaucratic process to engage their own governments in seeking U.S. waivers.

As globalization makes further inroads, MNCs would like to take advantage of emerging opportunities, no matter where they are, without being constrained by a nation's laws. It is a problem that nations must face, and the only solution is to let a multinational organization make laws that would then apply to all MNCs worldwide.

Paris Court Orders to Yahoo!

In November 2000, a Paris court ordered the Internet company Yahoo! to block French users from accessing Nazi memorabilia sold on the company's U.S. sites.[14] A disturbing precedent is set by courts' imposing sanctions outside their normal jurisdiction, applying national laws to global on-line services. The Paris court ruling, based on French antiracist laws, gave Yahoo! three months to make sure the French did not have access to the relevant auction on its site. If it failed, it would be fined $13,000 a day.

Yahoo! had agreed to block the sale of Nazi memorabilia, such as swastika flags and coins, on its French-language portal after an earlier court ruling, but it argued in court that this ban could not be extended to U.S. sites because that would breach the constitutional right to freedom of speech in the United States. In addition, technically there was no fail-safe way to block the access of only French nationals. The company decided to appeal to a higher French court and to ask a U.S. court to refuse to endorse the judgment on the grounds that the French court has no power to impose sanctions on the U.S. site of a U.S. company. At the time of preparing this book, the matter was still pending.

Meanwhile, industry groups are concerned about the implications of the French ruling. Businesses are lobbying regulators to try to limit the number of national courts and laws that can claim jurisdiction over Web sites based in other countries. After all, MNCs cannot be subject to every nuance of every law in every country.

Local rules do not make sense in a globalizing world. For example, in France, if you are poor or technologically illiterate, you will not be able to buy a Nazi military uniform. If, however, you are rich enough to travel abroad or cunning enough to disguise your nationality over the Internet, you can purchase what you like. Thus, the French judgment in the Yahoo! case is damaging in many respects. First, it is based on confusion about the location of transactions. Any government has the right to restrict sales of provocative material in its jurisdiction. But if citizens travel abroad, they may purchase any goods that are lawfully sold in the country they are visiting. A French person's completing an Internet transaction on a U.S. auction site is akin to that person's buying at an auction in the United States. France should not have the right to stop such a sale. But the French government should be able to restrict the import of Nazi memorabilia or its ownership in France. Second, the court decision is likely to be ineffective. Serious French collectors of Nazi materials will disguise their physical location. An electronic filter would have to be extremely complex to be effective, and its use would inevitably make Internet shopping or auction participation slow and costly. Finally, if Internet sites now withdraw all Nazi material, many pressure groups will be encouraged to bring similar suits in other countries. Commerce on the Internet then would be possible only if it met with the approval of every nation's consumer regulations. That situation would hinder the growth of Internet businesses.

The case highlights a question engaging regulators and governments around the world: To what extent should national courts be able to impose domestic laws on global media? If the judgment is taken to its logical conclusion, the result would be that every jurisdiction on the planet could regulate everything on the Internet. It would be nearly impossible to regulate content on the Internet if regulations had to apply to almost two hundred different countries.

Unocal Opens Twin Corporate Headquarters in Malaysia

In March 1997, a federal district judge in California ruled that Unocal, an oil and natural gas company, could face trial in the United States for human rights violations in Myanmar (formerly Burma), where it has a $340 million stake in a natural gas project.[15] A month later, the Clinton administration imposed sanctions against Myanmar that prohibited further investment by U.S. companies. Faced with this political pressure at home and drawn by the lure of growth opportunities abroad, the $5.3 billion company took a radical step: it de-Americanized itself. Legally, the company is headquartered in El Segundo, California, but in company literature

Unocal claims it "no longer considers itself a U.S. company" but a "global energy company." In practice, it is slowly moving assets, research spending, and management to Asia. The company opened what it calls twin corporate headquarters in Malaysia. Many senior executives were transferred to Malaysia, although the CEO remained in California. In addition, the company sold off its U.S. refining operations and gas stations. According to experts, Unocal might decide to spin off its Asia headquarters into an entirely separate company, and by doing so, it might be able to bypass U.S. sanctions. A security analyst has said, "They have structured their operations now so it would be easy for them to pull out of the U.S. if that's what they need to do."

Other MNCs are watching what action the U.S. government will take to discourage Unocal from doing business in Myanmar. The human rights case appears tenuous: Total (a French company) has been building and running the Myanmar operation; Unocal is just an investor. What implications will the Unocal case have for Total? If Total is pushed too much by the U.S. government, it may start thinking about a new home.

Summary

The three cases just discussed clearly show that the mission of MNCs is to extend their business. In that pursuit, they seek business anywhere in the world. If local laws impose any restrictions, MNCs explore ways to bypass those laws. In a globalizing world, a single government's laws do not apply to all multinationals. As such, the laws remain at best ineffective. Thus, there is a dire need for one set of global laws, applicable to all companies without any exception. The governments will be forced to give up their sovereignty in this matter as globalization progresses.

THE FUTURE OF THE NATION-STATE

If capital and skilled labor could be instantly transported and transformed around the globe, nations would still survive.[16] In the real world, of course, labor and capital are firmly tied down and likely to remain so. Financial capital has become extremely mobile, but the physical kind has not. This distinction is often overlooked. Once a multibillion-dollar microchip assembly plant has been built, it tends to stay put, even if government decides to tighten the tax screws a little. Labor, even the highly skilled, jet-setting, multilingual kind, is less mobile than is often supposed. Most people are anchored by culture, family, and neighborhood. Governments reinforce these ties by regulating migration. Even within the European Union, where official barriers to the movement of labor have been removed, relatively few people move from country to country.

This is not to say that free flows of capital and labor do not exist. Their existence has made revenue-seeking governments shift their pattern of taxation. The basic principle of efficient fiscal ranching is obvious: tax immobile factors of production more heavily than mobile ones. Following that principle means going easy on taxing the rich because, given sufficient cause, they can escape more readily than the less rich. It also means, where possible, taxing the income generated by sunk capital but offering tax breaks for new investment to attract uncommitted financial capital. More broadly, because capital of all kinds is more mobile than labor, it means shifting the overall balance of taxation so that the taxation falls more heavily on workers and less heavily on owners of capital.

By and large this scenario has been occurring, though some governments have shown more imagination than others. Ireland, for instance, is a tax-free zone for artists, which makes it an attractive home for best-selling authors and other creative types. The tax authorities there seem less inclined to offer special deals to, say, window cleaners or postal workers. Ireland also has been able to establish an extremely low tax regime for inward direct investment in manufacturing and internationally traded services, despite EU rules to discourage that sort of thing. The government says it applies these rules equally to new investment and existing operations, thus violating one of the maxims of efficient ranching; but because Ireland embarked on this policy at a time when it was a farm economy with hardly any incumbent manufacturing or traded-services companies, the principle was upheld at least in spirit, if not in letter.

As a matter of fact, corporate tax rates have been coming down across the advanced industrial economies and beyond. The fall is not particularly dramatic, but neither is it insignificant. On average, the standard rate of corporate income tax in the OECD countries fell from 43 percent in 1986 to 33 percent in 2000. Personal income tax has come down as well: in the OECD, the average top rate was 59 percent in 1975 and 42 percent in 2000. But rates lower down the scale have been raised. The marginal tax rate for workers on two-thirds of average earnings was 32.6 percent in 1978 and 38.4 percent in 2000. In addition, governments have increased taxes on consumption, such as value-added tax (VAT).

Overall, governments have taken steps to discourage capital moving out, but despite the gale of global market forces, the aggregate tax burden continues to rise. It seems that governments' ability to tax is intact. It will take more than today's global market to stop it.

For the time being, then, the state's power to tax, spend, and borrow seems under no serious threat. But globalization has much further to go, which may change the situation. Perhaps the history of the nation-state has come to a turning point. In the future, the need for mobility and communication among economies, rather than within them, will gain the upper hand. This demand will give rise to an increasingly homogeneous global culture similar to the homogeneous national cultures that developed in the past. This shift, in turn, not only will promote economic integration but also, however slowly, will blur the political boundaries between nations.

Governments are aware of the threat of globalization. In the short run, they encourage regional market agreements, because this step helps them preserve their power. As labor and capital become more mobile, governments are drawn into competition with one another. The effect of this competition will be to reduce the state. At the present time, such reduction is almost invisible with the nation-state in full control, and prudent governments will do what they can to stop further reductions from occurring. For example, they may seek harmonization with competing nations and set up a cartel, as corporations did in the past. One way of pursuing harmonization is to develop regional trade agreements that are preferable to the multilateral approach to trade liberalization as carried out under the WTO.

The regional agreements allow nations to negotiate side agreements on labor and environmental standards, and thus bring their trading partners' policies more closely in line with their own. It is easier to deal with a small number of partners than with a large number of members of a body like the WTO. Eventually, different regional agreements, pursuing similar policies, could become a global policy through a multilateral organization.

Although a supranational government is a remote possibility, individual governments will surrender some power or sovereignty to regional groups or multilateral agreements. In that way they can successfully counter the globalization threat without losing their grip. In fact, such steps allow governments to pool power in order to retain and increase it, in just the same way that a firm in a cartel gives up the freedom to sell all it could in order to gain a share in the group's fatter monopoly profits. So far, the state's freedom of action has barely been touched by the global market; should this freedom become more circumscribed, nation-states may resort to cartel-type rule.

The proposed GBC is quite in line with the current thinking of the governments. It harmonizes policies relative to MNC operations globally, making it easier for MNCs to operate without being constrained by local rules and regulations. At the same time, the GBC proposal preserves the power of the state, if not increasing it.

Many scholars feel that MNCs are becoming stronger at the cost of governments.[17] For example, it has been said that 51 of the 100 biggest economies in the world today are corporations. Such statements do not make sense. Such comparison of corporate power with state power is based on invalid criteria. National income, the measurement used to examine state power, is a measure of value added. It cannot be compared with a company's sales (which are equal to value added plus the cost of inputs). The power of even the biggest companies is nothing compared with that of governments—no matter how small or poor the country. The value added of Microsoft is a little over $20 billion a year, about the same as the national income of Uruguay. Does this fact make it remotely plausible that Bill Gates has more sway over the people of Uruguay than their government does? Take another nation, Luxembourg, a small state. It collects 45 percent of its GDP from its citizens. But Microsoft cannot tax the citizens of Luxembourg, conscript them if it decides to, arrest and imprison them for behavior it disapproves of, or deploy physical force against them at will. Big companies do have political influence. They have the money to lobby politicians and, in many countries, to corrupt them. Even so, the idea that companies have a power over citizens that is even remotely as great as the power of governments, no matter how big the company and how small or poor the country, is fatuous.

CONCLUSION

The recent advances in technology are not only making the movement of money and ideas far easier and cheaper than it has been before but are doing it in ways that governments find hard to interfere with. This situation has slowly trimmed the power of the state, and the trimming process has only begun. This situation does not mean that the nation-state will lose the means of functioning as a separate entity in the world. Nor does it mean that maneuverings among nation-states will cease to be an important component of geopolitics. What it does mean is that the technological revolution, like the movement toward universal free market democracy, is indeed diminishing the authority of the state in some important ways. In place of the state, a supranational entity is needed to fill the leadership gap. This is where the GBC fits in.

Today, MNCs can successfully replace some of the nation-state's authority. MNCs are not poised to dissolve the institution of the nation-state but merely to supersede its power in areas concerning the rules and regulations of the global market. Nation-states need to give up some of their discretionary power in this regard. They have no authority to pass laws that apply to corporations simultaneously conducting business in several countries. It is not unreasonable to expect individual governments to bow to a global institution on global matters; otherwise, MNCs find themselves in the precarious position of being forced to implement their nation-state's policies. As long as we lack an international organization to set global rules for global corporations, companies will find loopholes in laws imposed by nation-states in order to pursue their interests. But using loopholes is not a lasting solution, and the present world situation brings increasing pressure to handle global affairs appropriately.

Networks of production and finance have broken free from national borders and have become truly global, but they have left the rest of the system far behind. Nation-states and the institutions they have developed often try to dictate the terms of international exchange by just negotiating among themselves, an unfeasible arrangement when economic life is no longer embedded in a broad framework of shared values and institutionalized practices. Economics has become global, whereas politics remains largely local. As a result, globalization becomes the scapegoat for domestic policy failures.

Many people believe that government has overreached itself and should become smaller and promise less. Perhaps it is time for governments to admit that they are unable to handle the challenges of globalization of markets. Consider the following example. The biggest constraint on the spread of the global economy is not likely to be commodity inflation or product shortages. Rather, the main problem will be finding enough highly skilled and computer-literate workers to staff rapidly growing information industries. Europe and Japan will have to find a lot of highly skilled workers— quickly—as they try to beef up their new global industries. According to the London-based International Data Corporation, the demand for skilled workers will exceed supplies by at least 30 percent in Western nations.[18] It will be necessary to draw on the enormous supply of college-educated workers in countries such as India and China to fill the gap. Asia accounted for two-thirds of the global increase in college and other postsecondary enrollments in the 1990s. Indian universities turn out 122,000 engineers every year, compared with 63,000 in the United States. And engineers make up some 40 percent of China's enormous crop of annual graduates.[19]

The growth of the U.S. high-tech industry has been fueled by a steady flow of highly educated immigrants and foreign students. Between 1985 and 1996, foreign students accounted for two-thirds of the growth in science and engineering doctorates at U.S. universities. Most of these students planned to stay and work in the United States. Like many other aspects of the global economy, however, opening the doors to foreign workers will not be easy in many countries. Restrictive immigration policies enforced by nation-states are counterproductive.

As mentioned before, the nation-state has not been with us forever. It was an invention of the seventeenth century. It has served a useful purpose for a long time without much change or challenge to its authority. The institution of the MNC has been occupying a unique position in the economic life of people over the last 50 years. Today MCNs have reached a stage where they can be a global force for good in the lives of billions of people. The nation-states can play a crucial role in helping the MNCs improve living standards by revising their role in making global business regulations.

People normally prefer a linear progression of change, meaning that established institutions continue. Developments in the twenty-first century are not likely to be linear, but rather revolutionary. Existing institutions, relations, and ways of doing things will change drastically. History is witness to this likelihood. Empires have risen and fallen; species have emerged and vanished. The nation-state, which has played a central role over the last 200 years, could be forced in the twenty-first century to yield ground to a new institution, the MNC or global corporation. The rules of the game will be different with this shift of power to a new institution, and the shift will happen because MNCs are capable of delivering what people need: jobs, the wherewithal to buy goods and services, and innovations for a better and more comfortable life. People in the most remote corners of the world know what the good life is because of today's communications system. They want that life and are willing to work for it. Under the circumstances, the decline of the nation-state is not surprising, because it was created to meet the needs of a much earlier historical period. Nation-states do not have the will, the incentive, the credibility, the tools, or the political base to play an effective role in the emerging borderless economy.

NOTES

1. Kenichi Ohmae, "Putting Global Logic First," *Harvard Business Review,* January/February 1995, p. 119.

2. T.A. Stewart, "Welcome to the Revolution," *Fortune,* 13 December 1993, p. 66.

3. *Economist,* 31 December 1999, p. 17.

4. Richard D. Whitley, *Business Systems in East Asia: Firms, Markets and Societies* (London: Sage Publications, 1992), p. 13.

5. Peter Dicken, *Global Shift,* 3d ed. (New York: Guilford Press, 1998), pp. 88–90.

6. Michael Porter, *The Competitive Advantage of Nations* (New York: Free Press, 1990), chap. 3.

7. R.P. Appelbaum and J. Henderson, eds., *States and Development in the Asian Pacific Rim* (London: Sage Publications, 1992), chap. 1; also see C. Johnson, *MITI and the Japanese Economic Miracle: The Growth of Industrial Policy, 1925–1975* (Stanford, Calif.: Stanford University Press, 1982), pp. 19–20.

8. Thomas L. Friedman, *The Lexus and the Olive Tree* (New York: Farrar, Straus and Giroux, 1999), chap. 5.

9. *Economist,* 20 September 1997, p. 7.

10. Ibid., p. 12.

11. "Globalization and Its Critics," *Economist,* 21 September 2001, p. 10.

12. Ibid.

13. Bhushan Bahree, "Shell Looks Close to Deal with Iran over Oil Fields," *Wall Street Journal,* 21 September 2000, p. 26.

14. Jean Eaglesham and Robert Graham, "French Court Ruling Hits Yahoo!," *Financial Times,* 21 November 2000, p. 20.

15. "A Company without a Country?" *Business Week,* 5 May 1997, p. 40.

16. Subhash C. Jain, *International Marketing Management,* 6th ed. (Cincinnati: South-Western College Publishing, 2001), chap. 2.

17. *Business Week,* 31 January 2000, p. 77.

18. Ibid.

19. "Global Capitalism," *Business Week,* 6 November 2002, p. 80.

Chapter 8

A MANIFESTO FOR THE FUTURE

Globalization is a great force for good. It widens choices in all realms, because it makes resources go further. Policies to relieve poverty, protect workers displaced by technology, and support education and public health are all more affordable with globalization. Despite these benefits, popular support for globalization is lacking. In the developed countries, support for further trade liberalization is uncertain; in some countries, voters are downright hostile to it. Governments of rich countries present economic integration to voters as an unfortunate, but inescapable, fact of life—as a constraint on their freedom of action.

Governments in developing countries feel that they have been short-changed by developed nations in the name of globalization. They made appropriate responses to global capitalism but were disappointed with the results. The developed countries used poor labor conditions and neglect of the environment in developing nations as excuses for not accepting their exports, whereas the latter had opened their markets in good faith. Thus, developing countries see globalization as nothing more than a strategy by the rich nations to exploit them.

MNCs agree that capitalism without responsibility is undesirable. But when these companies say they will no longer put profits first, they never explain how they will implement that commitment, and the result is that people think the MNCs are dissimulating. The multinationals leave the impression that globalization is a cause of democratic paralysis. Globalization has undermined the role of elected governments while giving multinationals who promise everything the freedom to dedicate themselves to earning more profits.

The result is confusion. The public stands neither firmly in support of nor firmly against globalization. They are puzzled, anxious, and suspicious. This climate is bad for democracy and bad for economic growth.

PROPOSITIONS

This chapter offers propositions for a more purposeful discussion of globalization.

1. GLOBALIZATION WILL CONTINUE.

Globalization is the latest stage in the long accumulation of technological advances that have given human beings the ability to conduct their affairs across the world without reference to nationality, governmental authority, time of day, or physical environment. Globalization has occurred because of many things, among which technological advances stand out. These advances have broken down physical barriers to worldwide communication that used to limit the extent of any connection or cooperative activity that required traversing long distances.

People often ask whether globalization will regress, as happened before World War I. Although anything is possible, it would be difficult for nation-states to erect barriers to stop further progression of globalization, for two important reasons. First, today's communications revolution is more extensive than ever before. As a result, the human activities carried on without hindrance across the world have increased manifold. People of one nation are connected with the people of other nations in so many ways that they are not ready to go back to the isolation of earlier days. Second, globalization has created such economic interdependence among nations that any defection will have serious consequences. No nation can afford to take such a risk.

The process of globalization will continue. As people increasingly use the Internet, particularly in developing countries, it will make inroads in the furthest corners of the world. All major players in the globalization game—that is, nation-states, MNCs, and multilateral institutions—are aware that retrenchment is counterproductive, and they are not willing to risk the upheaval that reversing globalization might create.

Emergencies such as the 9/11 tragedy may slow down the process, but globalization is a wave of the twenty-first century that promises to bring about worldwide well-being and prosperity to rich and poor. The agreement among the members of the WTO in November 2001 at Doha, Qatar, to launch a new round of trade talks succinctly depicts the position of nation-states on globalization and its future.

2. WHAT DEFINES GLOBALIZATION IS NOT WESTERN (OR MORE SPECIFICALLY, U.S.) HEGEMONY. RATHER, GLOBALIZATION IS THE KEY TO THE ECONOMIC SUCCESS OF MANY DEVELOPING NATIONS.

Beginning in the fall of 2001, the violent protests against globalization disappeared. It is difficult to say to what extent this development is an after-effect of the September tragedy, but its welcome interlude offers an opportunity to examine afresh globalization and the complaints it has engendered.

One of the biggest complaints against globalization has been that it perpetuates inequality: the rich get richer and the poor poorer, in line with Karl Marx's argument that capitalism would enrich the ruthless few and impoverish the many. This argument has been long discounted in rich nations, but it is now being resurrected for the globe as a whole.

Over the past two decades, the number of people living in absolute poverty has fallen rather than risen, as mentioned in chapter 5. Globally, inequality among households probably has decreased, as has inequality among countries. Above all, globalization, where successful, has reduced poverty and inequality. This conclusion is supported by the following statistics. In 1820, 900 million people, or about 85 percent of the world's population, lived on the equivalent of a dollar a day, converted to today's international purchasing power. The numbers in extreme poverty peaked at about 1.4 billion in 1980, or at about 30 percent of the world's then much increased population. But over the last 20 years, as globalization has made inroads, the number of people in absolute poverty has fallen for the first time, to 1.2 billion, or 20 percent of the world's population. In addition, inequality among the world's households peaked in 1980. Thereafter, lessening international inequality has offset the rising internal inequality within a sizable number of nations. Furthermore, there has been no general rising inequality among developing countries.

The noteworthy feature of the past two decades is the large number of big developing countries that have participated successfully in the global industrial economy. Significant achievements have been registered during this period: manufactures rose from less than a quarter of developing countries' exports in 1980 to more than 80 percent by 1998; the countries that strongly increased their participation in the world economy have doubled their ratios of trade to income; and the growth of per capita income in this group of successful countries increased from 1 percent a year in the 1960s to 4 percent in the 1980s, and to 5 percent in the 1990s.[1]

It is heartening to note that the 24 countries in the World Bank's group of successfully globalizing countries include many of the world's biggest nations, with an aggregate population of 3 billion. The unfortunate truth is that about 2 billion people live in countries that are neither globalizing nor developing. The aggregate growth of these countries was negative in the 1990s. In fact, they are being progressively marginalized within the global economy.

Yet the belief that globalization is meant to enrich only the rich nations is false. Globalization is not a U.S. strategy to spread commercial Americanization over the world. In fact, it is an answer to the decades-long quest to make the poor less poor, or even prosperous.

The above explanation clearly outlines the benefits of globalization. Globalization has been responsible for accelerated economic growth in a group of successfully globalizing countries with very large populations. The numbers of desperately poor people and the extent of inequality among the world's households have both been reduced for the first time in some 160 years. A warning is appropriate here. It would be naive to conclude that globalization alone is enough to eradicate a nation's poverty. Many nations suffer from deeper problems: poor climate and geography, inadequate education, rampant disease, collapsed or deeply corrupt and predatory governments, and a failure to diversify beyond primary commodities that face stagnant world markets.

If critics of globalization are concerned about the plight of the poor, they should welcome what has been achieved over the past two decades and resolve to help the world do far better in the future. Briefly, then, what defines globalization is not U.S. hegemony; globalization concerns integration more than dominance. Of course, the new economy driven by advanced technology has boosted U.S. competitiveness and corporate reach. But globalization is equally defined by the fact that the son of Chinese prime minister Zhu Rongji is running the Hong Kong operations of an investment bank jointly owned by Morgan Stanley; the fact that Masayoshi Son, a Korean Japanese, financed the birth of Yahoo!; and the fact that Timothy Berners-Lee, a British computer scientist working in Switzerland, invented the World Wide Web. Globalization is symbolized as appropriately by sushi in Chicago as by Pepsi in Paris, and as well by the use of Hindi in Silicon Valley as by the use of English on the Internet.

3. NATION-STATES MUST GUARANTEE ECONOMIC FREEDOM BEFORE GLOBALIZATION CAN WORK TO THEIR ADVANTAGE.

Broadly, economic freedom means the ability to do what you want with whatever property you have acquired, as long as your actions do not violate other people's rights to do the same. Goods and services do not fall from heaven. They are created, and their creation depends on property rights and incentives. If property rights are guaranteed, people are not hemmed in by government regulations and trade barriers or fear of confiscation; if savings are protected against inflation and cash is stashed at will, economic freedom prospers. The freer the economy, the higher the growth and the richer the people. Countries that have maintained a fairly free economy for many years have done well.

Economic freedom is not an argument for raw laissez-faire. It is a broad concept that requires a great deal from government if it is to work its magic on living standards. Governments must set a clear and predictable regulatory and macroeconomic climate by protecting property rights, enforcing the law, avoiding inflation, and reducing taxes. The economic freedom must be administered to give people an incentive to invest, and not just in factories or farms but in education and training as well.

Exhibit 8.1 rates the economic freedom of more than one hundred nations. These rankings are based on 37 variables that have been worked out by the Fraser Institute using data that go back to 1970.

The rankings show the importance of economic freedom for national growth and development. The countries with low scores can be divided into two groups. In one group, the problem is that there is no real or sustained government because of anarchy, civil war, or broader conflict. In the other group, the problem is that the government stands in the way of growth, either because it steals money or because it fails to provide the necessary freedom and opportunities.

4. MNCS, THROUGH TRANSFER OF PRODUCTION FACTORS, INNOVATIONS, MARKET MAKING, AND GLOBAL MANAGERIALISM, BRING ABOUT WORLDWIDE ECONOMIC PROSPERITY.

An efficient system of industry and commerce, with its potential to alleviate poverty, is essential to human well-being. MNCs, given adequate freedom and incentives, can indeed manage industry and commerce effi-

Exhibit 8.1
Index of Economic Freedom, 2001 Rankings

FREE	MOSTLY UNFREE		REPRESSED
1 Hong Kong	42 Hungary	Guinea	Mauritania
2 Singapore	Kuwiat	Madagascar	Russia
3 Ireland	Lithuania	87 Kenya	130 Kazakstan
4 New Zealand	Panama	Qatar	Togo
5 Luxembourg	46 Costa Rica	Zambia	132 Bangladesh
U.S.	Latvia	90 Algeria	133 India
7 U.K.	48 Belize	Cameroon	Suriname
8 Netherlands	Greece	Paraguay	Ukraine
9 Australia	Guatemala	93 Brazil	Yemen
Bahrain	Morocco	Gabon	137 Equatorial
Switzerland	Oman	95 Bulgaria	Guinea
12 El Salvador	Sri Lanka	Burkina Faso	Haiti
MOSTLY FREE	54 Israel	97 Cape Verde	139 Azerbaijan
13 Chile	Poland	Djibouti	Tajikistan
14 Austria	56 Jamaica	Gambia	REPRESSED
Canada	Malta	Guyana	141 Bosnia
Denmark	Samoa	Houndas	Guinea-
Estonia	59 Cambodia	Mozambique	Bissau
Japan	Dominican Republic	Nigeria	Syria
U.A.E.	Lebanon	104 Fiji	144 Vietnam
20 Belgium	Slovak Republic	Lesotho	145 Burma
Germany	63 Benin	106 Croatia	146 Belarus
Taiwan	Jordan	Ecuador	Zimbabwe
23 Bahamas	Slovenia	Nicaragua	148 Turkmenistan
Cyprus	Tunisia	Pakistan	149 Uzbekistan
Finland	Turkey	110 Albania	150 Laos
Iceland	68 Armenia	Nepal	151 Iran
27 Czech Republic	Botswana	Nigeria	152 Cuba
Thailand	Colombia	Tanzania	153 Iraq
29 Argentina	Mali	114 China	Lybia
South Korea	Mauritius	Georgia	155 North Korea
Sweden	Mexico	Indonesia	Angola
32 Italy	Nambia	Malawai	Burundi
Portugal	MOSTLY UNFREE	Papua New	Congo
34 Uruguay	75 Ivory Coast	Guinea	(Democratic Republic)
35 Barbados	Malaysia	Venezuela	Sierra Leone
Bolivia	Mongolia	120 Chad	Somalia
Spain	Saudi Arabia	Egypt	Sudan
38 Norway	Swaziland	Moldova	
39 France	Uganda	Rwanda	
Peru	81 Philippines	124 Ethiopia	
Trinidad	Senegal	Kirgiz Republic	
& Tobago	South Africa	Romania	
	84 Ghana	127 Congo (Republic of)	

Source: Gerals P. O'Driscoll Jr., Kim R. Holmes, and Melanie Kirkpatrick, "Who's Free, Who's Not," *Wall Street Journal*, 1 November 2000, p. A14.

ciently. After all, these corporations have played a major role in the fivefold increase in economic output since 1950. The last 50 years have given us many innovations that today seem essential. These innovations include jet airplanes and with them commercial travel, computers, microwave ovens, electric typewriters, photocopying machines, televisions, clothes washers and dryers, air conditioners, freeways, shopping malls, facsimile machines, birth control pills, artificial organs, and chemical pesticides. This list contains only a few of the extraordinary accomplishments of the last half century. These achievements amply demonstrate the significance of the MNCs in our world. The MNCs organize human ingenuity and other factors of production to create new goods and services. Through market making, they bring these goods and services to our doorsteps and thus make our lives comfortable and exciting. We have arrived at a time in history when it seems that MNCs truly have the knowledge, technology, and organizational capability to achieve bold goals, including the elimination of poverty, war, and disease. This twenty-first century should be a time filled with the hope that all human beings will be freed forever from concerns of basic survival and will have the security to pursue new frontiers of social, intellectual, and spiritual advancement.

5. MNCS ADHERE TO THE CAPITALISTIC SYSTEM AND, THUS, PURSUE PROFIT MAKING WITH A VENGEANCE.

MNCs are driven by a single imperative—the quest for long-term financial gain. There is nothing wrong with this goal. After all, it is the basis of capitalism. Capitalism may not be the best system, but the alternative of socialism is even worse.

The economic gains of the past 50 years tell much about the success of these corporations.[2] The percentage of economic output traded among countries rose from just under 9 percent to over 22 percent between 1965 and 2000. Overall, trade has been expanding at roughly twice the rate of economic output. From 1983 to 1997, worldwide foreign investment grew four times faster than world trade. Given that as much as 70 percent of world trade is controlled by just 500 corporations and a mere 1 percent of all multinationals own half the total stock of foreign direct investment, a few large corporations have come to occupy a dominant economic position in the world.[3] But this situation should not be a problem. After all, there are large, small, and very small nations, too. Although MNCs have as their basic purpose the enhancement of shareholders' wealth, they realize that their long-term success requires following responsible capitalism, which means meeting the needs of different stakeholders. Basically, MNCs have a commitment to sustainable development, to balancing economic progress with social responsibility.

People turn against MNCs because they do not know much about them. A lack of transparency relative to what MNCs do, how they do it, when they do it, where they do it, and why they do it creates a distorted image of global corporations. Significant contributions are often underappreciated because they are unpublicized.

6. NATIONAL GEOGRAPHIC BOUNDARIES LOSE SIGNIFICANCE IN THE CONTEXT OF GLOBALIZATION.

The political boundaries of nation-states are too narrow and constricted to define the scope and activities of modern business corporations. By and large, these companies have achieved a global vision of their operations and tend to opt for a world in which not only goods but also all the factors of production can shift with maximum freedom. Thus, foreign companies should have complete freedom to choose whether they participate in a local market by importing goods or by establishing a local production facility. They should be governed by the same laws and be accorded the same rights as domestic firms. They should be allowed to undertake any activity that is legally permissible for domestic firms.

MNCs are truly global institutions and should be regarded as such. Many U.S. companies claim that they are not U.S. corporations but rather world corporations that happen to be headquartered in the United States. As has been noted:

> Though few companies are totally untethered from their home countries, the trend toward a form of "stateless" corporation is unmistakable. The European, American and Japanese giants heading in this direction are learning how to juggle multiple identities and multiple loyalties. These world corporations are developing chameleon-like abilities to resemble insiders no matter where they operate. At the same time, they move factories and labs around the world without particular reference to national borders.[4]

A global corporation like this cannot operate by following the rules and regulations of the particular nation-state where it happens to register and begin its business. These corporations have a global perspective and should be ruled and controlled only by global regulations. The role of the nation-state as an institution will decline as global corporations spread their sphere of activities even to those areas such as education that traditionally have been the domain of the nation-state. Government activities should be limited to the enforcement and protection of life, liberty, and property. In other words, the nation-state is no longer relevant as an economic unit, and its role should be redefined.

7. MNCS ESTABLISH GLOBAL NETWORKS TO REALIZE EFFICIENCY IN OPERATIONS AND SERVE THE MARKET WELL.

MNCs spread their operations around the globe to acquire efficiencies of scope and scale. Doing so involves integrating a firm's global operations around vertically integrated supplier networks. The point may be illustrated with reference to Otis Elevator.[5] When the company set about to create an advanced elevator system, it contracted out the design of the motor drives to Japan, the door systems to France, the electronics to Germany, and the small geared components to Spain. It handled system integration from the United States. In a fully globalized economy, many nations that own the right to products and processes do not have to produce anything. They can simply license rights to products and processes to different contractors worldwide, coordinate their activities, and thus make as much money—or probably more—than if they undertook to produce the goods themselves. To an extent, Nike is an example of a company that follows such a strategy.

MNCs are the servants of demanding consumers around the world. They attempt to provide the best values to consumers through the widest choice of goods and services. Consumers do not care where a product is produced, as long as it provides the quality they are seeking. In that regard, multinationals are truly democratic in serving their customers.

8. GLOBALIZATION WILL PROCEED SLOWLY, FROM REGIONALISM TO GLOBALIZATION.

In the post–World War II period, the creation of the European Union proved the feasibility of economic integration among nations to their mutual advantage. Today the European Union is a viable world economic force with as large a market as that of the United States. If the present trend continues, the European Union will continue to grow as Eastern European nations join the group. Because of the EU program, Western European nations are doing more together than ever. New agreements on matters important to future European development covering space, broadcasting, and computer research have been negotiated among countries and companies. But expanding trade has been, and continues to be, the greatest achievement of the common market. The rate of expansion in European trade during 1990s was seven times the rate of economic growth.

With Western Europe setting an example, attempts at regional integration have been made in Asia, North America, and elsewhere. However, these attempts have not been as extensive or far-reaching as the ones in Europe. It is interesting to note that despite the slow emergence of globalization, regional integration in two vast regions, Asia and the Americas, is high on the agenda. For the first time in history, East Asia is creating its own economic bloc, which could include preferential trade arrangements and an Asian Monetary Fund. The membership of the bloc will comprise the so-called ASEAN + 3: the 10 members of the Association of Southeast Asian Nations (ASEAN), plus Japan, China, and South Korea. In addition to implementing free trade among members, the new group is contemplating moving toward trade systems of cooperative exchange to shield itself from the huge fluctuations in the currencies of the major industrial countries; this arrangement would be similar to Europe's moves toward monetary integration in the 1970s to defend itself against wide fluctuations of the dollar.

Japan began this movement. Traditionally, Japan relied on the multilateral frameworks of the GATT and the WTO, but in the past few years it began to pursue bilateral trade agreements with Singapore, Mexico, and South Korea. South Korea made similar policy shifts and has been negotiating actively with Chile as well. China, another country that had eschewed regional approaches, stunned everyone at the fourth annual ASEAN + 3 summit in late 2000 by proposing a China-Asia free trade area, which the Southeast Asians, fearing Chinese domination, immediately broadened to include Japan and South Korea. Thus, a study of a possible East Asia free trade area, which would be a world-shaking development, was launched at the summit.[6] The new study will build on the one already under way for the creation of a free trade area in North and East Asia (China, Japan, and South Korea), a development that itself is of major significance. In short, the East Asian Economic Group is beginning to take shape, albeit slowly and in subregional stages. There can be little doubt that these new movements will result in the evolution of an East Asian economic bloc.

As far as the Americas are concerned, scholars have maintained that the United States—preeminent but not hegemonic—cannot maintain its global leadership without the cooperation of its southern neighbors. A core group

of South American countries—Argentina, Brazil, Chile, and Uruguay—
have made great strides in recent years toward regional integration and are
poised, despite their short-term economic problems, to make steady political and economic gains over the next decade. The right incentives are critical, however, to ensure that these nations become fully democratic,
market-oriented allies of the United States. To this end, the best incentive
that the United States can provide is an expansion of the North American
Free Trade Agreement (NAFTA) to the Southern Cone, making these South
American nations members of the pact alongside the United States,
Canada, and Mexico. As a matter of fact, NAFTA should extend the membership to other nations in the region as they meet qualifying criteria on
lines similar to the ones used by the European Union in adding new members. This so-called Super NAFTA would offer great advantages to all its
participants, help stabilize and enrich the Americas, and further the process
of hemispherical integration.[7]

Leaders in both the United States and Latin America have often spoken
about the need to form a regional trade group. President George W. Bush's
announcement in April 2001 that 34 nations in the region—practically all
the nations in the New World except Cuba—will create the Free Trade
Area of the Americas (FTAA) by 2005 is a major step forward.[8] The
planned FTAA is likely to turn the region into a powerful force in international economic diplomacy. With 800 million people, a third of global
economic output, and more than a quarter of total exports, such an organization would be the world's largest trading group.

Although the FTAA may not become a reality by 2005, at least a beginning is feasible if the major nations in the region, Argentina, Brazil, and
Chile, join the NAFTA countries to form the FTAA. Later on, other nations
can join under the established criteria and timetable. Despite the gloomy
conditions in Argentina toward the end of 2001, there are reasons in 2003
to hope for the formation of the FTAA. For the first time since the countries
of South America won their independence, the priorities of local governing
elites and public opinion are converging with U.S. priorities. The United
States will have to take the lead for the FTAA to evolve.

In addition to the above three regional groups, it is conceivable—
although quite unlikely, at least in the short run—that a free trade agreement will materialize among nations along the Indian Ocean. Such a
regional bloc would comprise South Asian countries and the African
nations of Kenya, Mauritius, Mozambique, Somalia, Tanzania, and South
Africa. It would be a market of almost 1.5 billion people. The traditional
enmity between India and Pakistan, however, makes such an agreement

impossible. But if India and South Africa take the lead, they can form an Indian Ocean regional agreement.[9]

As mentioned above, the three large trading blocs—the European Union, ASEAN + 3, and FTAA—will economically integrate the nations regionally. Even if the Indian Ocean regional agreement never takes place, the first three will comprise 3.5 billion people and almost 80 percent of the world gross product. Adding the Indian Ocean market to the equation, over 83 percent of the world population would be covered, accounting for more than 90 percent of world GDP.[10]

While the process of global integration continues, more activities will occur at the regional level. In the long run, regions will negotiate with one another to make global agreements. The regional integration will facilitate globalization.

9. GLOBALIZATION SEEKS GLOBAL ASSIMILATION.

Culturally, globalization is akin to the kind of immigrant assimilation that has occurred in the United States and other countries for years. People from different parts of the world integrate themselves into a new, larger society to advance themselves economically, often giving up a part of their old culture along the way. The process is difficult, causing guilt, anger, and blame. But nearly everyone, given the option, chooses mobility with economic improvement over poverty, and modernity with economic improvement over tradition.

10. A SUPRANATIONAL GLOBAL ORGANIZATION IS NEEDED FOR SMOOTH PROGRESS TOWARD GLOBALIZATION.

For centuries the nation-state has been solely responsible for protecting its people and providing them a decent life. However, effective management of a global economy in the interest of its multiple participants requires nation-states to give up their sovereignty in areas where their actions are counterproductive or less than optimum to a worldwide organization. Some may argue that this relinquishment is under way at regional and international levels. For example, Western European nations have empowered the European Union to act on behalf of all the members in matters of common interest. Similarly, as members of the WTO, nations must abide by the trade agreements.

All these attempts at creating regional or multilateral bodies have been made by nation-states. In other words, nation-states have decided what powers can be delegated to a regional or multilateral organization, how this organization will function, and who else might join it.

The IMF, the World Bank, GATT (now the WTO) and the International Labor Organization are all associations of states. Therefore, an individual nation-state's political interests are always present when multilateral issues are discussed. Besides, over time the situation has changed, and some of the existing institutions are no longer able to deliver what they were supposed to. The contemporary conflict that afflicts the WTO is an example. At least part of its original purpose was to advance the interests of its member states in health matters and to restrain the disadvantages that followed from the commercial priorities of the drug companies. Current developments now mean that world health may best be improved by global cooperation among the World Health Organization and drug companies on issues of R&D and manufacture. This position means abandoning the basic assumption that war between nation-states and drug companies is inevitable.[11]

The proposed GBC will be different in the sense that MNCs will play the primary role in its establishment and work, whereas the nation-states will occupy a secondary position. Nation-states look at issues first from a political angle and then from other angles. In the interest of boosting economic prosperity for the 2 billion poor people and the 3 billion people who hardly survive economically, it is important that economic concerns be the focal points of the working of the new organization.

As the twenty-first century progresses, it will become clear that any troubles, failures, and frightening anxieties chiefly arise from the absence of mechanisms for managing a global economy. If a global organization along the lines of the GBC that this book promotes is created, the benefits of globalization will predominate. Otherwise, there is a great risk of economic and political chaos. In the new organization for managing the global economy, the nation-state will continue to play a significant, if lesser, role. It will be the guardian of local economic rules and of transparent and uncorrupt domestic administration; but even more important, the nation-state will be an institution that will seek out ways of engaging with the new sources of economic power, the MNCs, and influencing them as is desirable.

It is difficult to accept the fact that nation-states in many areas will become subsidiaries to MNCs. It is because the global markets are just beginning to see that their own effectiveness and convenience can be secured only if, possessing legitimate authority, they generate their own cooperative systems of regulation to combat their chaotic volatility. As that happens, a kind of role reversal will occur. Nation-states, which used to be the source of cooperation, have already become serious competitors at many levels for the inward investment that globalization has made available; in contrast, companies and the global markets in which they operate, which used to compete, have become the readier source of much effective cooperation. There are tentative signs of this development in the global stock market, in global banking, and in the management of the Internet. The GBC provides a unique way to formalize such cooperation among all the major players, with MNCs assuming a leadership role. Globalization of markets and corporations calls for globalization of politics and for multiple supranational governance structures.

11. THE FREE FLOW OF INFORMATION HAS GIVEN NEW POWERS TO CONSUMERS WORLDWIDE.

Traditionally, governments monopolized information so that people received what their government wanted them to know. Governments were able to fool, mislead, or control the people, because only the governments possessed real facts about things happening around the world. Today, people are able to get the information they want on worldwide events and happenings. Thanks to television networks such as CNN, the Internet, and increasing overseas travel, people are aware of many more things today than ever before. For example, a government once might have subsidized inefficient industries to avoid social unrest that would be brought on by unemployment. A government may still adopt such a policy today, but people would know what the policy would cost them.

In the past, people in developing countries viewed MNCs as modern colonizers similar to the East India Company of the past. In today's world, people know better. People's interests lie in maximizing their benefits; the idea of buying a domestic firm's product in the name of patriotism becomes irrelevant.

The better informed people are, the more they will want to make their own choices and the less these choices will be in line with politically determined national interests. In other words, in the normal course of things a nation cannot avoid globalization, because its people want what globalization will bring them. Worldwide, people want a good living standard, which they perceive to be obtainable through global corporations, not the government. It would be the height of arrogance for governments to protest against the people's choices.

12. GLOBALIZATION IS NOT A THREAT TO A NATION'S CULTURE.

Any social unit has traits that its members revere. Over time these traits become so ingrained that they develop into cultural values of the unit. The cultural values of a group do change, although the transition happens very slowly.[12] The change occurs as people gain more information, experience new things, and come into contact with other people. These three kinds of interactions serve as the agents of change. The interactions provide a new perspective, but that does not mean people accept everything they are exposed to. Sometimes they accept new things; sometimes they don't. On some occasions, they experiment with new things and give them up. In other words, globalization does not constitute a cultural threat to any culture or society.

Take the case of yoga. Even though it originated in a developing country, India, millions of people in Western nations have started practicing yoga because they have found it healthy. They did not reject it simply because it represents old values or is associated with a poor nation. People in Islamic countries have not taken to drinking alcohol simply because it represents a Western notion and might mean becoming outgoing and modern. Their religion, Islam, does not permit drinking, and most Muslims strictly adhere to this value. Hindus have not taken to eating beef even though many U.S. products are held in high esteem in India and the Big Mac represents the United States. What Indians like about McDonald's is its efficient way of providing inexpensive food for the average person in a clean environment. Because Hindus do not want traditional hamburgers, McDonald's created a meatless variety for them, and they fully enjoy these alternatives with the spicy sauce that the company provides in its Indian outlets. McDonald's has not challenged India's values. It has simply introduced a new technology to serve food. Thus, the notion that globalization challenges a nation's culture is a misunderstanding.

13. GLOBALIZATION'S SKEPTICS FEAR CAPITALISM.

The main intellectual problem of individuals opposed to globalization is their aversion to capitalism. They fail to understand that economic freedom is the best, and perhaps the only, way to attack poverty and control concentrations of economic and political power. The alternative to capitalism, socialism, has failed to prove its virtues, which has become amply clear after the breakdown of the Soviet Union. Thus, critics should discard their false or wildly exaggerated fears about the mixed economy—that is, about capitalism as it exists in the West, with safety nets, public services, and moderate redistribution in place.

Under this form of capitalism, economic growth does not hurt the poor, as critics allege. In developing countries, capitalist growth is indispensable if people are ever to be raised out of poverty. Growth in mixed economies is compatible with protecting the environment: the environment in rich nations is cleaner than in poor ones. Further, when prices are adjusted to reflect the costs of pollution or are allowed to reflect the scarcity of natural resources, good stewardship will go hand in hand with growth. Above all, mixed capitalism does not put poor nations at a disadvantage; it helps them.

14. GLOBALIZATION IS NOT A THREAT TO POLITICAL SOVEREIGNTY AND DEMOCRACY.

It is commonly believed that conditions that establish the market's confidence in any particular economy and its government (e.g., balanced budgets, moderate taxes, light regulations, and privatization) are necessary for any economy to prosper. Thomas Friedman refers to the adoption of such policies as putting on the golden straitjacket. He notes:

> Two things tend to happen: your economy grows and your politics shrinks. The Golden Straitjacket narrows the political and economic choices of those in power to relatively tight parameters. That is why it is increasingly difficult these days to find any real difference between ruling and opposition parties in those countries that have put on the Golden Straitjacket. Once a country puts on the Golden Straitjacket, its political choice gets reduced to Pepsi or Coke—to slight nuances of policy, slight alterations in design to account for local traditions, some loosening here or there, but never any major deviation from the core golden rules.[13]

The policies of Friedman's golden straitjacket are almost universally accepted as the right ones from the standpoint of economic growth. But the critics complain that in the pursuit of economic growth, political sovereignty and democratic legitimacy are lost. Their argument, however, does not hold ground. As long as voters prefer balanced budgets, moderate taxes, privatization, and the other conditions on their merits, democracy has not been weakened.

What is important about globalization is not the triumph of markets over national governments. Both proponents and opponents of globalization agree that the driving force today is markets, which are subordinating the role of government. The truth is that the size of government has been shrinking relative to the economy almost everywhere. As the oversight role of the nation-state decreases with the expansion of markets globally, a global institutional framework is needed to prevent crisis. The Asian financial crisis of 1997–99 showed that unfettered liberalization of capital markets without proper global regulation could lead the world to the brink of disaster. And the incredibly dynamic performance of the U.S. stock market makes a strong case for enforcing strict accounting rules plus antitrust policies to keep markets open and competitive. Globalization should not be the ideological darling of one group or the demon of others, but rather a market system operating under global rules and regulations.

15. GLOBALIZATION HAS LITTLE ASSOCIATION WITH ENVIRONMENTAL DESTRUCTION.

Critics frequently blame globalization for destroying the environment. The evidence shows that global economic integration has little to do with the environment. It is government policies that fail to protect it. For example, the reasons behind the export of lumber from old-growth Alaskan forests to Japan mostly involve the U.S. government's subsidizing Alaskan loggers to sell more lumber to generate local jobs. The nuclear and mining disasters that befouled much of Eastern Europe and Russia occurred under communist governments. The cutting down of much of the Amazon forest is part of the Brazilian national government's strategy of developing the hinterland. The forest fires that pour smoke over Southeast Asia every year are set by land-hungry peasants with the support of politicians. As a rule, those countries with the cleanest environments tend to be the most developed. It would be wise for environmentalists to remember that in the 1950s and 1960s, long before globalization, the skies over U.S. cities were filled with black smoke from coal, and the rivers ran black with pollution.

Ultimately, consumers decide which products to buy and from where to buy them. Companies must listen to consumers, because one disaster can damage a brand's reputation forever. As long as consumers care for the safety of the environment, respect for human rights, and the just treatment of labor, global corporations will have to respond to those concerns in a positive manner. A few years ago, Levi Strauss gave up not only a good source of quality production but also a potentially large market in Asia based on the conviction that better working conditions produce better products.

LOOKING AHEAD

In the twenty-first century, a new world order should become a reality and be characterized as follows:

- The world's money, technology, and markets are controlled and managed by gigantic corporations.
- A common consumer culture unifies all people in a shared quest for material gratification.
- There is perfect global competition among markets and localities to offer their services to investors at the most advantageous terms.
- MNCs are free to act solely on the basis of profitability without regard to national or local consequences.
- Relationships, both individual and corporate, are defined entirely by the market.
- There are no special loyalties to places on emotional grounds.

Limitless affluence for the entire human population of the world is a vision of the global economy. It has an entrancing appeal for everyone who wants to live a comfortable life. The institution of the MNC has the capability to make it happen. Nation-states should actively join the global corporations in this noble task.

NOTES

1. "Grinding the Poor: A Survey of Globalization," *Economist*, 29 September 2001, pp. 10–13.

2. Martin Wolf, "A Stepping Stone from Poverty," *Financial Times*, 19 December 2001, p. 17.

3. "The Global Economy: War of Words," *Economist*, 1 October 1999, pp. 3–9; and United Nations, *World Investment Report*, 1999.

4. "The Stateless Corporation," *Business Week*, 14 May 1990, p. 98.

5. Michael E. McGrath and Richard W. Hoole, "Manufacturing's New Economies of Scale," *Harvard Business Review*, May/June 1992, pp. 94–102.

6. C. Fred Bergsten, "America's Two-Front Economic Conflict," *Foreign Affairs*, March/April 2001, pp. 16–27.

7. Felipe A.M. de la Balze, "Finding Allies in the Back Yard," *Foreign Affairs*, July/August 2001, pp. 7–13.

8. Guy de Jonquieres and Edward Alden, "American Ties," *Financial Times*, 20 April 2001, p. 12.

9. Subhash C. Jain and Pervez N. Ghauri, "Commentary: Indian Ocean Rim Trade Bloc: Prospects and Problems," *International Executive*, September/October 1996, pp. 583–98.

10. World Bank, *World Development Report, 2002* (Washington, D.C.: World Bank, 2002).

11. Richard Lanhorne, *The Coming of Globalization* (New York: Palgrave, 2001), pp. 31–33.

12. See Subhash C. Jain, *International Marketing,* 6th ed. (Cincinnati: South-Western College Publishing, 2001), pp. 146–155.

13. Thomas L. Friedman, *The Lexus and the Olive Tree* (New York: Farrar, Straus and Giroux, 1999), p. 87.

BIBLIOGRAPHY

Accordino, J.J. *The United States in the Global Economy.* Chicago: American Library Association, 1992.

Aceves, W.J. "Lost Sovereignty: The Implications of the Uruguay Round Agreements." *Fordham International Law Journal* 19 (1995): 427–74.

Adam, C. "Internationalization and Integration of Financial and Capital Markets." In *Handbook on the Globalization of the World Economy,* ed. A. Levy-Livermore, pp. 557–81. Northampton, Mass.: Edward Elgar, 1998.

Adler, N., and S. Bartholomew. "Managing Globally Competent People." *Academy of Management Executive* 693 (1992): 52–65.

Aggarwal, R. "Managing for Economic Growth and Global Competition: Strategic Implications of the Life Cycle Of Economies." *Advances in International Comparative Management* 2 (1986): 19–44.

Aggarwal, R., and T. Agmon. "The International Success of Developing Country Firms: Role of Government-Directed Comparative Advantage." *Management International Review* 30, no. 2 (1990): 163–80.

Aggarwal, V. *Institutional Designs for a Complex World.* Ithaca, N.Y.: Cornell University Press, 1998.

Aghion, P., and J. Williamson. *Growth Inequality and Globalization.* Cambridge: Cambridge University Press, 1998.

Agnew, J., and S. Corbridge. *Mastering Space: Hegemony, Territory and International Political Economy.* London: Routledge, 1995.

Alexander, T. *Global Apartheid: An Overview of World Politics.* Cambridge, England: Polity Press, 1996.

Ali, A., and R. Camp. "Competitiveness and Global Leadership." *Competitiveness Review* 3, no. 1 (1993): 21–33.

————. "Global Managers: Qualities for Effective Competition." *International Journal of Manpower* 17, no. 6/7 (1996): 5–18.

Amin, A., and N. Thrift. *Globalization, Institutions, and Regional Development in Europe.* Oxford: Oxford University Press, 1995.

Attali, J. "The Crash of Western Civilization: The Limits of the Market and Democracy." *Foreign Policy,* Summer 1997, pp. 54–64.

Bailey, D., G. Harte, and R. Sugden. *Making Transnationals Accountable—A Significant Step for Britain.* London: Routledge, 1994.

Barber, B. *Jihad vs. McWorld.* New York: Times Books, 1995.

Barnet, R., and J. Cavanagh. *Global Dreams: Imperial Corporations and the New World Order.* New York: Simon and Schuster, 1994.

Barnet, R.J. "Lords of the Global Economy." *Nation,* 19 December 1994, pp. 754–65.

————. "Homogenization of Global Culture." In *The Case against the Global Economy,* ed. J. Mander and E. Goldsmith, pp. 71–77. San Francisco: Sierra Club Books, 1996.

Barnet, R.J., and R.E. Muller. *Global Reach: The Power of the Multinational Corporations.* New York: Simon and Schuster, 1974.

Barnevik, P. "The Logic of Global Business," interview by W. Taylor. *Harvard Business Review,* March/April 1991, pp. 91–105.

Barry Jones, R.J. *Globalization and Interdependence in the International Political Economy.* London: Pluto Press, 1995.

Bartlett, C.A. "Managing across Borders: New Organizational Responses." *Sloan Management Review,* Fall 1987, pp. 45–53.

————. "Managing across Borders: New Strategic Requirements." *Sloan Management Review,* Summer 1987, pp. 7–17.

Bartlett, C.A., and S. Ghoshal. *Managing across Borders: The Transnational Solution.* 2d ed. Boston: Harvard Business School Press, 1989.

————. "Tap Your Subsidiaries of Global Reach." *Harvard Business Review,* November/December 1986, pp. 87–94.

Bergsten, F.C. "Globalizing Free Trade." *Foreign Affairs* 75, no. 3 (1996): 105–20.

Birkinshaw, J.M., and N. Hood. *Multinational Corporate Evolution and Subsidiary Development.* London: Macmillan, 1998.

Black, S., H. Gregersen, and M. Mendenhall. *Global Assignments.* San Francisco: Jossey-Bass, 1992.

Blair, M.M. *Ownership and Control: Rethinking Corporate Governance for the Twenty-first Century.* Washington, D.C.: The Brookings Institution, 1995.

Blumberg, P.I. *The Megacorporation in American Society: The Scope of Corporate Power.* Englewood Cliffs, N.J.: Prentice Hall, 1975.

Bora, B. "The Role of Multinational Corporations in Globalizing the World Economy: Evidence from Affiliates of US Multinational Companies." In *Handbook on the Globalization of the World Economy,* ed. A. Levy-Livermore, pp. 147–67. Northampton, Mass.: Edward Elgar, 1998.

Boudreau, M.C., K.D. Loch, D. Robey, and D. Straud. "Going Global: Using Information Technology to Advance the Competitiveness of the Virtual Transnational Organization." *Academy of Management Executive* 12, no. 4 (1998): 120–28.

Boyer, R., and D. Drache, eds. *States against Markets: The Limits of Globalization.* New York and London: Routledge, 1996.

Brewer, T.L., and S. Young. "The Multilateral Agenda for Foreign Direct Investment: Problems, Principles and Priorities for Negotiation at the OECD and WTO." *World Competition* 18, no. 4 (1995): 67–83.

———. *Multilateral Investment Rules and Multinational Enterprises.* Oxford: Oxford University Press, 1998.

Bryan, L., and D. Farrell. *Market Unbound: Unleashing Global Capitalism.* New York: Wiley, 1996.

Bryan, L., J. Fraser, J. Oppenheim, and W. Rall. *Race for the World: Strategies to Build a Great Global Firm.* Boston: Harvard Business School Press, 1999.

Buckley, P.J., and M. Casson. *The Future of the Multinational Enterprise.* London: Macmillan, 1976.

Burbach, R., O. Nunez, and B. Kagarlitsky. *Globalization and Its Discontents.* London: Pluto Press, 1997.

Burtless, G., R.Z. Lawrence, R.E. Litan, and R.J. Shapiro. *Globaphobia: Confronting Fears about Open Trade.* Washington, D.C.: The Brookings Institution, 1998.

Cairncross, F. *The Death of Distance: How the Communications Revolution Will Change Our Lives.* Boston: Harvard Business School Press, 1997.

Calvet, L. "A Synthesis of Foreign Direct Investment Theories and Theories of the Multinational Firm." *Journal of International Business Studies,* Spring/Summer 1981, pp. 43–59.

Cantwell, J.A. "The Changing Form of Multinational Enterprise Expansion in the Twentieth Century." In *Historical Studies in International Corporate Business,* ed. A. Teichova, M. Levy-Leboyer, and H. Nussbaum. Cambridge: Cambridge University Press, 1989.

Caufield, C. *Masters of Illusion: The World Bank and the Poverty of Nations.* New York: Henry Holt, 1996.

Caves, R.E. *Multinational Enterprise and Economic Analysis.* Cambridge: Cambridge University Press, 1982.

Certon, M., and O. Davies. "50 Trends Shaping the World." *Futurist,* September/October 1991, pp. 22–29.

Charkham, J.P. *Keeping Good Company: A Study of Corporate Governance in Five Countries.* Oxford, England: Clarendon Press, 1994.

Chayes, A., and A.H. Chayes. *The New Sovereignty: Compliance with International Regulatory Agreements.* Cambridge: Harvard University Press, 1995.

Cleveland, H. *Birth of a New World Order.* San Francisco: Jossey-Bass, 1993.

Comeaux, P.E., and N.S. Kinsella. *Protecting Foreign Investment under International Law.* Dobbs Ferry, N.Y.: Oceana Publications, 1997.

Cowling, K., and R. Sugden. *Beyond Capitalism: Towards a New World Economic Order.* New York: St. Martin's Press, 1994.

Cox, K.R. *Spaces of Globalization: Reasserting the Power of the Local.* New York: Guilford Press, 1997.

Diamond, J. *Guns, Germs, and Steel: The Fates of Human Societies.* New York: W.W. Norton, 1997.

Dicken, P. "Global-Local Tensions: Firms and States in the Global Space-Economy." *Advances in Strategic Management,* no. 10B (1994): 217–47.

———. *Global Shift.* 3d ed. New York: Guilford Press, 1998.

Diehl, P.F. *The Politics of Global Governance: International Organizations in an Interdependent World.* Boulder, Colo.: Westview Press, 1996.

Dobbin, M. *The Myth of the Good Corporate Citizen: Democracy under the Rule of Big Business.* Toronto: Stoddart, 1998.

Doremus, P.N., W.W. Keller, L.W. Pauly, and S. Reich. *The Myth of the Global Corporation.* Princeton, N.J.: Princeton University Press, 1998.

Dorrenbacher, C., and M. Wortmann. "The Internationalization of Corporate Research and Development." *Intereconomics* 26, no. 3 (1991): 139.

Drucker, P. *The Concept of the Corporation.* New York: Mentor, 1983.

———. "The Global Economy and the Nation State." *Foreign Affairs,* September/October 1997, pp. 36–45.

———. "Multinationals and Developing Countries: Myths and Realities." *Foreign Affairs,* Fall 1994, pp. 121–34.

Dunning, J.H. "The Eclectic Paradigm of International Production: A Restatement and Some Possible Extensions." *Journal of International Business Studies* 19, no. 1 (1988): 1–25.

———. *Multinational Enterprises and the Global Economy.* Workingham, Mass.: Addison-Wesley, 1992.

———, ed. *Governments, Globalization, and International Business.* New York: Oxford University Press, 1997.

Edwards, M. *Future Positive: International Co-operation in the 21st Century.* London: Earthscan, 1999.

Feketekuty, G., and B. Stokes, eds. *Trade Strategies for a New Era: Ensuring U.S. Leadership in a Global Economy.* New York: Council on Foreign Relations, 1998.

Fisse, B., and J. Braithwaite. *Corporations, Crime and Accountability.* New York: Cambridge University Press, 1993.

Frank, R. *Luxury Fever: Why Money Fails to Satisfy in an Era of Excess.* New York: Free Press, 1999.

Frank, R., and P. Cook. *The Winner-Take-All Society.* New York: Free Press, 1995.

Franko, L.G. *The Threat of Japanese Multinationals.* Chichester, England: Wiley, 1983.

Friedman, T. *The Lexus and the Olive Tree*. New York: Farrar, Straus and Giroux, 1999.

Fukuyama, F. *The End of History and the Last Man*. New York: Free Press, 1992.

Funabashi, T. "Tokyo's Depression Diplomacy." *Foreign Affairs* 77, no. 6 (1998): 27–37.

Gardner, R.N. "The Case for Practical Internationalism." *Foreign Affairs* 66, no. 4 (1988): 827–45.

Giddens, A. *Runaway World: How Globalization Is Reshaping Our Lives*. London: Profile Books, 1999.

Goldsmith, E. "Global Trade and Environment." In *The Case against the Global Economy*, ed. J. Mander and E. Goldsmith, pp. 78–91. San Francisco: Sierra Club Books, 1996.

Graham, E.M. *The Global Corporations and National Governments*. Washington, D.C.: Institute for International Economics, 1996.

Grant-Wisdom, D. "The Economics of Globalization." In *Globalization, Communications and Caribbean Identity*, ed. H.S. Dunn, pp. 2–17. New York: St. Martin's Press, 1995.

Gray, J. *False Dawn: The Delusions of Global Capitalism*. London: Granta Books, 1998.

Greider, W. *One World, Ready or Not: The Manic Logic of Global Capitalism*. New York: Touchstone Books, 1998.

———. *Who Will Tell the People: The Betrayal of American Democracy*. New York: Simon and Schuster, 1992.

Guehenno, J. *The End of the Nation State*. Minneapolis: University of Minnesota Press, 1995.

Gummett, P., ed. *Globalization and Public Policy*. Cheltenham, England: Edward Elgar, 1996.

Hakanson, L. "International Decentralization of R&D—The Organizational Challenges." In *Managing the Global Firm*, ed. C.A. Bartlett, Y. Doz, and G. Hedlund. London and New York: Routledge, 1990.

Hampden-Turner, C., and A. Trompenaars. *The Seven Cultures of Capitalism*. New York: Doubleday/Currency, 1993.

Heilbroner, R. *21st Century Capitalism*. New York: W.W. Norton, 1993.

Henderson, J. *The Globalization of High Technology Production*. London and New York: Routledge, 1989.

Hewson, M., and T.J. Sinclair. *Approaches to Global Governance Theory*. Albany, N.Y.: M.E. Sharpe, 1999.

Hormats, R. "Making Regionalism Safe." *Foreign Affairs* 73, no. 2 (1994): 97–108.

Hu, Y. "Global or Stateless Corporations Are National Firms with International Operations." *California Management Review*, Winter 1992, pp. 107–26.

Huntington, S. "The Clash of Civilizations." *Foreign Affairs* 72, no. 3 (1993): 22–49.

———. *The Clash of Civilizations and the Remaking of World Order.* New York: Simon and Schuster, 1996.

Irwin, D. *Against the Tide: An Intellectual History of Free Trade.* Princeton, N.J.: Princeton University Press, 1996.

Jones, G. *The Evolution of International Business.* London: Routledge, 1996.

Kanter, R.M. *World Class: Thriving Locally in the Global Economy.* New York: Simon and Schuster, 1995.

Kaplan, R. *The Ends of the Earth: A Journey at the Dawn of the Twenty-first Century.* New York: Random House, 1996.

Khor, M. "Free Trade and the Third World." In *The Case against Free Trade: GATT, NAFTA, and the Globalization of Corporate Power,* ed. R. Nader, pp. 97–107. New York: Earth Island Press, 1993.

Kobrin, S.J. "The MAI and the Clash of Globalizations." *Foreign Policy,* Fall 1998, pp. 97–108.

Korey, W. *NGOs and the Universal Declaration of Human Rights.* New York: St. Martin's Press, 1998.

Korten, D. *When Corporations Rule the World.* San Francisco; Berret-Koehler Publishers/Kumerian Press, 1995.

Kotkin, J. *Tribes: How Race, Religion, and Identity Determine Success in the New Global Economy.* New York: Random House, 1992.

Krugman, P. *Pop Internationalism.* Cambridge: MIT Press, 1996.

Kung, H. *A Global Ethic for Global Politics and Economics.* New York: Oxford University Press, 1998.

Kuttner, R. *Everything for Sale: The Virtues and Limits of Markets.* New York: Knopf, 1997.

Lall, S. *The New Multinationals.* Chichester, England: Wiley, 1983.

Landes, D. *The Wealth and Poverty of Nations: Why Some Are So Rich and Others Are So Poor.* New York: W.W. Norton, 1998.

Lawrence, R.Z., A. Bressand, and T. Ito. *A Vision for the World Economy: Openness, Diversity and Cohesion.* Washington, D.C.: The Brookings Institution, 1996.

Laxer, J. *False God: How the Globalization Myth Has Impoverished Canada.* Toronto: Lester Publishing, 1993.

Levitt, T. "The Globalization of Markets." *Harvard Business Review,* May/June 1983, pp. 92–102.

Lowe, J. *The Secret Empire: How 25 Multinationals Rule the World.* Homewood, Ill.: Irwin Professional Publishing, 1992.

Mander, J. "Megatechnology and Trade, and the New World." In *The Case against Free Trade: GATT, NAFTA, and the Globalization of Corporate Power,* ed. R. Nader, pp. 13–22. New York: Earth Island Press, 1993.

Mander J., and E. Goldsmith, eds. *The Case against the Global Economy.* San Francisco: Sierra Club Books, 1996.

Mattera, P. *World Class Business: A Guide to the 100 Most Powerful Global Corporations.* New York: Henry Holt, 1992.

McGrew, A.G., and P.G. Lewis. *Global Politics: Globalization and the Nation-States*. Cambridge, England: Polity Press, 1992.

Nader, R., ed. *The Case against Free Trade: GATT, NAFTA, and the Globalization of Corporate Power*. San Francisco: Earth Island Press, 1993.

O'Farrell, P.N., P.A. Wood, and J. Zheng. "Internationalization of Business Services: An Interregional Analysis." *Regional Studies* 30, no. 2 (1996): 101–18.

Ohmae, K. *The Borderless World*. New York: Harper Perennial, 1991.

———. *The End of the Nation State*. New York: Free Press, 1995.

———. *Triad Power*. New York: Free Press, 1985.

Ozawa, T. "Foreign Direct Investment and Economic Development." *Transnational Corporations* 1, no. 1 (1992): 27–54.

Pauly, L.W. *Who Elected the Bankers: Surveillance and Control in the World Economy*. Ithaca, N.Y.: Cornell University Press, 1997.

Pauly, L.W., and S. Reich. "National Structures and Multinational Corporate Behavior: Enduring Differences in the Age of Globalization." *International Organization* 51, no. 1 (1997): 1–30.

Pfaff, W. *The Wrath of Nations*. New York: Simon and Schuster, 1993.

Porter, M. *The Competitive Advantage of Nations*. New York: Free Press, 1990.

Porter, M.E. *Competition in Global Industries*. Boston: Harvard Business School Press, 1986.

Prahalad, C., and Y. Doz. *The Multinational Mission: Balancing Demands and Global Vision*. New York: Simon and Schuster, 1987.

Reich, R.B. "Who Is Them?" *Harvard Business Review*, March/April 1991, pp. 77–89.

———. "Who Is Us?" *Harvard Business Review*, January/February 1990, pp. 53–64.

Rhinesmith, S.H. *A Manager's Guide to Globalization*. New York: McGraw-Hill, 1996.

Rifkin, J. *The End of Work: The Decline of the Global Labor Force and the Dawn of the Post Market Era*. New York: G.P. Putnam's Sons, 1995.

Ritzer, G. *The McDonaldization of Society*. Thousand Oaks, Calif.: Pine Forge Press, 1993.

Rodrick, D. *Has Globalization Gone Too Far?* Washington, D.C.: Institute for International Economics, 1997.

Rosow, J.M. *The Global Market Place*. New York: Facts on File, 1988.

Rubner, A. *The Might of the Multinationals: The Rise and Fall of the Corporate Legend*. New York: Praeger, 1990.

Rugman, A.M. *Multinational Enterprises and Trade Policy*. Vol. 2. Cheltenham, England: Edward Elgar, 1996.

———. "Negotiating Multilateral Rules for Investment." In *G8's Role in the New Millennium*, ed. M. Hodges, J. Kirton, and J. Daniels, pp. 143–58. Aldershot, England: Ashgate, 1999.

Rugman, A.M., and J.R. D'Cruz. *Multinationals as Flagship Firms: Regional Business Networks*. Oxford: Oxford University Press, 2000.

————. "The Theory of the Flagship Firm." *European Management Review* 15, no. 4 (1997): 403–11.

Safarian, A.E. *Multinational Enterprise and Public Policy.* Cheltenham, England: Edward Elgar, 1993.

Sen, A. *On Ethics and Economics.* Oxford, England: Basil Blackwell, 1987.

Senge, P. *The Fifth Discipline.* New York: Doubleday/Currency, 1990.

Sera, K. "Corporate Globalization: A New Trend." *Academy of Management Executive* 6, no. 1 (1995): 89–96.

Shuman, M. *Towards a Global Village: International Community Development Initiatives.* London: Pluto Press, 1994.

Skinner, Q. *Liberty before Liberalism.* Cambridge: Cambridge University Press, 1998.

Slaughter, A. "The Real New World Order." *Foreign Affairs,* September/October 1997, pp. 16–26.

Stewart, T. *Intellectual Capital: The New Wealth of Organizations.* New York: Doubleday/Currency, 1997.

Stopford, J. "Multinational Corporations." *Foreign Policy* 113 (winter 1999): 13–24.

Stopford, J., S. Strange, and J.S. Henley. *Rival States, Rival Firms: Competition for World Market Shares.* Cambridge: Cambridge University Press, 1991.

Strange, S. *The Retreat of the State: The Diffusion of Power in the World Economy.* England: Cambridge University Press, 1996.

————. *States and Markets: An Introduction to International Political Economy.* London: Pinter, 1988.

Stranger, R. *Japanese Manufacturing Investment in Europe.* London: Routledge, 1993.

Sutherland, P.D. *Answering Globalization Challenges.* Washington, D.C.: Overseas Development Council, 1998.

Sveiby, K.E. *The New Organizational Wealth: Managing and Measuring Knowledge-Based Assets.* San Francisco: Berret-Koehler Publishers, 1997.

Thomsen, S. "Japanese Direct Investment in the European Community: The Product Life Cycle Revisited." *World Economy* 16, no. 3 (1993): 301–15.

Thurow, L. *Head to Head.* New York: William Morrow, 1992.

Thurow, L.C. *The Future of Capitalism.* New York: William Morrow, 1996.

————. "The Revolution upon Us." *Atlantic Monthly,* March 1997, pp. 97–100.

Tolentino, P.E.E. *Technological Innovation and Third World Multinationals.* London: Routledge, 1993.

Tomlinson, J. *Globalization and Culture.* Cambridge, England: Polity Press, 1999.

United Nations Conference on Trade Development. *Globalization and Liberalization.* New York: United Nations, 1996.

————. *Transnational Corporations, Market Structure and Foreign Policy.* World Investment Report—Overview. New York and Geneva: United Nations, 1997.

————. *World Investment Report 1997: Transnational Corporations, Market Structure and Competition Policy.* New York: United Nations, 1997.

Vayrynen, R.V., ed. *Globalization and Global Governance.* Lanham, Md.: Johns Hopkins University Press, 1998.

Vernon, R. *In the Hurricane's Eye: The Troubled Prospects of Multinational Enterprises.* Cambridge: Harvard University Press, 1998.

Waters, M. *Globalization.* London: Routledge, 1995.

Weiss, L. *The Myth of the Powerless State.* Ithaca, N.Y.: Cornell University Press, 1998.

Weissman, R. "Stolen Youth: Brutalized Children, Globalization and the Campaign to End Child Labor." *Multinational Monitor,* February 1997, pp. 10–16.

Wells, L.T. *Third World Multinationals: The Rise of Foreign Investment from Developing Countries.* Cambridge: MIT Press, 1983.

White, D. *The Frontiers in the American Century.* New Haven, Conn.: Yale University Press, 1996.

Wilkin, P. "New Myths for the South: Globalization and the Conflict between Private Power and Freedom." *Third World Quarterly* 17, no. 2 (1996): 227–38.

Wilkins, M. *The Maturing of Multinational Enterprise: American Business Abroad from 1914 to 1970.* Cambridge: Harvard University Press, 1974.

Williamson, J.G. "Globalization, Convergence, and History." In *Historical Foundations of Globalization,* ed. J. Foreman-Peck, pp. 103–32. Northampton, Mass.: Edward Elgar, 1998.

World Bank. *World Development Report 2002.* Washington, D.C.: World Bank, 1999.

Wurm, C. *Business, Politics and International Relations.* Cambridge: Cambridge University Press, 1993.

Yergin, D., and J. Stanislaw. *The Commanding Heights: The Battle between Government and the Marketplace That Is Remaking the Modern World.* New York: Simon and Schuster, 1998.

Yeung, H.W-C. "The Political Economy of Transnational Corporations: A Study of the Regionalization of Singaporean Firms." *Political Geography* 17, no. 4 (1998): 389–416.

INDEX

About the Author

SUBHASH C. JAIN is professor of international business, director of the Center for International Business Education and Research (CIBER), and director of the GE Global Learning Center at the University of Connecticut School of Business in Storrs.